Get Off Your Assets

Get Off Your Assets

*A Woman's Guide to Avoid Getting Screwed
in Your Gray Divorce*

Neale Godfrey

ROWMAN & LITTLEFIELD
Lanham • Boulder • New York • London

Published by Rowman & Littlefield
An imprint of The Rowman & Littlefield Publishing Group, Inc.
4501 Forbes Boulevard, Suite 200, Lanham, Maryland 20706
www.rowman.com

86-90 Paul Street, London EC2A 4NE

Copyright © 2025 by Neale S. Godfrey

All rights reserved. No part of this book may be reproduced in any form or by any
electronic or mechanical means, including information storage and retrieval systems,
without written permission from the publisher, except by a reviewer who may quote
passages in a review.

British Library Cataloguing in Publication Information Available

Library of Congress Cataloging-in-Publication Data

Names: Godfrey, Neale S., author.
Title: Get off your assets : a woman's guide to avoid getting screwed in
　your gray divorce / Neale S. Godfrey.
Description: Lanham : Rowman & Littlefield, [2025] | Includes
　bibliographical references and index.
Identifiers: LCCN 2024025768 (print) | LCCN 2024025769 (ebook) |
　ISBN 9781538187937 (cloth ; alk. paper) | ISBN 9781538187944 (ebook)
Subjects: LCSH: Divorced women--Finance, Personal. | Older women--
　Finance, Personal.
Classification: LCC HG179 .G6284 2025　(print) | LCC HG179　(ebook) |
　DDC 332.0240086/53--dc23/eng/20240808
LC record available at https://lccn.loc.gov/2024025768
LC ebook record available at https://lccn.loc.gov/2024025769

♾™ The paper used in this publication meets the minimum requirements of American
National Standard for Information Sciences—Permanence of Paper for Printed Library
Materials, ANSI/NISO Z39.48-1992.

Dedication

This dedication is for every woman contemplating a gray divorce, navigating one with resilience, or emerging anew from the experience. Remember, you are not alone. I offer this dedication as a tribute to your bravery and unwavering determination—not only to liberate yourself from an unfulfilling marriage, but also to craft a fresh, forward-looking chapter of your life. Cheers to all you remarkable *women warriors* who are now reclaiming the realms of Earning, Spending, Saving, and Sharing on your own terms.

I penned this book in response to your requests, wondering why it took me so long to deliver these words to you. But the wait is over. The moment is here.

I stand with you, shoulder to shoulder, as a beacon of support. Your trust is cherished, and my faith in your journey is unshakable.

With belief in your strength,
Neale

Contents

Preface   xi

SECTION 1: BEFORE YOUR GRAY DIVORCE   1

Chapter 1	What Is a Gray Divorce?	3
Chapter 2	'Til Death Do You Part	9
Chapter 3	A Leopard Can Change His Spots	11
Chapter 4	Busting the Money Marriage Myths	13
Chapter 5	History of Women and Our (Financial) Rights	21
Chapter 6	Gender Roles Are Tough to Shake	27
Chapter 7	Don't Pass This Baggage onto Your Kids	37

SECTION 2: WHEN YOU ARE CONSIDERING OR KNEE-DEEP IN YOUR GRAY DIVORCE   41

Chapter 8	Design Your New Life	43
Chapter 9	Know Yourself and Your Financial Personality	51
Chapter 10	Building Financial Security to Let You Sleep at Night	57
Chapter 11	No Magic Money Log	59
Chapter 12	A Budget Does Not Have to Be an Instrument of Torture	61

viii ～ Contents

Chapter 13	"Wish I May, Wish I Might"	67
Chapter 14	Wash That Man Right Out of Your Life	71
Chapter 15	FICO—More Than a Cute Name for a Dog	75
Chapter 16	Put Together Team-You	85
Chapter 17	How Do You Find Your Divorce Team?	87
Chapter 18	Choosing the Right Financial Advisor	95
Chapter 19	Get Your Money Act Together	101
Chapter 20	Show Me the Money—Some Things to Consider	107
Chapter 21	Initiating the Divorce	115
Chapter 22	How Do You Legally Divvy-up Assets and Income?	119

SECTION 3: YOUR FINANCIAL LIFE AFTER GRAY DIVORCE   **129**

Chapter 23	Choose Your New Butter Dish	131
Chapter 24	'Til Debt Do We Part—The Golden Years Are Tarnishing	135
Chapter 25	Refinancing Your Mortgage	141
Chapter 26	Reverse Mortgages	143
Chapter 27	"The Bag Lady Syndrome"—How to Leave Your Shopping Cart Behind	147
Chapter 28	Never Own Anything Bigger Than Your Hat	153
Chapter 29	Time to Get Off Your Assets and Learn to Vision Your New Life	157
Chapter 30	Financial Goals—Why Die on the Vine When You Can Replant?	163
Chapter 31	Women Beat Men at Investing	167
Chapter 32	Financial Wellness Later in Life	171
Chapter 33	Before the Plunge—Prenups	179
Chapter 34	Giving Is Part of Living	195
Chapter 35	Retirees, "Let the Force Be with You" (and Your Grandchildren)	199

Contents ～ ix

Chapter 36	When Your Kids Are Concerned, Can You Step Away from Your Wallet?	203
Chapter 37	Adult Children Returning to the Empty Nest	205
Chapter 38	The End or New Beginning?	209
Notes		211
Bibliography		229
Index		241

Preface

You had a long-term marriage. You had kids. You bought your dream house. You set up your investment accounts with your husband. You have been saving for your grandchildren's college education. You pretty much have been doing everything right. You are now looking forward to your "golden years" to wind down and enjoy those put-off hobbies and long-dreamed-of trips.

You know that your relationship with your spouse has not been filled with the same fireworks that existed in the beginning. You understand that life dampened the romance. It's supposed to, right? Let's face it, who feels like putting on that sexy lingerie, lighting candles, and sprinkling rose petals on the bed after a long day at work? Especially since your day could have included taking the dog to the vet after cleaning up the vomit on your new dress or getting a flat tire on the way to the office when your boss noted that she did not appreciate the dog was more important than the meeting you missed. Or, how about finding out that your mother is going to get kicked out of her nursing home for giving the staff a hard time, again?

You get it. Sexy lingerie? Are you kidding? And don't take this guilt on yourself. Your partner is just as guilty of letting the flames flicker out and die. He missed many cherished moments to work or play golf with his buddies; he didn't help with the dog vomit. He forgot your anniversary on occasion and, when reminded, felt that a new lawn mower was the romantic gift of your dreams.

Or, maybe you did give up your career to raise the kids and be a great homemaker who never missed a special occasion. You may have given xii ~ Preface

Martha Stewart a run for her money when you were a class mother for both kids. You did find that your life and your husband's went on different tracks. He didn't talk about work; you didn't ask or share much about the trials and tribulations of managing the kids and home. You both let your relationship get back-burnered to everyday pressures. You both felt the fire fizzle out. In fact, 73 percent of divorced people cite the reason for divorce as "lack of commitment." Life got in the way. And you felt like a Halloween-hussy in the sexy underwear and questioned why menopause caused underarm fat that could not be tucked into your bra.

Now, after thirty years of marriage, when the kids are gone (and the dog, too), you look across the breakfast table and realize you don't have much to say to your partner. You no longer can talk about the daily life you both juggled. You don't hate each other, and this may have nothing to do with infidelity with perhaps one of you finding the newer, younger, cellulite-free version of the other . . . it just may be because you are not content; maybe you're bored or unfulfilled. Most importantly, you know that you deserve to be happy.

I'm going to refer to this as the "Please Pass the Butter Syndrome." It's an old reference to just waking up one day, looking across the breakfast table and being overwhelmed with the sadness and emptiness of your life. You don't despise this man. He just represents the "same old, same old." You want more than to keep waking up to the repeat of "Groundhog Day," passing the butter and feeling the despair. If you do want more . . . keep reading.

Avoid the Crisis Divorce—How to Get Your Ducks in a Row

My goal is also to help you be proactive if you find yourself in a divorce. We never want to face the fact that a divorce is imminent. We don't want to think of saying "I Do" with the thought of really considering, "I Don't." But you may find yourself in that situation. And if you do, and you do not have your financial ducks in a row, you will probably be dealing with a catch-up or even an overwhelming situation. That will put you at a distinct disadvantage and may make you feel insecure and at your wit's end. You will have to juggle your emotions, your finances, and frankly, a massive upheaval in your life, all at the same time. You are going from "Mrs." to "Ms.," so your identity is also changing. This book will help you to get those ducks in a row, even if you are not thinking or considering a split up.

Preface ~ xiii

Forest for the Trees

Our human nature is not to believe that he may want a divorce. Or, that you may want a divorce. We can even ignore some signs that may lead to "butter being passed." It's so hard to listen to our tiny angel that may be whispering in our ear, "Hey, this marriage is essentially dead." One of your friends or family members could have dropped some hints to you gently—or not so gently—that things don't seem to be going well in your marriage. You could ignore those warnings, too.

I could be considered the Queen of Denial in my first divorce. My parents divorced when I was sixteen. It devastated my family and especially my mother. I was determined that this was never going to happen to me. Ever! I was going to keep my family together, do or die.

To give you some background, at this point, my then-husband and I were married for thirteen years. We had a young daughter, and I was pregnant with our son. We met when I was sixteen and in high school. I had a crush on him. We didn't start dating until we were in college and married shortly after graduation.

He was the one I went to laugh and cry with. He was my best friend and the go-to guy for any discussion or problem. I trusted him and knew he would never violate that trust. I come to the world by giving trust. You must really show me that you are not trustworthy, especially if I am banking on that trust as the basis of the relationship. So, anything I saw that did not support that thesis, I rejected.

Here is a big one: He used to jog in the evenings when he got home from work. He started to jog longer and longer. Then, he started to jog with a bottle of wine. He told me that he really got thirsty when he jogged and loved to have some wine along the way. Okay, a red flag?

Not for me. I bought into that and thought that it might be cute, or so I told myself. Obviously, it was nagging at me, so I ran this by a friend, who said, "Wait a minute, he is jogging with a bottle of wine? Either he is an athletic alcoholic or is meeting someone with whom he is sharing the wine."

I got defensive and told her that she was wrong on both counts. I walked off in a huff telling myself that he would never cheat on me. That was preposterous. I even stopped speaking to her for a while, because that was such a mean thing to say to me.

You know the end of the story. She was right on both counts, and it was just that I refused to look at the situation. I didn't want to look at it. Did I know? I obviously suspected but couldn't let my story be altered.

xiv ～ Preface

Or shattered. I was willing to look away and rewrite things the way I wanted them to be written.

I had missed the forest and the trees. Yes, we divorced, and he later married his wine-drinking-jogging buddy. And I rewrote my story to be one of gratitude for finding out then. I tried to understand my denial, and not believe that "da' Nile isn't just a river in Egypt." All kidding aside, these lessons are hard and hurtful, and I get it. And yes, my friend and I are still friends to this day.

Warning: Danger Ahead

There may also be impending divorce warning signs you don't want to ignore (besides your husband jogging with a bottle of wine).

#1 – Being Shut Out – Communication is the basis of a healthy relationship. When communication breaks down, and you are feeling shut out or shutting him out, this may be the start of the end. You may think that it is not worth it to bother, or he may not care to even talk to you. You are drifting apart and seeking your support structure somewhere else.
#2 – "R-E-S-P-E-C-T" – I feel that when that goes, so goes the marriage. If you feel contempt for each other, and the harsh, hurtful words fly, it's hard to come back from that. You may have been lied to, which means you no longer trust him. Financial infidelity falls in this realm; that one partner feels it's okay to lie to the other about finances.
#3 – Guest Bedroom Syndrome – When you stop sleeping together and having intimacy, and one of you ends up on the couch or in the guest room, this is a big signal that a divorce could be around the corner. It can start subtly like you no longer hold hands or kiss each other good night.

"Miserable Husband Syndrome"[1]

This one was new for me, although my third husband suffered from it, and I didn't know that it was a syndrome that often leads to divorce. Basically, it's when your husband goes from being a congenial guy to being annoyed, angry, depressed, sad, moody, and kvetching all the time.

When I first met my then, soon-to-be husband, I was impressed with how cool he was in most situations. He was happy and madly in love with me. But as the pre-honeymoon bliss wore off (which was an architectural trip he wanted to take), things changed, and his true nature blossomed. Miserable Husband Syndrome raised its head, but I ignored it.

Here is an example:

We were meeting friends for dinner, and I was so excited to introduce my fiancé to them. He was coming from Brooklyn, and I was driving in from New Jersey. There was traffic. There is always traffic. I was always early, but he was always late.

The meal was fabulous, and the friends were near and dear. It was a magical evening. We left, and I was giddy about the food, atmosphere, friends of my heart, and so on, as I regaled how great it was to see our buddies and to introduce them to what I thought would be my forever soulmate. All my husband did was complain about the traffic he was in three hours before. He couldn't move off that. He was stuck. He complained about how it was crawling at five miles per hour, that he hated being locked in his car with nothing to do, and that it was a waste of his time. (By the way, he was retired and didn't do anything all day.) He knew that this was a special evening for me.

I made mental excuses; he was tired; maybe he was getting sick. I felt sorry for his inconvenience, and maybe next time, I'll pick a restaurant in New York that he likes. Maya Angelou said it best: "You may not control all the events that happen to you, but you can decide not to be reduced by them."[2] I became reduced and ignored the red flag . . . but we do that for people we love, sometimes, until our heads blow off.

I did feel that it was essential to explain my philosophy of life. I told him that I come to the world with my glass half full and that his glass always seemed to be half empty. I tried to explain that the night was fabulous and that we needed to move on from the traffic.

With Miserable Husband Syndrome, you will notice that this behavior becomes second nature to the person who suffers from it. As the relationship progressed and we were married, I found this negativity debilitating. He was always complaining. He felt that I was not supportive of him unless I sympathized with his grief, his victimhood. Then he revealed the big one. He had brought up the night he suffered in the traffic again. He said that his late wife always supported his position. She shared his grief and would have been so sorry that he had to wait in traffic.

Oops. I missed the headline . . . and the article . . . and any subtext.

You need to know how you feel in the relationship; that is my point. And you need to recognize that moods and attitudes can change, for the better or worse. These can affect behavior and can become the new normal. That stress may be too much for you. Obviously, you can become the Miserable Wife, and you may also have to look in the mirror and decide if that is the person you have morphed into and want to be.

xvi ⁓ Preface

You need to consider the words of Eckhart Tolle, when he said; "When you complain, you make yourself a victim. Leave the situation, change the situation, or accept it. All else is madness."[3]

The Pandemic Held up a Magnifying Glass to Marriage

The pandemic exacerbated this new divorce phenomenon. You were stuck at home looking at each other and maybe annoying each other even more. Did you explode when he ordered your take-out salad with carrots, when even the long-gone dog knew you hated carrots because he would always get yours plopped in his dog bowl? You questioned, "How could I live with this man for thirty years, and he doesn't know me?" We can blame some of the rising gray divorce rates on Covid, but the issues were festering way before the lockdown.

CNBC reported that the pandemic was straining many marriages—some to the breaking point.[4] It looks like many more couples were asking to "Please pass the butter." Sales of online self-help divorce agreements rose by 34 percent in 2021 as compared to the year before. Tensions grew as couples were stuck inside with their partners. Family divorce lawyers also said they were seeing the same increase.

There are many reasons for this. During the first ten months of the pandemic, women—particularly women of color—lost more jobs than men. Over this period, women lost 5.4 million jobs, nearly 1 million more than men. In December 2020, it became even more dramatic when women lost 156,000 jobs, and men gained 16,000.[5] The International Monetary Fund called it a "she-cession" because women had to leave the workforce at a higher rate than men.[6] McKinsey & Company found that a third of mothers had considered leaving the workforce or downshifting their careers during the pandemic.[7] Childcare and care for sick family members fell on women. The strain on relationships was more significant, and divorces rose.

The "Please pass the butter" syndrome is not just unique to the United States. According to the McKinsey report, a British law firm's divorce filings were up 122 percent from July to October 2020. Similar patterns were seen in China, and even in Sweden, where restrictions were laxer.

'Tis the Season

Interestingly, according to a study by the University of Washington, divorce rates rise every time couples spend a lot of time together.[8] Associate Sociology Professor Julie Brines and doctoral candidate Brian Serafini, as reported in 2016, found quantitative evidence of a seasonal, biannual pattern of filings for divorce. They discovered that after the summer and winter holiday months of being together, divorces rise. After the holiday season in January, the divorce rates or inquiries begin to increase, and January seems to be dubbed the informal "divorce month."

The study further cemented the theory that too much time together may bring on "Please pass the butter" syndrome. They found that winter and summer holidays are "culturally sacred times for families" to spend time together. Couples may even be trying to mask their contempt for each other, and many may see the holidays as a time to mend broken relationships.

But we know that holidays may also be emotionally charged, and negative feelings can be ignited. The holidays can be a time of sadness as expectations, and visions of sugar plums dancing in our heads don't pan out but come crashing down into clear view as plum jam. As the study suggests, many couples regroup, get their finances in order, find an attorney, or summon the courage to file for divorce by the spring. Sadly, suicides also tend to peak at that time of year.

The Good 'Ol Days

In your parents' day, couples often just "sucked it up" and went on silently in an accepted martyrdom "for the sake of the kids." Today, you may be deciding to do something about this, and to do something may be to get divorced. You are living longer and want to "live" longer. In fact, "gray divorce" is on the rise. Really on the rise. The *Wall Street Journal* reported, "The Divorce Rate Is at a 40-Year Low, Unless You're 55 or Older."[9] The Council on Contemporary Families states that "For married individuals aged 65 and older, the risk of divorce has more than doubled since 1990."[10] In 1990, one out of ten Americans who got divorced were over fifty. Now, one out of four in this age demographic gets divorced. An epidemic? Yes. Will the divorce bug bite you in your later life?

The facts are sobering. And I'll keep repeating them because they profoundly affect Baby Boomers. According to the Center for Disease Control (CDC), the divorce rate in America is 2.5 per 1,000.[11] That means that there are over 2.4 million divorces per year. Or, every thirty-six seconds. (We will discuss this further, but there are some critical reasons for the phenomenon that don't include wedded bliss for our younger generations. Millennials are getting married later and living together in greater numbers without getting married.)

xviii ～ Preface

When you take a closer look, the divorce rates for people over age forty-five continue to rise since the 1990s. Interestingly, marriage rates for older people have fallen. A University of Michigan study showed that 74 percent of senior citizens in 1974 said they expected to get married again whereas in 2020, only 71 percent said they expected to remarry.[12] Many older couples decide not to get married because they don't want to lose financial support, like spousal Social Security benefits or a former spouse's pension.

Now hold on to your hats. Looking at the stats for first marriages, only 41 percent are likely to end in divorce. The percentages go up with second marriages, with 60 percent divorcing. But when you look at third marriages, 73 percent will divorce. (I can attest to that one!)

Hey, it may be that Bill and Melinda Gates or Jeff Bezos and MacKenzie Scott, or even Al and Tipper Gore metaphorically said to each other: "Please pass the butter. . ." Of course, many nonbillionaires face this situation, but it's fun, or possibly comforting to think that even the ultra-rich have the same problems as we have.

Competitive Marriage Syndrome[13]

Many of us were covertly or overtly told that, as a woman, we were supposed to take a backseat to a man. I remember my mom telling me to always let the boys win at sports and not appear too intelligent in front of my dates. Ouch. These were conflicting messages because she raised me always to support myself and not to rely upon a male for that. I guess "support" also meant not to surpass what he could provide.

These mixed messages are tough to incorporate into our lives. She raised me to never to be afraid and to know that I could be anything and do anything. But the flipside came when my first husband wanted a divorce and my mother immediately said, "Of course he does. You are more successful and earn more money."

One woman even told me that, when she was discussing her divorce with her therapist, he said, "Of course your husband wanted a divorce. You were smarter, more successful, and earned more. No man would be able to deal with that. You should make sure that if you ever marry again, you don't earn more than he does."

The good news is that she never went back to that doctor.

In today's world, these subtle, or not so subtle, messages can still be seen. Women are out there in every profession and are successful. Very successful. That means that in many cases they are more successful than their spouses.

Preface ~ xix

I'd like to believe that we have grown up enough where this is not even an issue, but I'd be naïve to suggest that.

A University of Chicago Booth School of Business study found that when a wife earns more than her husband, those marriages are 50 percent more likely to end in divorce.[14] The study explains several reasons for this tension. There are the societal expectations of a traditional marriage, where the man is the breadwinner, and this leads to him digging in on gender roles, leading to arguments.

In 1960, only 3.8 percent of wives earned more than their husbands, but by 2020, a TD Ameritrade survey, as reported in *USA Today*, found that the number of female breadwinners jumped to 21 percent and the number is increasing.[15]

The *American Sociological Review* reported that when a wife outearns her husband, he is more likely to cheat. In fact, about 15 percent of men in the study who were 100 percent financially dependent on their wives had affairs.[16] There seems to be a masculinity threat, as they feel they are "feminized" in their inability to earn a larger salary. The affairs may be a way for men to prove themselves as "virile" by engaging in sexual conquest.

Another study by the American Psychological Association found that often men's self-esteem is reduced if their partner is more successful, whereas women's self-esteem is not affected by their partner's success.[17] Men are three times more likely than high-earning wives to stray; high-earning wives had the lowest cheating rates of any population. Among the wives who earned a higher paycheck, only 5 percent cheated.

Our society is slow to change. Many men still define their identity in terms of career and their earning power. They may feel threatened when their financial superiority is questioned and may start to sabotage the relationship.

Be Honest

How many people roll their eyes when they find out that the man is staying home to take care of the kids? Or they may do even a more exaggerated eye roll that turns into a lip-purse when they find out that he is a day worker, and she is a corporate executive? Come on, fess up. These old cultural stereotypes are Velcro to us. But we can tear them off.

We need to shake off this old baggage and be who we are and appreciate our spouse for his choice of career. We all need the words of Michele Obama to resonate with us. She notably said, when looking at owning her success,

xx ～ Preface

"Am I good enough? Yes, I am."[18] Stand in that place and never apologize for being successful and being who you are. Own it. Money is not life's report card for women (and don't raise your children to think that it is).

Women Hang On

Even if a man is cheating on his wife, women tend to hang on longer than men in the same situation. Why?

Women may still love their spouse and may be willing to forgive him. Or, they could just be naïve and listen to his excuses and lies, and take on the blame for his behavior, believing it was their fault. We know that women hang on because of the children. A mother may be more willing to sacrifice her own self-esteem and happiness for the sake of the kids. She may be afraid of the effects a broken family may have on the kids. One big reason, and the one that I'm going to focus on, is that women may be financially dependent upon their spouse and feel that they can't survive financially without him.

Interestingly, other stats show that women and men cheat at the same rate within a marriage, although the reasons given are different.[19] The most common reason a woman gives is emotional dissatisfaction. Not surprisingly, 60 percent of affairs begin at work. Seventy-four percent of men say that they would be more likely to cheat if they knew they wouldn't get caught. Sixty-eight percent of women said they would do the same.

As discussed above, many women do hold on to their cheating husbands. The above stats on the income disparity skew toward cheating husbands giving justification because their wives earn more.

Many of you may stand by the adage that, "If he cheated once, he will do it again." *Psychology Today* has reported this fact.[20] Many women, when they catch their husbands cheating, can even get embarrassed and scared to be viewed as weak if they don't kick him to the curb. I'm not going to sit in judgment about what decision you make. I only want you to be protected economically. By the way, the magazine notes that "They (men) may or may not be a cheater again."

Women hold on to cheating husbands because:

- They still love their husband.
- They are concerned about the impact on the kids.
- They don't want a broken family.
- They can't deal with the pressure from friends and family who want them to stay together.

- They are scared that they can't survive financially on their own.
- They fear the whole divorce process, and they don't think they can navigate it.

I'm going to help you with the last two points. It may seem impossible now, but sometimes your hardest moments can lead to your greatest success and empowerment. Just keep going, one step at a time. You will come out of your gray divorce much stronger. A plan will help you move forward and help you to decide if you want to proceed with a divorce.

Rosa Parks said, "I have learned over the years that when one's mind is made up, this diminishes fear; knowing what must be done does away with fear."[21] I hope to diminish the economic fear and help you navigate your process to financial freedom. One step you will take is to design your own Money Map. Think of that as your guiding light or GPS for your financial future.

Now What?

I'm not going to deal with the psychological impact on your life. I know it sucks. Really sucks, but that is not the focus of my book. I'm a money expert who has coached millions of women, kids, and their families over the years to take charge of their financial lives. That's what I'm going to do here. I'm going to deal with the monetary impact of gray divorce.

I'll give you advice if you are just thinking about divorce. I'm also going to hopefully head you off at the pass before you or your spouse asks you to "Please pass the butter." But, if you are knee-deep in "passing the butter," I'll also be there to give you valuable suggestions about how you can get off your assets and look at the monetary impact of gray divorce while you are in the throes of it; and then when you are finished and can take a deep breath and start fresh. I will speak to you in an objective, dispassionate way so you can protect yourself and move forward and design a wonderful new life. (Okay, maybe not so dispassionately, because I am passionate about being there for women who are going through this.) My goal is to help you to become financially resilient during any stage of gray divorce. This is my mission, my commitment.

Regardless of your stage in this gray-divorce journey, you will come away with a plan, your plan. Pablo Picasso said it best, "Our goals can only be reached through a vehicle of a plan, in which we must fervently believe, and upon which we must vigorously act. There is no other route to success."[22]

xxii ⌒ Preface

My book is also for your adult kids who see you going through the process, in addition to friends who are your support structure during this challenging time. As a spouse, you may not be looking at your divorce in a realistic way and need advice from loved ones who may be seeing a potential trainwreck that could be on the horizon for you.

Here is the tough part. You have been used to exploring problems together with your spouse. You have been each other's support structure. You had each other's backs during tough times. But this is not the time to turn to him. This is not the time to do this together. You need to be strong and fearless. It's not wise to be each other's advisors. I will help you to find another support structure: Team You. You must understand that we are talking about money. Money is the business side of any relationship. Your kids can also take some tips and hopefully learn from your experience, and you can give them some advice.

I know you can do this. Keep in mind the words of former head coach of the Seattle Seahawks football team, Pete Carroll, "Each person holds so much power within themselves that needs to be let out. Sometimes they just need a little support, a little nudge, a little direction, a little coaching, and the greatest things will happen."[23]

It may feel like I'm taking a while to get into the meat of the issue in dealing financially with gray divorce. That's because I intentionally am. You need the background to understand how you feel and start to look at how you got here and why. Holding the mirror up to yourself will empower you to shed the old paradigms and give you strength to know that you can and will move forward to design your best life.

Note to readers: I want to be sensitive to any person's sexual or gender bias, whether they are same sex or other sex coupled in any manner or form. I am writing mostly to women, but that designation refers to attitudes and feelings, not to biology or any other social construct. I will refer to women and wives in this book, as the people I'm speaking to. But in no way will I define that for you. You get to define that and hopefully you will resonate with this knowing that I refer to men and women, and husbands and wives with the utmost of respect of how you define these titles for yourself.

Why Am I Qualified to Support and Nudge You through Your Gray Divorce?

Besides being a money expert, I've been married three times and have been divorced three times, and two of those have been gray divorces. The most recent marriage and divorce was unique in the way it happened. My almost eighty-year-old husband totally blindsided me as he texted me that he wanted a divorce. Yup, TEXTED me. It was a quick, "Please pass the butter," and his kids were coaching him on the passing, and they were holding a sharp butter knife. So, I get it. I've also spoken to hundreds of women over the years who have shared their stories with me and some of the lessons they would have liked to have known before, during, and after their gray divorce. Their first comment is always, "Neale, where was your book when I was going through my divorce?" That's what this book is about. I'll be there with you every step of the way.

If you are one of many women who have left the money decisions to him, this book is for you. If you are one of most women who earned less than he did, this book is for you. If you are not sure what you should be financially considering before, during, or after your gray divorce, this book is for you. If you are comfortable hearing all this advice from a trusted expert in the money field, who has been helping people to raise financially responsible children for the last thirty-five years and has been through this: This book is for you.

The book will contain lots of quizzes to help you explore your financial personality, the baggage you carried into your relationship, the baggage you collected during your relationship, how prepared you are financially for a divorce, what you need to concentrate on, goal setting, and so on. It will also contain worksheets so that you can feel confident going into a meeting with your team and explore the right questions leading to the right answers. I have collected stories over the years from real people experiencing gray divorce, and these are important to include so that you know you are not alone and can identify with others who have been down this path.

Let's get started.

Who the Hell Am I?

My explanation may seem drawn out; however, in today's world, there are many "so-called experts" popping up. Thousands of followers on Instagram or TikTok is not an indicator that someone knows anything about a respective topic. It's important for you to have confidence in the person who is speaking to you. I'm not just an Influencer, I'm real; I know my stuff and I care.

Dubbed "The Goddess of Money" by a national talk show host, I have indeed been advising, coaching, and supporting people for almost fifty years to design their financial lives. I began my professional career in 1972 joining The Chase Manhattan Bank to become one of the first female executives

xxiv ～ Preface

in banking in the United States. I did become an executive and headed up a $10 billion division. I left after thirteen years after smashing into and not through the glass-ceiling and became president and CEO of The First Women's Bank. We needed a women's bank because the Fair Credit Reporting Act had not been enacted. Before 1974, women couldn't get credit under their own name. My first credit card at Chase had my husband's name on it because I legally could not have credit! (My then-husband had no credit because he was a law student.) The graduate students I mentor at Columbia University are always shocked to hear this anecdote.

While at The First Women's Bank, I was immersed in the women's movement, dealing with the icons such as Gloria Steinem, Betty Friedan, Muriel Siebert, Bella Abzug, and even Madonna. I was deemed to be the highest-ranking woman in finance in the United States and became a public face for the women's money movement. When I was the president of The First Women's Bank, there were fifteen thousand commercial banks in the United States; however, there were six female bank presidents. I was the only one who did not inherit my bank from a deceased male father or husband.

As an advocate for empowering women and their children to take charge of their financial life, I saw women uncomfortable in handling their own money. My research showed that it was because we were not taught anything about money as kids.

At this time, I went through my first divorce and became a single mom of two young kids. I learned about all the protections I should have put in place before and during my thirteen-year marriage; but naivety and youth had gotten in my way. I looked for books to teach my own kids about money so they could be raised with all the lessons I missed. There were no books to teach kids about money; it was not a topic we taught at home or at school. My then three-year-old child quipped, "Mommy, why don't you write the books?" Out of the mouth of babes. In response to this need to educate our kids about money . . . I did. I created the topic of teaching kids about this important topic when I opened a real bank for kids at FAO Schwarz in NYC in 1988 and an Institute for Youth Entrepreneurship in Harlem to bring at-risk kids into the economy. Princess Diana even opened accounts for the royal children at The First Children's Bank!

In total, I have written twenty-eight books, including curricula, lesson plans, and teacher's guides. I'm a *New York Times* #1 best-selling author. I morphed into becoming an entrepreneur, who created this topic of teaching kids and their parents about money as my life's work. The exciting news is that this is now a mainstream topic. No one will ever ask, "Why is it important to raise financially responsible kids?"

Preface xxv

But my job is not finished.

You may have seen me in and on various media. I have appeared extensively on TV, radio, and in other media throughout my career. I appeared on *Oprah* thirteen times. I was also a regular on *Good Morning America*, *The Today Show*, CNBC (I had my own show), CNN, and Fox, and starred in my own PBS Special: *Your Money, Your Children, Your Life.*

I have also been a national spokesperson for companies and organizations who share my passion to educate women and our next generation to be financially independent. Some of those are Microsoft, Fidelity, Lincoln Financial, UPS, American Bankers Association, MasterCard, Coca-Cola, AIG, Aetna, Hartford Insurance, among others.

I have been honored with such awards as Woman of the Year, Banker of the Year, UN Child Advocate of the Year, Muriel Siebert Lifetime Achievement Award in Financial Literacy, UN Femme Award, 50 Best Female Entrepreneurs in NJ, Outstanding Service Toward Financial Literacy, United Negro College Fund, Women of Influence Award, Commerce and Industry Association of NJ, National Honoree, Women in Business, and Garden State Woman of the Year. I have served on the boards of UNICEF, UNWomen, NY Board of Trade, YPO Women's Business Network, YPO Metro, Morris County Chamber of Commerce, National Urban League Guild, and New Jersey's State Employment and Training Commission Council on Gender Parity in Labor and Education. I am a member of YPO and previously of CEO. I also am an advisor to such companies as GreenLight, DriveWealth, OneEleven, Toekenz, and EarlyBird.

I am currently an Executive in Residence and an Innovation Fellow at Columbia Graduate School of Business. I mentor at a graduate level. I also assist with teaching and mentoring in a class called "Think Bigger: The Innovation Method." I am also part of a program, V-WISE, out of Syracuse University, Whitman School of Business, working with female vets to help them to become entrepreneurs.

I wrote five times a month for *Forbes* from 2010–2018 and reached over 8 million readers. I was a syndicated columnist for the Associated Press and *Huffington Post*. I now write a monthly column for *Kiplinger Magazine*. My article on gray divorce in *Kiplinger* garnered so much interest that Lisa Kiplinger, my editor, reached out to tell me it was time to write this book.

But with this, I've been married and divorced three times, and two of them, as explained, were gray divorces. The first divorce made me gray, but that is another story. This all means that I have "Been there, done that, and got the t-shirt." I can relate my personal stories and have the expertise to give you guidance and real financial advice. I explain all of this because you need xxvi ～ Preface

to have confidence in the person who will take you on this very personal journey of yours.

Totally, I have served over 20 million women, parents, and kids via my books, articles, and programs. I'm now ready to help you with your gray divorce.

Enough about me . . .

Is Gray Divorce a Real Problem?

I said this before, but it is worth repeating. Every thirty-six seconds, there is a divorce in America, which translates to more than 876,000 divorces per year.[24] Almost 50 percent of all marriages in the United States will end in divorce.[25] Here is the shocker: 73 percent of third marriages will end in divorce (that's where I fit).[26] Almost one out of every four divorces in the United States are "gray."

The good news is that the overall divorce rate has declined, but the bad news is that the divorce rate for older generations (gray divorce) has increased.[27] (It's not a real decline, because other factors are in play, as stated before, like Millennials are getting married later.) The significant fact is that 66 percent of wives are the ones who most often file for gray divorce.[28] That number has grown to 75 percent in recent years. AARP has reported that 66 percent of women who divorce after age forty say that they initiated their divorce.[29] Even prepandemic, in 2017, about 1 million couples called it quits.

Do Women Need Financial Advice in a Gray Divorce?

Yes. In fact, it's YES. UBS Global Wealth Management found that 54 percent of women over fifty-one years old say they leave their money decisions to their spouses.[30] This is particularly tough when you are going through a divorce and may not have a handle on the past and current financial situation in your family. This really means that most women facing gray divorce will be financially navigating all of this in the dark. Also, Nationwide Advisory Solutions found that 62 percent of women have a plan to help protect themselves against outliving their savings, which is great, versus 76 percent of men.[31] Unfortunately, I feel women think they have a plan, like counting on their partner; consequently, they don't really have a plan.

The numbers show clearly that the economic cost of divorce (all divorce) falls more heavily on women. After separation, women experience a sharper decline in household income and a greater poverty risk than men. A women's standard of living is estimated to decline by 27 percent in divorce, where

Preface ~ xxvii

a man's is expected to increase by 10 percent. We can easily conclude that women would welcome some sound advice before they find themselves in this situation. This is why I'm here.

We know that women live longer and will therefore have greater health-care challenges and costs. This is borne out by the fact that the study cited above also found that women are more reliant upon Social Security as their primary source of guaranteed income. We know that almost 94 percent of women will be financially responsible for themselves at some point, according to a Bank of America study,[32] but this process is accelerated in a divorce.

Women suddenly find themselves dealing with issues of abandonment, grief, anger, and fear. On top of that, many women are having to all of a sudden take on financial responsibilities as well. The world of money may be totally new to them, or at least a new world for them. It's filled with jargon that only exacerbates their insecurities.

Then there are the surprises. Some women have found out that their husbands have high debt, outdated documents, and even hidden accounts. My mom faced her gray divorce at almost fifty when she suddenly found out that her husband, my dad, had borrowed tons of money from his mother and her parents. We almost lost our home because he had remortgaged it, unbeknownst to my mother. In one day, she found out that we were facing bankruptcy. Were it not for my father's brother, Uncle K, who stepped in and paid the mortgage, we would have been left homeless.

I was a child of sixteen and watched my mom dissolve and later pick herself up. She was alone. She had to reinvent her life. If you asked her, she would have said that it was important for women to get involved in the family finances. In fact, nearly 60 percent of divorcees or widows regret they had not been more involved in the money side of their married lives.[33] A whopping 98 percent of them urge other women to become more involved early on in their marriage. That is how I was raised, because I watched my mother dissolve, and I don't want that to happen to you.

Many men have been paying more attention to their finances than women. Women will tend to focus on the latest emergency facing the family. Their kids need new sports equipment, or the prom is coming up. What gets tapped into? A woman's money set aside for her retirement is tapped. One result? Men have over three times more retirement savings than women.[34]

One other reason women save less is that they earn less, and if women drop out of the workforce to raise kids, they also have less. It's better today than it was when it comes to gender pay parity; but we are still not there. Today, women earn 82 cents for every dollar a man earns.[35] It's even worse for people of color, and it's not okay.

SECTION 1

BEFORE YOUR GRAY DIVORCE

SECTION I

BEFORE YOUR GRAY DIVORCE

CHAPTER 1

~

What Is a Gray Divorce?

Gray divorce is basically, divorce after fifty. But, it's not so simple. It's important to give a contextual reference for you so that you can identify with the situation you are in: thinking about gray divorce; are you in it now; or have you been through one.

Why do two people in a long-term relationship decide to part ways, and maybe begin to "pass the butter?" Most marriages find a rhythm; a cadence and stay in the daily perpetual motion of their lives. But something has changed with the metronome of long-term marriages. Today, many older couples are making the decision to leave. That is why the divorce rate of couples over fifty has doubled since 1990.

Couples are not simply drifting apart. They are making the overt choice to change the course of their lives. They have come to the realization that their marriage doesn't work for them. They have lots of life to live and want the space and time to gain happiness and fulfillment. It may be an individual choice or as a couple, like in the case of Bill and Melinda, who seemed to have reached it together.

Some psychologists feel that many couples are reevaluating their relationship in real time, which is a relatively new phenomenon. Many of you may no longer remain tight-lipped and sucking up a maybe, dull, loveless existence. You may feel you don't have to live out what could seem like a life sentence of boredom, or living with a tightwad, or an overspender, or an unfaithful or controlling spouse.

Scott Galloway, in his article in *Medium*, "The Case to Rebrand 'Divorce,'" calls this "conscious uncoupling."[1] He also mentions that divorcing couples should be aware of the fact that the financial cost of divorce is expensive as well. The median US divorce costs $7,500. I also love how

4   ～   Chapter 1

Galloway mentions that there still is a lingering stigma and shaming around divorce. He mentions that "Frequently on administrative forms, the options for marital status are single, married, divorced. (How is 'divorced' a status? Isn't that just single?)"

The other thing is that the taboo and stigma of divorce, although still there, is fading. People understand that you can redesign your life, change it, and experience a new phase, or new things with new people. You may even be beginning to question the thought around "'til death do us part." That may be a myth to question: That there is only one person out there for you . . . forever.

You now can accept that you can reinvent yourself and discover new talents and new things to make you happy. The rules can be broken. There is a lot of life to still live, and you should live it. Some things just come with an expiration date, and you must look at that maybe old, stale box of marriage.

Quiz: Are You Ready for a Gray Divorce?

Take this short quiz to see if you may be a candidate for a gray divorce. Some of it is fun. You might need to laugh and cry through this process.

Just answer Yes or No to these questions.

ARE YOU READY FOR A GRAY DIVORCE?

1. Do you and your husband feel it hard to find conversation now that the kids have flown out of the nest? — Yes / No

2. When you think about really considering divorce, do you immediately reach for your antacid? — Yes / No

3. Has the flame gone out of your relationship? — Yes / No

4. Do you fight over the same things you have been fighting about for years without any resolution? — Yes / No

5. Are you bored hearing your husband talk about the same old things he has always talked about? — Yes / No

6. Do his habits, which you used to overlook, now drive you nuts? — Yes / No

7. Have you tried marriage counseling, and it hasn't worked? — Yes / No

8. Is irreconcilable anger or abuse part of your relationship? — Yes / No

9. Do you hide bills from him or things you have bought because you don't want to suffer his wrath or judgement? — Yes / No

10. Are you emotionally exhausted by trying everything you can to save the marriage, but you feel you are at the-end-of-your-rope? — Yes / No

11. If you ask about money issues, does he brush you off by saying that "You never cared before," or "Don't worry, you are taken care of."   Yes   No

12. Have you found your old wedding dress in the closet, and rather than wanting to save it for an heirloom to pass down to your kids, you now want to have it used as kindling?   Yes   No

13. Have you rewatched the movie *Under the Tuscan Sun* because Diane Lane is your new hero? (The Italian lover sounds fun, coupled with fabulous food. You can skip the Vespa, but the new dream sounds promising and not a shared dream with the boring old guy across you at the breakfast table.)   Yes   No

14. Have you put off this divorce conversation because you fear how your kids, friends, and spouse may react?   Yes   No

15. Do you think you should suck it up because you are not smart or gutsy enough to live on your own?   Yes   No

Results: Obviously, this is a quiz to help you start looking at your plight in life. There are no right or wrong answers. Like any life decision, you must weigh its importance for yourself. There will be ramifications, maybe seismic ones. But that is not a reason to stay put in a life that you know is not right for you. Any divorce is situational, and your situation will be unique. You want to be as self-reflective as you can and avoid any knee-jerk reactions because you may be coming from a place of hurt, anger, and hopelessness.

CHAPTER 2

'Til Death Do You Part

Not so much. I will continue to repeat this. In the past twenty-five years, the divorce rate for Americans over the age of fifty has doubled, and more than tripled for those over the age of sixty-five.[1]

"At a time when divorce rates for other age groups have stabilized or dropped, fully one out of every four people experiencing divorce in the United States is 50 or older, and nearly one in 10 are 65 or older," according to a report by Susan L. Brown and I-Fen Lin,[2] sociologists at Bowling Green State University. Back in 1990, fewer than one in ten persons who got divorced were over the age of fifty. The research went on to note that it wasn't just remarried older people who were getting divorced—more than half of all gray divorces are with couples who have been married for over fifty years.

As a side note, it's interesting that our Millennial kids are getting married later and divorcing less than my generation is. Obviously, if there are fewer marriages, there will be fewer divorces. In 2018, a record 35 percent of Americans ages twenty-five to fifty, or 39 million people, had never married.[3] The Baby Boomer parents are reversing these stats for themselves.

"He slurps his soup, she nags him about not putting the dishes in the sink, he doesn't understand me . . ." I get that. I thought after twenty years, the "soup slurping" and "dirty dishes left on the table" just get to be part of the daily married-life-ballet. You have history, kids, family, illness, and frankly have lived through a lot of drama that life throws your way.

Regardless of whether you are initiating your divorce, the feelings will be intense for everyone involved. Throw a dose of *guilt-gasoline* on the fire; it flares and even gets more heated. You will have to be resilient. Get out the fire-extinguisher, and don't fan the flames.

10 ～ Chapter 2

You may start feeling like a strange person trying to get this new life via your new divorce. I always take solace in the fact that I am not the only crazy out there. *Marie Claire* has compiled some of the weirdest reasons to divorce that may make you feel sane and collected.[4]

Weird Reasons for Divorce That Should Make You Feel Sane

- Former White House Communications Director Anthony Scaramucci's wife divorced him as soon as she found out that he was going to work for Donald Trump. By the way, he didn't last long, but the divorce did.
- A UK woman filed for divorce because her husband wanted her to dress up like a Klingon and speak to him in Klingon.
- A woman divorced her husband after he told her he didn't like the movie *Frozen*. The woman concluded that his indifference toward Elsa shows that there is something wrong with him as a human being.
- Judge Judy divorced her first husband because he viewed her career as a hobby.
- A ninety-nine-year-old Italian man filed for divorce after he found out that his ninety-six-year-old wife had written to her lover in the 1940s. It is thought that this couple holds the record for the world's oldest divorce. Talk about gray divorce?

CHAPTER 3

～

A Leopard Can Change His Spots

There are several factors that are converging today to make us reevaluate divorce. The stigma of divorce is disappearing. Even Pope Francis and the Catholic Church are reexamining their posture toward the church's stance on divorce.[1] People are also living longer and the prospects of remaining in an empty relationship doesn't bode well for many people today. People are allowed to act to change their future. In her study, Brown references, "one reason for this (gray divorce) is the increasing economic independence of women. Many women no longer must choose between a bad marriage and poverty."

Are people expecting more of a sense of happiness and fulfillment today than they were before? I think so. And it seems that couples are just not willing to put up with an "Irish Divorce," which is a bad marriage. The Urban Dictionary describes this term with words like: "the not-divorce marriage," "abandoned," "deserted," "dumped," "loveless marriage."[2] You may have grown up seeing your parents or your friend's parents going through the motions of marriage, and not engaged in a loving partnership. Have you ever been out at a restaurant and seen couples eating and not interacting at all? Many of you may just have thought that was the way advanced married couples act; that this was the way it was supposed to be. It's not.

The advent of easy online dating may also have given older people hope for a better relationship down the road. The prospect of living with someone you no longer love and respect appears to not be a sacrifice worth making for many. Online dating is accepted and is the norm for all age groups. Seniors are also meeting via activities and travel, and just being out-and-about.

A report shows that 29 percent of seniors have gone on a date with someone they met online.[3] What's interesting is that 45 percent of Millennials said the same; not a huge difference. We are more comfortable with the

12 ～ Chapter 3

Internet and what it has to offer, as 87 percent of those over the age of fifty use it.

Where are you in the gray divorce process?

- Thinking about it
- Knee-deep in the process
- Coming out of it

When you think of your financial situation, do you feel any of the following emotions?

- Confident
- Excited
- Terrified
- Overwhelmed
- Confused
- I want to burst into tears
- I'm so angry
- I feel betrayed by my ex
- I need ice cream

This is partly fun, but it should also be provocative to make you think about your feelings. You may be feeling all these things together; it's natural, so don't worry.

CHAPTER 4

Busting the Money Marriage Myths

Let's take a moment to examine some of the *marriage myths* you may be carrying around and that are nagging at you that somehow this divorce is "Your Fault." Some of the financial stories that people have shared with me may resonate with you.

- *Myth:* You'll live happily ever after.
- *Myth:* You'll be able to change your partner's annoying habits.
- *Myth:* The man should handle the money.
- *Myth:* He told me not to worry, I'd be taken care of.
- *Myth:* Women are not good with money.
- *Myth:* If he loves you, he should know your needs.
- *Myth:* If you are in love, you shouldn't argue about money.
- *Myth:* All financial assets should and will be split evenly.
- *Myth:* Kids will make the marriage better, in fact, they can fix a bad marriage.
- *Myth:* Combining families with kids should work if you and your husband love each other.
- *Myth:* The finances of blended families will just work themselves out.

Back to the Future

Many of these money and marriage myths are based upon the way we were raised. We watched our parents just assume roles. Then you grew up and moved out and, suddenly, you hear your mothers' words coming out of your mouth. It may be more than that . . . you may see your mothers' actions taking over, as well. Some things are great, like "Clean up your room. An uncluttered room is an uncluttered mind." Or, "A penny saved is a penny

14 ～ Chapter 4

earned." But the issue is that these little nuggets of advice can morph into rules, and you can carry this unexamined baggage into your marriage. These assumptions and rules may set your patterns for life.

Let's take a break and look at how you grew up and how the money patterns were established in your life. These may be baggage that you are carrying around that you may want to examine.

YOUR PARENTS AND MONEY

1. **Finances in my home were managed by:**
   a. Dad.
   b. Nobody! My parents handled the finances as they came up, and whoever got the angriest won.
   c. My parents. We discussed everything and made up a budget and savings plan together.

2. **My mother:**
   a. Had no money in her own name.
   b. Had a joint checking/savings account with my father.
   c. Had her own bank account(s).

3. **My parents:**
   a. Never talked about money.
   b. Argued a lot about money.
   c. Discussed financial decisions.

4. **My mother's response when I asked to buy something was:**
   a. "Ask your father."
   b. "We can't afford it."
   c. "Let's see how it fits into our budget and what you're going to contribute."

5. **Our household budget was made by:**
   a. Dad.
   b. Mom, but she had to negotiate and cajole for every expense.
   c. The family: money was considered a shared resource.

Busting the Money Marriage Myths ~ 15

6. Discussion of money in front of the kids:
   a. Was never done.
   b. Was something Mom did behind Dad's back.
   c. Was done openly.

7. If the family next door purchased the latest technology:
   a. Dad would decide that we could or couldn't get one. There was no discussion.
   b. Mom would bust Dad's chops until we got one.
   c. There'd be a family discussion of where it fit into our budget and how everyone would contribute.

8. When Dad was offered a new job:
   a. We would move at Dad's convenience.
   b. We did move, and Mom never forgave Dad; we wouldn't move, and Dad never forgave Mom.
   c. We discussed and planned the move until we reached a mutual family decision.

9. The picture we had of our family's overall condition was:
   a. We were well off and Dad would provide for us.
   b. We were having financial difficulties. Mom never seemed to have confidence in Dad.
   c. Mom and Dad were open about what we could afford; we knew we had a plan that would keep us clothed, housed, and educated.

10. When the subject of money came up, my father's response to my mother would likely be:
   a. "Don't worry your pretty little head about it."
   b. "Get off my back."
   c. "Let's sit down and discuss it."

16 ~ Chapter 4

No Worries

You are just looking back to see how you were raised and reflecting on what you took into your future money life with your husband. There are no right or wrong answers.

How to Look at the Quiz

If many of your answers were *a*, you probably came from a rigidly traditional household where the father controlled the purse strings and money was not talked about. The baggage from this household contains lace collars and high button shoes that Grandma wore, alongside Grandpa's starched collars. To break free from that notion that there's safety and security in not knowing anything about money, you are going to have to find new patterns for yourself that will reflect your new financially independent self.

If most of your answers were *b*, you probably came from a household with a transitional, but still rigid household, where money was not a comfortable subject. This is the dark side of old traditions. This one can even be harder to shed, because you may be afraid that conflict, danger, and hurt may result if you start taking too much of an interest in the details of your own financial life. This one leads to financial infidelity, a dangerous situation to be in for any marriage.

If more of your answers were *c*, you probably came from a household with a more relaxed, open attitude toward money. This doesn't mean you won't have any problems with money, but you may find it easier to bring them to the surface and deal with them. You were able to communicate about money in a safe place within the relationship. This one will be our focus.

Busting the Money Marriage Myths ~ 17

What Did I Know About My Family's Finances?

When I was growing up:

1. I knew how much my parents earned.
   Yes ☐ No ☐

2. I understood the cost of a new car.
   Yes ☐ No ☐

3. I knew whether my family owned or rented our home. Yes ☐ No ☐

4. I knew the amount of my family's monthly mortgage or rent payment. Yes ☐ No ☐

5. I understood my family's insurance coverage.
   Yes ☐ No ☐

6. I knew how much it cost to outfit me for grade school each year. Yes ☐ No ☐

7. If my family had financial difficulty, I knew about it, and understood the seriousness of our challenges.
   Yes ☐ No ☐

8. My parents discussed the provisions made for us (kids) in case anything happened to them.
   Yes ☐ No ☐

9. By the time I was in junior high, I was involved in my family's monthly budget and bill paying.
   Yes ☐ No ☐

10. By the time I was in high school, I was involved in my family's monthly budget and bill paying. Yes ☐ No ☐

18 ～ Chapter 4

If you answered *no* more often than *yes*, you grew up in a household where you were basically kept away from the household's fundamental driving mechanism—family finances. This is, to one degree or another, the way most of us of the fifty-plus generation was brought up. So, it's not surprising if some of these habits were carried into your marriage. Now suddenly, in a divorce, especially a gray divorce, you may find yourself behind the wheel of an immense machine and out in traffic. Don't beat yourself up. You were never given a learner's permit to navigate that new and large financial vehicle.

Financial Infidelity

Hidden money issues can tear the love out of a marriage. Financial infidelity is when you or your spouse may lie about money, or at least be secretive about it. It's a form of cheating, or "money adultery."

Have you or your spouse ever:

- Spent money without telling the other?
- Bought something and even told the kids or grandkids, "Don't tell your father (grandfather)?"
- Hidden bills from the other?
- Hidden assets from the other?
- Hidden cash from the other?
- Had a credit card that the other did not know about?
- Had a gambling problem and lied about it?
- Borrowed money from friends and not told your spouse?
- Had an investment or savings account that your spouse did not know about?
- Lied about the amount of money you earn, so you can hide some of it?

You get the point. This is financial deception, and it can lead to distrust and make any divorce even messier. A Harris Poll conducted for the National Endowment for Financial Education found that 85 percent of respondents said financial deception harmed or negatively affected their relationship. It's noteworthy that 52 percent said that this deception was worse than physical infidelity.[1]

When the poll asked why people lied, 38 percent said that they believed that some aspects should remain private and 34 percent said they had a fear that their spouse/partner would disapprove.

A look back may shed some light on how you want to move forward. You can't change the past, but you can change the future. And during this divorce process, you both will have to come clean with what financially has and has not been shared.

You are now going to have to deal with all your money issues, even if you don't want to. And it's important that you are prepared to do so. The time to learn the Heimlich maneuver is not when you're choking at the dinner table; it's before you sit down to eat. We need to listen to the words of Beyoncé, who said, "I truly believe that women should be financially independent from their men. And let's face it, money gives men the power to run the show. It gives men the power to define value. They define what's sexy. And men define what's feminine. It's ridiculous."[2]

Handling your own money and having the power over your own life and future is "The New Sexy." You can do it.

CHAPTER 5

~

History of Women and Our (Financial) Rights

Before you start to beat yourself up for being financially illiterate, or fearful of his reaction, and succumbing to the myth that men should handle the money, you must understand that this notion was built into the fabric of our nation and therefore into our daily lives and consequently into our behavior. Even considering women as financial equals is recent. So recent, that I still have shoes that are as old as the 1973–1974 Equal Credit Opportunity Act[1] that gave us the right to have our own credit in our own name.

If your kids start to mumble under their breath that you are out of date and trying too hard, show them this list:

Milestones for Women and Money

1963

The Equal Pay Act demanded equitable pay for the same work, prohibiting sex-based wage discrimination between men and women.

1971

Reed vs. Reed: The Supreme Court ruled it unconstitutional for states to give preference to males over females when appointing administrators of estates.

1974

The Equal Credit Opportunity Act made it illegal to require women to have a male co-signer when applying for credit, allowing women to get credit on their own.

1981

The Supreme Court overturned state laws that gave husbands unilateral control of jointly owned property.

2023

Women still earn 82 cents for every dollar a man earns. As a society, we haven't improved much from 2002, when women earned 80 cents to the dollar a man earned.

Breaking up Is Hard to Do

While we are at it, I'll outline the history of divorce. You may "lose" your head over the following timeline (pun intended).

1760 BC
The oldest codified divorce law was traced during the reign of King Hammurabi of Babylon. A man could divorce his wife by simply saying; "You are not my wife." He had to pay a fine and return the dowry. Women could also get a divorce, but it was a lot more complicated as she had to file a formal complaint, which was hard to prove because she needed witnesses, and you can imagine other men were not willing to testify.

1533
Henry VIII tried, unsuccessfully to force Pope Clement VII to annul his marriage to Catherine of Aragon. (The term was "annulment" and not "divorce" in those days.) The Pope refused and Henry broke with the Roman Catholic Church and declared himself the head of a new church, the Church of England. That new church granted the annulment. Henry VIII then married Anne Boleyn. Later, he didn't want to bother with divorcing her, so he just had her beheaded.

1643
This was the first recorded divorce in the American colonies. The divorce was granted to Anne and her husband Denis Clarke of the Massachusetts Bay Colony on the grounds that Denis abandoned his wife to be with another woman.

1839
The *Married Women's Property Acts* was enacted by individual states in the United States. It helped rectify some of the difficulties women faced with coverture. That is an English common law system that didn't allow a woman to own property, enter contracts, and otherwise act autonomously from her husband's will and authority.

1848
New York adopted a law in 1848 and women were allowed to own property. Before this, women were almost considered property of men, as in England.

1857
The Divorce and Matrimonial Causes Act, a divorce law, was enacted in England. Ordinary people could now get divorced. Before that, men could easily divorce if there was adultery, but women could only divorce if the man's adultery was compounded by another matrimonial offense.

24 ~ Chapter 5

1950s
The system of Family Court was established in the United States, and now hears divorce cases because the other courts couldn't accommodate the overflow. Heretofore, it could take a very long time to end a marriage.

1969
The Divorce Reform Act was passed, allowing couples to divorce after two years of separation, that is, no-fault divorce. California was the first state to enact no-fault divorce.

2010
New York was the last state to enact no-fault divorce.

2023
The steps to getting a divorce today are governed by state law and it can take time to understand these laws. The divorce takes place when the court legally ends your marriage by the signing of a divorce decree. In addition to ending your marriage, most divorces outline how your marital property is divided and other considerations. There are different types of divorce, including fault and no-fault divorces, and contested and uncontested.

There are standard marriages, common-law marriages, and domestic partnerships.

Standard marriage – A specific legal status that the state and federal government gives to couples. Some examples pertain to tax benefits and Social Security benefits.

Common-Law Marriage – A common-law marriage is an alternative to traditional marriage. Essentially, a couple who lives together for a specific period and presents themselves as married has certain rights. With a common-law marriage, the couple has never formally married, and they do not have a legal marriage license. A common-law marriage can become legal, depending upon the state. Once a common-law marriage is established, it is just as valid and legally binding as a traditional, legal marriage. This means that the divorce process will now be the same.

Domestic Partnerships – There are also domestic partnerships. These arrangements are not just for same-sex couples. Domestic partnerships are made up of two people of any gender, which includes male, female, or nonbinary people, who are living together. This term is often used in health insurance to describe who may be covered by a family health-insurance policy. There were glaring differences between domestic partnerships and legal marriages until the US Supreme Court declared that same-sex marriages were equal to opposite-sex marriages in the groundbreaking case *Obergefell v. Hodges* in 2015.[2]

The ending of a domestic partnership is not the same as a divorce. Not all domestic partners have to divorce. In most cases, depending upon your state, those partnerships that have lasted for fewer than five years, don't have children, and meet other financial and property requirements can fill out a "termination of domestic partnership" form with their Secretary of State.

Lots of Rules and Steps

Depending upon your state and its rules, here are some steps that you may encounter in a legal or common-law divorce:

- *Separation* – Divorce can't usually take place overnight. Many states require a waiting period, which is a certain amount of time required between when you leave the marital residence and/or the time you file for divorce. In some states, you must live apart, but in others you can do this in the same house.

  If you are legally separated, you have a written agreement or order about money and support, and custody, if applicable. This can be good if you have a spouse who is not being cooperative and denies the support you need.

  During your exploratory research with your attorney/mediator, you will understand the procedures required for your state.
- *Grounds for Divorce* – This is when you and your attorney decide if you want to file a petition to the court asking for a fault or no-fault divorce. All states allow no-fault divorces. This means that neither you nor your spouse are alleging any specific wrongdoing as justification for the divorce. It is a classic "Please pass the butter" divorce where you just want to move on with your life and there was no blame for the breakup.

  Fault divorces can be more complicated and therefore more expensive. You may consider this if you believe that your spouse is to blame for your breakup and if you think that this will influence the decision by the court on the asset split.
- *Filing for Divorce* – This is when the actual paperwork is filed with the court so that the formal process can begin. If your state requires a waiting period, you will have to prove that you have been separated for the required length of time before filing. If you don't really separate, you may have to start the process all over again.

26   ~   Chapter 5

- *Serving the Petition for Divorce* – When you file for divorce, your spouse must be formally notified. The sheriff can serve your spouse, or you can hire a process server. If you don't know where your spouse is, you still need to attempt to prove you tried to find him. The court may give you permission to publish notices in local newspapers.
- *Response or Default Divorce* – In most cases, when your partner is served, they have a set period to respond. If they do not respond, you can petition the court for a default or uncontested divorce. The court can decide how to proceed, but usually they award you what you want and finalize the divorce.

  If your spouse does respond, they will submit an "answer" to your petition and they have the right to agree or disagree with your claims.
- *Temporary Hearings* – In some cases, a temporary hearing will be held after the petition for divorce is filed but before the official court proceedings begin. The court will address issues that are important and can't be resolved until the trial begins. These matters could include custody of kids, temporary support, a restraining order if there was violence, restricting use of joint assets, and the splitting of expenses.
- *Discovery and Preparation* – Your attorney will begin to compile evidence and documentation once the case begins. They may have to subpoena documentation.
- *Settlement or Trial* – The final step involves the negotiation of the divorce settlement. If the divorce is uncontested, this process usually moves more quickly than if it is contested. If you cannot come to an agreement on the issues, you will need to have a trial. During the trial, each party will argue their case and the decision by the court will be made.

CHAPTER 6

~

Gender Roles Are Tough to Shake

Gender roles are ingrained in us from the time we were little kids. I'm guilty of falling back into these old paradigms. These all play on women's ability to step up to the plate to make financial decisions.

Let's look more closely at how you may have been raised: *Men were expected to be the financial provider.*

Obviously, I am a feminist. I have lived it all my life. That doesn't mean that I burned my bra, but I did march for a woman's right to choose about what happens to her body. I was never seen singing "I Am Woman Hear Me Roar." (Okay, I may have hummed it sometimes in business meetings.) I'm all in favor of a woman's right to earn her own salary (or not) and make her own choices. But even with all this autonomy and independence, old baggage can slip into my behavior.

One case in point was that I was raised to believe that "men were supposed to pay for dinner." In fact, when I was dating later in life, one of my dates asked me to split the bill . . . that was it for him. I'm not talking about someone who could not afford dinner, or a situation when I was young when we all pooled our change to buy food. I'm just talking about a situation where, when the bill came, he pushed it over to me and said, "Do you want to pay your half in cash or use a card?"

I was frankly really put off and probably heard the words of my mother saying, "Dump this man." Seriously, I stopped dating this person and told all my friends what a jerk-loser this guy was. They, of course, supported me. But if I really look at this, I was carrying around some old baggage and outdated paradigms.

My father handled the money, and my mother was sort of a stay-at-home-mom. She did work part time, and we had a nanny until things hit the fan.

28 ∼ Chapter 6

I grew up with a man handling the finances. I shook off this part of the money baggage paradigm when I started to earn money at age ten. I was a saver, even at that age. But my mother's etiquette training came from her baggage based upon the books by Emily Post,[1] the self-proclaimed guru of behavior in polite society. This self-absorbed socialite set rules that still influence us today at home and in the workplace.

Men Are the Breadwinners

Even today, many men are the main breadwinners, and that was certainly the case when I grew up. Obviously, the gender pay gap affects this, but also many women have had career breaks to raise the kids. But women are coming into their own. The stigma of women earning more than their husbands still haunts us.

It should be noted that prepandemic, two-thirds of mothers were either breadwinners or cobreadwinners for their families.[2] But women are still carrying baggage into their relationships feeling that "men should earn more." A 2018 paper from the United States Census Bureau entitled "Manning up and Womaning down: How Husbands and Wives Report Their Earnings When She Earns More" indicated that respondents told census people a different number representing their earnings than what employers reported to the IRS.[3] It was amazing. Women reported that they earned 1.5 percent less than they did, while their husbands inflated their own earnings by 2.9 percent.

Many men feel they should be the major breadwinners and say that "It feels natural to do this." And to be fair, the UBS study found that "71% of women want their husbands to provide them with a sense of financial security."

Again, I was certainly raised that way. What was interesting is that my mom, who later was "left" by my dad, raised me to be financially independent and have a career. She was trying to straddle two worlds, which many of you are doing. But even with her newfound need to make me equal, when I announced that I was going to marry my first husband, she said, "I'm not sure that this makes sense because you will always be more successful than he and that is not a good foundation for marriage."

Women Are Pulled in So Many Directions

Regardless of whether you have been working or not, you have many demands on your time. It may be that you feel you can do it all or it may be

Gender Roles Are Tough to Shake ⌒ 29

that your husband just relegated you to this role and you acquiesced; I'm not sure. Women take on most household duties, including childcare and chores.

I have written other books on this topic. In my book *Mom, Inc.: Taking Your Work Skills Home*, I recommend that women start to subcontract out some of the duties that they don't have to perform themselves. We don't have to be perfectionists and do every task. Of course, we can do it better . . . duh . . . but that is not the point. The point is to free up time for what is going to be more meaningful to us.

A wise Rabbi once told me that when I was pulled in so many directions to stop and examine the "pull." He said, "Ask yourself the question: *Does it matter profoundly?* If the answer is 'No,' look hard at this. You know that someone else can do that task." I had a bracelet made for myself with this saying on it, so I could always be reminded of this advice.

Gender Disparity Is Alive and Well

Women are still way behind men when it comes to earning money. We all have heard of the gender parity issues. They are real, and unfortunately still alive and well. I keep talking about my first real job at Chase. Yes, I'm venting, but it's important for you to have real stories.

When I began my career at age twenty-one and found myself at The Chase Manhattan Bank, I experienced it. I was accepted into the Global Credit Training Program, which was Chase's prestigious program to teach future executives how to lend money and to become *real bankers*. Chase decided to take a risk and hire a few women (very few); I was one of them. I was brought in at the same salary as the men; $11,000 a year. (Oh, go with me people . . . it was 1972. I Googled this and the Wage Index[4] [whatever that is] indicated that in 1972, the average wage was between $7,000 and $8,000 a year.) After about two weeks of being in the training program, the head of personnel called me in and said that I was taking the job of a man, and that Chase was going to reduce my salary to $6,500 a year. I asked what I had to do to earn what the men were earning, and she said; "Graduate first in the credit class." I did, and she didn't raise my salary. She went on to explain that I would never earn what the men did, because they were entitled to a career in a man's world, and I was not.

She was a woman of her word. I never earned what the men were earning. In fact, if you look at my lack of equal salary, bonuses, and future pension, this has cost me over $2 million dollars in lost income.

I'm not expecting a call from Jamie Dimon, CEO of JPMorgan Chase, to apologize for this and to write me a check . . . or maybe, I am?

30 ～ Chapter 6

Why am I jawing on about this? Because women still earn less than men and therefore will get less Social Security and pensions and will not have the retirement savings that men have. In 1972, women earned sixty-three cents for every dollar a man earned. It's better today, but we are still not there. Today, women earn eighty-two cents for every dollar a man earns. It's even worse, in some cases, for people of color.[5] Black women make sixty-three cents, Hispanic women make eighty-seven cents, Native American women make fifty-eight cents for every dollar a man earns.

Former Governor Chris Christie invited me to join his New Jersey Gender Parity Committee during his time as New Jersey governor. He asked me what my goals were on the Committee. I said, "That we don't need a gender parity committee and that women automatically get paid what men do." He felt that I was snarky in my retort. But isn't that the only point?

Pew Research Center reports that there is no single explanation for why progress toward narrowing the pay gap has stalled out.[6] Women generally begin their careers closer to wage parity with men but lose ground as they age. It's interesting, because women are more likely to graduate from college than men but the pay gap between college-educated women and men is not any narrower than the one between women and men who do not have a college degree.

One factor is clearly motherhood. Mothers ages twenty-five to forty-four are less likely to be in the labor force than women of the same age who do not have kids. This can reduce the earnings of some working mothers.

We Have Come a *Short Way,* Baby

We are making strides, but we are still behind men. There are only a little more than 10 percent of Fortune 500 companies run by women.[7] Many feel that they are still being pushed out of large corporations, even though the shove may be more subtle. The new world of entrepreneurship has seen great strides for women. Women started 49 percent of new businesses in the United States in 2021, up from 28 percent in 2019.[8] But still women receive less venture capital (VC) for those start-up businesses than their male counterparts. In 2018, of the $130 billion in VC given out, women only received a measly 2.2 percent.[9] In 2019, that number only rose to 17 percent of VC money going to females.[10] Gender bias is alive and well. We still have a *long way to go, baby*.

Where does that leave us as we face gray divorce? The Bureau of Labor Statistics shows that the median income for men who are sixty-five years and older is $53,000 today, and the average income for women of that age is approximately $39,000.[11]

Gender Roles Are Tough to Shake ～ 31

The Secret to Long Life: Dump Him

If you look at the stats for fifty-five to sixty-four-year-olds, the divorce rate climbed from 5 per 1,000 to 15 divorces per 1,000 marriages and for those sixty-five and older, it rose from 1.8 to 5 since 1990. This is mostly the baby boomer generation. We followed the script. If you went to college, part of your "job" was to graduate with a "Mrs." The stats bear witness to this; in 1970, there were almost 77 marriages for every 1,000 unmarried women. In 2017, the rate had dropped to approximately 32 marriages for every 1,000 unmarried women, a decrease of 58 percent.[12]

In my day, *nice girls* didn't live with men before marriage. Hell, *nice girls* were supposed to be married as virgins; forget living together, you were not even supposed to have sex before marriage. We know that many women didn't get that memo, but many did.

Remember the myth that married people live longer? Well, marriage seems to help men live longer, not women.[13] This is not the "big reveal" for women. The truth is that single women tend to live longer than married women. These are findings from Dr. Friedman in his book *Longevity Project: Surprising Discoveries for Health and Long Life* from the Landmark Eight-Decade Study.[14] He also found that women who act by leaving unsatisfying marriages also live longer.

The other thing to look at is that female suicides decrease by 8 percent to 16 percent when there is a divorce.[15] These stats cover all divorces, but we need to look at how many unhappy women can stay in a marriage that is not working or is abusive.

Here is one woman's story. I'll call her Ann.

I was giving a speech in Ohio some years ago and I was discussing "How to protect yourself in a divorce." This story was one of the catalysts for me writing this book, because it was so poignant, and frankly, universal.

I noticed that in the audience of about two hundred people, there was a woman who burst out in tears and got up abruptly and left. Sometime later she came back into the room and sat in the back, and I could see she was still dabbing her eyes as tears flowed down her cheeks.

After the speech, she lingered behind and sheepishly came up to me as I was packing up my things. I looked up at her and could feel her pain.

I asked her name, and she said it was Ann. I was trying to figure out a way to continue our conversation because I knew she wanted to talk. I said that I was dying for a cup of coffee and asked if she would like to join me. She acted surprised and said she would like that.

32 ～ Chapter 6

It took Ann a few minutes to share her story. She was sixty-three years old and had gotten married when she was nineteen. She and her husband had met when they were freshmen in high school. Ann always dreamed of becoming a nurse and her husband, Ray, was going to be a doctor.

The plan was to get married after she became a nurse and had worked for a while and Ray would be in medical school. Ann loved her nursing school and was first in her class while Ray was in undergraduate school studying biology.

Ann glanced down as she continued. She looked embarrassed as she told me, "I got pregnant during nursing school, and we had to get married." She went on to explain that she wanted to hire a neighbor to watch their daughter so she could finish school.

Ray said, "It's your job to raise our child, you can go back to nursing school later."

Well, Ann explained that "later" never happened. She got part-time work to help Ray pay for medical school, working in a local grocery store. She got pregnant with their second child, and her dream of becoming a nurse got pushed off even farther.

Ray graduated from medical school, and they moved to another city so he could do his internship and then residency. She was far away from her original nursing school, and she knew that too much time had passed for her credits to transfer. Whenever she brought this up to Ray, he would get angry and tell her that it was his job to earn the money and her job to raise the kids. She tried to explain to me that she loved being a mom, it was just that she also wanted to be a nurse.

One year turned into the next. She was a good mom. She told me all about raising two great kids; the holidays, the vacations, and how her kids excelled in sports and academically. She has no regrets.

When the kids were in high school, Ray's schedule got busier. He now had to work nights and would sometimes not come home until late. He seemed to have a short fuse and was always criticizing her. (You know where this is going.) She knew that they were drifting apart.

She told me that it was almost a cliché, but to earn extra money, Ray was paying their teenage son to detail the car. While diligently cleaning up the inside, he found a pair of women's undies in the glove compartment. Ray Jr., their unsuspecting son, brought the thong into the kitchen to chide his mom and said, "Hey, Mom, you left these in Dad's car, you wild and crazy lady."

Ann said she could not hide the look on her face, and her son said, "Mom, I'm really sorry, I thought they were yours."

Ann confronted Ray and he said that Ann had become dull and boring, gained some weight, and that he was entitled to a more exciting life. Ann said that this all unfolded over several months. She said that when she visited Ray at the hospital one day, it became obvious that he was having an affair with his head nurse. She said it was ironic.

They started the divorce process.

Gender Roles Are Tough to Shake ～ 33

Ann had always trusted Ray. That was the basis of their relationship. He broke the trust with his infidelity, but Ann told me that she questioned herself, and that maybe it was her fault. She had been uninterested in sex and "date night" had all but disappeared because Ray was working late, and her son needed to be taken to soccer games and she was exhausted. Their daughter had graduated from college and was living on her own.

Ann said that it was impossible to think that Ray would hurt her in a divorce. I could see how broken she was about all of this, even telling it as a story that happened years before. She said that it was hard to stop loving him; at least some of him. She kept saying, "I still loved the old Ray. And I believed that Ray would be fair to me."

She agreed to use Ray's lawyer. When I was giving my lecture earlier and said, "Never use your husband's lawyer," I had gone on to explain that "women look at divorce and money as a 'love and trust issue,' and men look at divorce and money as a 'business issue.' That's why women's standard of living goes down in a divorce, and men's goes up." She said that this resonated with her, and she felt so stupid. Ann realized that I had been describing her life and she was ashamed. That's when she dashed out of the room.

Well, Old Ray turned into New Ray and Ann got hurt. Really hurt. Ray said that he earned the money, and he was entitled to the lion's share. Ann was forced to leave the family home, which was put up for sale. She rented a small apartment near the high school where their son was going.

Ray earned $300,000 a year, and they had lived very well. Ray's attorney, who was also Ann's, said that alimony of $80,000 was more than fair for Ann. Ray had a lot of expenses, like liability insurance that he had to cover, and so forth.

Ann's Alimony	Gross Before Taxes = $80,000
Expenses	Annual Amount
Taxes	$18,000
Monthly rent @ $3,000/month	$36,000
Utilities, homeowners' insurance, phone, and internet @ $1,000/month	$12,000
Car lease @ $500/month	$6,000
Supplemental health insurance @ $500/month	$6,000
Food/sundries @ $500/month	$6,000
Total Expenses	$84,000

34 ～ Chapter 6

Let's look at some math here: Even though California is a 50-50 state in divorce, it's not that simple. Remember, alimony is deductible for Ray and taxable for Ann. She ran down her expenses quickly, but here is the summary, and we haven't even gotten to clothes, traveling to see her children, maybe an occasional night out, and certainly no emergency savings.

She started to sniffle again and said that she must dig into her part of the money from the sale of the house each month. She received $300,000 from the sale of the house (there was a huge mortgage) and she has been using at least $25,000 a year from that to make ends meet. She said she is scared.

A hug was in order, and that's what I gave her. We discussed her life moving forward and some of the things she could consider. I also shared a favorite quote by Jackie Joyner-Kersee: "It's better to look ahead and prepare than to look back and regret."[16] There was no reason for her to feel stupid. She was healthy and had two great kids and friends who also loved and supported her. And her story could help lots of other women.

I told her I was planning to write a book about gray divorce, and she quipped, "I needed that before I got into this mess." She did admit that besides the money panic, she really feels better without Ray. There is no one criticizing her or ignoring her. She admitted that if she had a better handle on her money and had a job, she would have left him first.

Pink, Blue, and Beyond

It's time to discard the gender stereotypes most of us grew up with. We hopefully have evolved beyond those. Interestingly a recent survey, that millennials are more likely to push back on gender stereotypes than Gen Z, but not when it comes to money.[17]

The *good news* is that 51 percent of those surveyed felt that traditional gender roles will seem outdated in ten years.

The *bad news* is that we are not there yet.

Scarlett O'Hara Should Be *Gone with the Wind*

You may have left the money issues to your husband, and just like Scarlett O'Hara: "You will worry about those money things some other time." Unfortunately, you are not alone. The UBS report found that 56 percent of married women still leave their investment decisions to men.[18] And here is the kicker: 61 percent of millennial women do so too, more than any other generation. We will explore some of the reasons why women, by default, have allowed or encouraged men to handle their financial lives. We will also explore why younger women are still carrying this baggage around and are maintaining the status quo, when they could and should be busting the myth that "Women are not good with money." Let's look at the reality. Women control about $22 trillion in wealth. That is 51 percent of the wealth we have in the United States.[19] That is considered *big bucks*, but many women still feel disempowered with money and are abdicating their role of responsibility.

Well, that time has come. You can't undo the past. But you can commit today to *kick the habit.*

Repeat after me: "I can take control of my financial life." We will bust some of these old myths: Together.

Ignore Those "Friends" Who Want to Give You Advice

Everyone is going to want to give you advice about your divorce and frankly about your life. You need to protect yourself from all that is flying around you. Some advice is good and helpful, and some is going to be hurtful, and frankly not only harmful, but stupid. I will discuss the helpful advice that you will get from *"Team You,"* but you are going to have to hold up your protective shield when you hear things, like:

- "Have you tried a couple's retreat?"
- "You know people change when they get older; you are getting older."
- "I just listened to a great podcast on *How to Save Your Marriage*. I decided to change my hair color because of it. It was inspiring. I'll send you the link."
- "I have a wonderful plastic surgeon; it is never too late for a facelift."
- "You are getting older, and I know that men find younger women attractive. Have you tried an open marriage?"
- "You know, you took marriage vows in a house of worship. Those vows said that marriage is forever. I'm not being judgmental."
- "A cousin of mine got a divorce. It was so stressful that he dropped dead. Is your husband in good health?"
- "Have you really tried to make your husband happy? He doesn't seem happy. I always make my husband happy."

Laugh this all off. Or better yet . . . run.

The Grass May Not Be Greener on the Other Side of the Fence

You may be feeling that divorce is your only option. It's not. It's common to take a "time out" to reassess how you feel and what it's going to feel like living separate lives for a while. There are informal and formal separations.

36 ～ Chapter 6

These may lead to a formal divorce, but this can be a valuable time to really explore how you feel without having to look at your partner every day.

The "time out" must be at least several months. A long weekend is not going to give you any idea about how you both will feel. Set down the rules for "disengagement" and really be introspective.

Gray divorce does not have to be a tragedy or a confession of failure. You may be empowered to design and obtain a more fulfilling life than you may now have. How wonderful not to feel that your present marriage is a life sentence. But also, I caution you. Maybe it's better to work on your present relationship and not assume that your spouse will be inflexible. The grass always looks greener on the other side of the fence, but sometimes, it's not. Remember, there are cow pies in the grass on both sides of the fence.

CHAPTER 7

~

Don't Pass This Baggage
onto Your Kids

Are our kids and grandkids facing all of this? Not exactly. People are waiting longer to get married today. In 1963, the average woman married at around age twenty noted Tera R. Jordan, associate professor of human development and family studies at Iowa University.[1] By 2017, the median age of marriage was twenty-seven for women and twenty-nine for men. In 2022, the average age for women to get married was thirty and the average for men was thirty-two (also down three years form 2021). I think that the pandemic has influenced these numbers, but the point is, people are getting married much later than they had in my day and for you who are facing gray divorce.

When I went to college in 1969, many of my female classmates were there to also get their "Mrs." Most wanted to be coupled by graduation. Even though I didn't go looking, I did find myself in a serious relationship and I skipped graduation and got married instead.

Money issues still play a big part in the cause of divorce. Couples that argue about finances at least once a week are thirty more times likely to get divorced.[2] Another study found that money issues were only second to infidelity, as a cause for divorce.[3] This is not surprising, but the larger the couple's debt, the more likely they were to say that money is what they fight the most about. Almost 50 percent of couples with $50,000 or more in consumer debt say that money is a top reason for arguments. Those arguments lead to stress, and you know where that goes. Finger-pointing and fights ensue. And conversely, when you lower your debt, and lower your stress, couples see a shift in their marriage.

You can still give motherly advice to your children who are thinking of marriage. It's important to know that nearly two-thirds of marriages do start off in debt, so these are issues that your kids are going to have to deal with. The big

37

38   ∽   Chapter 7

message is around communication and transparency. The issues need to be discussed and dealt with. Talking about issues can really make a difference. In fact, 94 percent of respondents who say they have a great marriage discuss their money dreams with their spouse. I would add each managing a budget, paying bills, and sharing the responsibility of investing will help things out.

I will discuss how you should NOT pass this legacy on to your kids (girls and boys) so together you can have real discussions about financial empowerment. This empowerment will directly give them the mojo to take charge of their financial lives. You are living proof that things do not always turn out as planned. You can still *mother* your kids . . . because they are your kids. Some advice is needed here so they do not repeat your errors; or at least learn from them.

Your offspring will hopefully be transparent and at ease discussing money issues with their prospective partners as easily as they can discuss sex. In the 1990s, I worked with Oprah for four and a half years and was on her show thirteen times. It was always a problem to get guests to discuss their money problems, but easy to get them to discuss their sexual problems. I never understood that.

One day, I asked a young woman in a couple why that was the case. I said, "Here you are, and you have had an intimate relationship with this guy and are considering marriage, but you don't know what he earns or the debt he has?" She didn't skip a beat and said, "Asking him about his money is personal." Obviously, I'm from another world. Taking your clothes off in front of a person and having sex is less personal than discussing your prospective partner's income and debt? And sharing your information with him is too personal?

Marriage or Living Together?

They may look and feel the same, but they are different. Pew Research Center[4] found that many Millennials are opting not to get married. This is another conversation you may want to have with your kids. More Americans live with a *special squeeze* than have married them. And what's great is that the stigma seems to be lessening in most cases; however, there are those who say that society is better off when couples get married.

What's interesting is that the married adults reported being more satisfied with their relationship and more trusting of their partners when they were married and not just living together. They may feel more secure.

Money issues play a big part in these relationships. About 40 percent of the cohabiters say that finances and convenience were a big reason for their decision. There may be a subtext that says, "I can't afford to live alone." And about 30 percent say that neither they nor their partner are ready financially to be married. More than half of people surveyed believed their partners could be trusted to handle money responsibly, and 40 percent of cohabiters felt the same way.

Most American adults want unmarried couples to have the same legal rights as married couples when it comes to health insurance, inheritance, or tax benefits. There are some things to consider if you opt to live together and not marry.

- *Check to See If Common-Law Marriage Is Recognized in Your State* – If your state recognizes it, you can enjoy the rights of married couples. But just know that a common-law marriage is not just created simply by living together. There are time restrictions.
- *Be Careful If You Buy a House* – The house belongs to the person or people on the deed, and the mortgage, if there is one. You can look at sharing the title by having your lawyer create a joint tenancy with the right of survivorship and tenancy-in-common. The difference is that with the right of survivorship, your interest in the home automatically transfers to the other owner when the other party dies.

  If you both apply for the mortgage, you are both responsible for paying for it, and you are both responsible even if you break up.
- *Make Sure You Create a Will* – The marriage certificate protects married couples even if they don't have a will. If you are married, without a will, your estate will eventually go to your spouse. If you are unmarried and die without a will, your estate will go to your next of kin, but that is not your partner.
- *Watch Out for Health Care* – Many corporations and the government will not offer health insurance coverage to unmarried couples. If you are married, the IRS doesn't tax your health benefits. But if you are providing a domestic partner with health care benefits, the portion applying to them could be taxable to you.
- *Look into an Advance Health Care Directive* – If one of you has a medical emergency and you don't have an Advance Health Care Directive in place, the other has no legal right to be given information or to make decisions about care.

40 ～ Chapter 7

Change Your Job Description

Your offspring may not feel as guilty as you have when it comes to divorce because of the "Please pass the butter" syndrome and have figured out some unique ways to deal with it, besides waiting to get married or not getting married at all. Many of our kids have cracked the code when it comes to divorce if there are kids in the picture. No one wants to deal with the guilt of leaving the children for the sake of your own happiness. No one wants to turn their kids' lives upside down. But how do you sacrifice your own life for another?

There is a new phenomenon called Parenting Marriage.[5] It is an arrangement where both parents get to see the kids every day: kids don't have to go back and forth between two homes, and you don't have to sell your home and figure out how to divvy up the assets. You may now be able to afford to divorce.

As *Psychology Today* puts it, you are changing the nature of your relationship by changing your job description to be coparents and not a couple. It can be weird, I'll admit. You are living together, but not together. You and he sort of have separate living quarters. If you have a big house, it obviously works best. You and he can live on separate floors . . . but you will run into each other and each other's new squeezes along the way.

I'm not going to spend lots of time on this topic; I just want you to know that our next generation has come up with some workable—or not-so-workable solutions—to the "blah" marriage.

I understand why they may just want to live together, but they need to know the pros and cons of each. Marriage is a legal union, and live-in or cohabitation relationships are mostly considered unofficial arrangements.

It may be time to think about a prenup, which I'll cover later when a new marriage might follow your gray divorce.

SECTION 2

WHEN YOU ARE CONSIDERING OR KNEE-DEEP IN YOUR GRAY DIVORCE

CHAPTER 8

〜

Design Your New Life

It's worth a minute to reflect at this point. You may be in the process of "passing the butter" and find yourself knee-deep in a horrible situation. You may be second-guessing yourself . . . big time. You may wake up at night as you question, "What have I done?"

Many say that divorce is "death by a thousand cuts," and that may feel exactly right. Your spouse, your kids, and many of your friends may be telling you what a selfish, horrible person you are. Then, you can be gripped by fear; fear of staying where you are, of moving forward, and of not moving forward. Fear can take over and bring you to your knees. Besides making you run to the bathroom every five minutes, fear can blind your vision and make you miss the warning signs of impending doom.

Muster your courage to move forward. Nelson Mandela said it best, "I learned that courage was not the absence of fear, but the triumph over it. The brave man [or woman] is not he who does not feel afraid, but he who conquers that fear."[1]

I've been there. Of course, you are sad, and you may have tried to tell, or have told, your loved ones about your thoughts on divorce. But they may not be able to get out of their own way, thinking about how it affects them.

You may not want to just "pass the butter," you may want to "face-plant" in the butter. Take a deep breath. You can move forward.

Completing Incompletions

And as you move toward designing your new money life, it's a good time to look at all those financial "incompletions" that you may have hanging around. This is a great exercise, no matter what your life looks or feels like.

44 ～ Chapter 8

It also gives you something practical to focus on and may lessen the fear, because you are moving forward . . . for you.

I'll ask you a series of questions that I want you to think about so that you can start to fill in your *Money Map*—your GPS for your future.

It's a good time to write down your thoughts and responses to these questions. You can record your answers or get out your tablet or write in Notes on your phone.

Here are the general questions:

- What do I want to start doing with or about money that I've never done?
- What money habits do I want to change?
- What do I want to stop doing with money?
- What do I want to say about money that I've never said?
- What do I want to learn about money?

Here are questions pertaining to a possible divorce:

- If I get divorced, what do I hope happens? (Think of this in the event of the best-case scenario.)
- What things or lifestyle will I gain if I get a divorce?
- What things or lifestyle will I lose if I get a divorce?

You get to examine this list and add to or subtract from it; it's your list.

As an aside, I do this exercise with women who are in all different phases of their life. Some are powerful female executives who handle every aspect of their financial lives and others are stay-at-home moms or women who have consciously relegated money issues to their partner. It does not matter; there is no judgment. What matters is that you know some of the nagging money issues you want to deal with. Those may be piddly, minor issues, and some may be massive ones that find you at 3:00 a.m., whisper in your ear, and wake you up. Those may be the issues that you push aside and tell them that you will deal with them after the holidays, or when the prom is over, or after your dog has completed his medicine because the vet said he has been eating too many carrots and is turning orange, or when you land your next promotion.

But these niggling issues don't just go away on their own. Complete the incompletions to make them go away. I call this *Your Financial Sock Drawer*. Why? Because if someone says to me to clean my whole house, the job is too daunting, and I'll never get to it. But if someone suggests for me to start with my sock drawer; I'm in. That is an incompletion that I can tackle and complete. I can do that.

Sock-It-to-Me!

Cleaning and organizing my home, or even my closets, does not bring me joy. The joy comes from seeing it done exactly how I want it, but not in the doing. It all seems overwhelming to me. The job is too big. I have a housekeeper, occasionally, and I could participate in the process; I don't. But she knows *not* to touch my stuff. I have many excuses as to why I don't complete my incompletions in my home. I know that if I suddenly take on an organizational project, it probably means my computer is not working.

Let's look at socks. Yes, socks. I, like many, have been waiting for the mismatched sock to return to my home to find its mate. It makes no logical sense to me. I bought two socks, two socks were worn, two socks were washed, but one magically disappeared when I was matching the pairs. I ponder where the other one went. I know if I decide to throw the mismatch away, its partner will magically reappear.

So, I created an entire sock drawer filled with the mismatched socks. When moving, I even took them with me, secretly hoping the other would find the new house and be reunited. I think of penguins who mate for life and travel thousands of miles to be reunited with their soulmate. My other socks only have to travel up one flight of stairs or move to a new house to find their *sole-mate (pun intended)*, not swim thousands of miles through frigid waters like those loyal penguins. I know this sounds ridiculous.

If I did organize my closets, I would feel happy . . . really happy, but I have just let it go. When I can't find something that I know is stuffed in there somewhere, I just buy a new one. Pathetic. That is why I started small, with my socks.

Clearly, this would show up on my *Life's Incompletion List* (not my *Financial Incompletion List*). My point is that you must take baby steps with your list. You must take a bite-sized slice of your financial life, one at a time, not the whole pie. A bite-sized piece is doable, not daunting. I can throw away the mismatched socks. I can do that! And then start cleaning another part of my house. And, I did.

Mark Twain said, "The secret of getting ahead is getting started. The secret to getting started is breaking your complex overwhelming tasks into small manageable tasks and then starting on the first one."[2] Undoubtedly, Twain started with his sock drawer.

46 ～ Chapter 8

How great will you feel when you finally tackle the sock drawer and throw away the mismatched socks? Or when you answer every email and your inbox is *empty*? Completing incompletions is a beautiful feeling. It's a feeling that you want to share with your besties and celebrate. Here is a chance to do the same with your financial life.

It is all about your choices, and now you get to choose what is important to you to deal with so that you can start dreaming about penguins swimming miles to find their rock nests in Antarctica with their mate waiting patiently for them. But don't let these cute animals take your focus off the Will that needs to be updated so that your kids are protected, or how you need to find new health insurance because you are being taken off your husband's policy as soon as the divorce is final. You will also start to understand why you made certain decisions, and you get to change those and move forward in a fresh way.

Hopefully, this new empowered clearing allows you to make choices for yourself that fit your new life.

Rewrite Your Story

Just start with the simple Q&A below. I've repeated these from above.

Ask yourself these questions and see what comes up for you. Write/record your answers so you can easily review them and refer to them:

Your Incompletion List

1. *What do I want to start doing with money?*
2. *What money habits do I want to change?*
3. *What do I want to stop doing with money?*
4. *What do I want to say about money?*
5. *What do I want to learn about money?*
6. *If I get divorced, what do I hope happens? Think of this in the best-case scenario.*
7. *What lifestyle aspects will I gain if I get a divorce?*
8. *What lifestyle aspects will I lose if I get a divorce?*

Now What?

Jot down your answers freely and let things come to mind. You should repeat the things that keep showing up when you ask yourself these questions. They are the incompletions or wishes that are most important to

Design Your New Life ～ 47

you. The repeated answers are the ones you will work on first. Circle those as your priorities and give yourself a deadline for dealing with those items. Don't make the deadline any more than two weeks because they will slip into the realm of "After I get my next promotion" or "When my closets are organized."

I'll give you some things to think about that should perhaps be on your list:

1. *What do I want to start doing with money?*
   A logical first step is understanding where I stand with all the things regarding my current money situation with my husband is the logical first step.
   Consider the following:

   - Health care
   - Insurance
   - Budget
   - Living arrangements
   - Investments
   - Wills, including a living will
   - Inheritances
   - After-life arrangements

Note: Do not list yourself to death (no pun intended). The list should highlight things you will get to. Remember when I said that organizing your whole house was too much of a daunting job, and most of us never get there. This is like your *financial sock drawer*: one sock at a time. You can start with one and get that completed, then move on to the next.

2. *What money habits do I want to change?*
   Consider the following answers:

   - I don't have to rely upon my spouse to consult with for my money decisions.
   - I don't have to look to my partner to handle paying bills and making investment decisions.
   - I don't have to use shopping as a way to handle stress or joy.
   - I don't have to think about my funeral; my kids can worry about that. (Oops, I want to take that burden off them.)
   - I don't need a hobby of surfing the Internet for deals to buy that I don't need.

48 ～ Chapter 8

3. *What do I want to stop doing with money?*
   Consider the following answers:

   - I have always been able to get my credit card out of my wallet faster than anyone in the adjoining five counties, but it's a skill I can now forego.
   - I can stop buying elaborate gifts for my friends and put a limit on gift buying.
   - I want to stop making impulse purchases that I know I don't need.
   - I want to stop splurging on gifts for my grandchildren and spend more time making memories with them.
   - I want to stop being "The Bank" for my adult children who are living beyond their means.
   - I want to stop falling off my budget as if it were my diet. (Come to think of it, maybe I also want to stop falling off my diet, as well.)

4. *What do I want to say about money?*
   Consider the following answers:

   - I can create and stick to my budget.
   - I can get a handle on my finances.
   - I can understand how investments work and what's best for me.
   - I can understand what "risk tolerance" means.
   - I want to explain to my adult kids, in the most loving way, that they need a budget and that I can't keep going into my emergency funds to pay for things they want.
   - I want to say to my financial advisors, "I'm still intimidated by all the financial language. Please stop using jargon and just explain it all to me."
   - I want to say to my kids: "This is my life, and I'm going to make my own decisions, even if they are hard for you to understand. I know what is best for me, and I'd like your support."

5. *What do I want to learn about money?*
   Consider the following answers:

   - I want to learn how to set realistic goals for my future.
   - I want to create a real budget that I can live within.
   - I want to understand how my investment plan will help me to reach my goals.
   - I want to be able to know that I will be okay financially.
   - I want to design a life containing my wishes, that I will love.
   - I want to make sure that my kids understand my wishes and that I've planned for my later life.

Design Your New Life ⟶ 49

6. *If I get divorced, what do I hope happens? Think of this in the best-case scenario.*
Consider the following answers:

- I can make decisions on my own and not have to be accountable to someone else.
- I won't have to put up with his complaining and can feel positive about life.
- I don't have to be a caregiver and will have time for myself and my needs.
- I can find the new hobbies and other things that I have always wanted to do and enjoy.
- I can design the life I want.

7. *What lifestyle aspects will I gain if I get a divorce?*
Consider the following answers:

- I can gain time for me.
- I can gain the freedom to live my life.
- I can gain the knowledge to handle my decisions and not be dependent upon him.
- I can gain control of my life.

8. *What lifestyle aspects will I lose if I get divorced?*
Consider the following answers:

- I may lose financial security.
- I may lose the comfort of being a couple.
- I may lose the ability to be "married" and face the stigma of being "divorced."
- I may lose some friends.
- I may lose some ease with my family who have been judgmental about my divorce.

Results:

You will note that you have repeated some items. Those are the ones that are bothering you the most. Those should be the first that you want to deal with. You will get to everything, but not all at once. The recurring themes here are around goal setting, budgeting, spending, investing, tough conversations with loved ones, and later-in-life planning. Literally, make a list of these incompletions and circle or check off all the ones that kept coming

50 ～ Chapter 8

up. Now list all your incompletions by importance, that is, #1, #2, #3. Set a realistic timeframe to complete them and celebrate your success.

The ones pertaining to your possible divorce are divorce-centric. You get to rewrite how you feel. You may not have completions around them to handle, but you may. For instance, taking charge of your finances reduces the worry of financial independence. Having the "talks" with family and friends reduces stress related to the stigma of divorce.

The big secret to this is to remember that starting something is the easy part, finishing it is the hard part, but also that is where the real reward is to be found. I like the words of Buddha Gautama: "There are two fatal errors that keep great projects from coming to life: 1) Not finishing 2) Not starting."[3]

CHAPTER 9

~

Know Yourself and Your Financial Personality

Quiz to Determine Your Financial Personality

We need to revisit all that baggage that you want to or have left behind and see where you are today. We are basically born or educated to have a financial personality; simplistically, you are either a *Saver* or a *Spender*. Many of us marry partners who have the opposite financial personality. You will take a short quiz to see how you have come into your relationship. The horse has left the barn regarding how you and your spouse each handled money. But it's important for you to know how you come to the world and may deal with money moving forward so that your future plans take that into account. And that you have not just adopted his financial personality because it caused less strife.

We have determined that the primary factor that governs how you treat money is the way you feel about money. This is what makes our financial habits so hard to break. You'd think that nothing in the world would be more rational than money. It can be counted; it can be measured; everything about it is an exact science. Right? Wrong. There's nothing more emotionally driven, nothing more deeply personal, than our attitude toward money. That's why it's become the last taboo.

But it's what women should think about and have to talk about.

Take this short quiz to start to examine your financial personality.

Financial
Personality Quiz

1. **The best thing about having a lot of money is that:**
   a. You can buy anything you want.
   b. You can be generous with family and friends.
   c. You can invest it and ensure your financial independence.

2. **The best thing to do with extra money is to:**
   a. Spend it.
   b. Save it.
   c. Invest it.

3. **People who spend money as fast as they earn it are:**
   a. Fun.
   b. Immature.
   c. Shortsighted.

4. **Investing money means:**
   a. Nothing to me.
   b. You could lose it. You're better off leaving these decisions to a man who understands those things.
   c. You could make more.

5. **Lending money is:**
   a. Okay, I guess.
   b. Something that could lead to trouble, but could be fine if it is given to family.
   c. Okay, if there's an arrangement for repayment.

6. **I'm happiest spending:**
   a. Yup, that's it.
   b. On someone else.
   c. When I buy something I really want, and know I can afford it.

7. **People who have more money than I do:**
   a. Are smarter than I am, but who cares.
   b. Are more selfish than I am.
   c. Are neither of the above.

8. **If I buy something for myself:**
   a. I feel great. Why not?
   b. I feel guilty. I should have been buying something for someone else.
   c. I feel fine. I've planned and budgeted for it.

9. **I would go into debt:**
   a. Any time someone wants to make me a loan.
   b. To buy a house or send the kids to college, but not for myself.
   c. If the downside wasn't disastrous and the upside was worth the risk.

10. **When it comes to investments, I say...**
    a. "Why invest? Live for today."
    b. "It's better to be safe than sorry. Be conservative."
    c. "Nothing ventured, nothing gained; within reason."

11. **My chief financial goal is:**
    a. To have enough money to live as well as possible right now.
    b. To be well-provided for.
    c. To be financially independent.

12. **If I buy something for myself and then see it on sale somewhere else:**
    a. I'm really ticked off.
    b. I feel guilty.
    c. I don't care, particularly if I've done my homework online and have gotten a good price.

13. Five years from now I expect to be:
   a. Five years older.
   b. Trying to keep the family home.
   c. Financially secure for the rest of my life.

14. To me, "the best" means:
   a. The coolest.
   b. The best bargain.
   c. The best suited to my needs now.

15. I feel best about myself when I:
   a. Buy myself something trendy.
   b. Buy something for my home.
   c. Resist the temptation to buy something I want, but don't need.

Know Yourself and Your Financial Personality ∼ 55

Results:

When it comes to financial personalities, as I have said, you are generally a *Saver* or a *Spender*. But we need to look further into women's financial personalities. Women essentially have two possibilities: we can be independent, or we can be dependent. The second possibility generally means that we have been dependent upon a man or partner. Dependence is dependence, but it comes in different forms. In this quiz, I've offered two different profiles of dependence and one profile of independence.

The quiz is overly obvious, but it is just supposed to make you think. If your answers to the quiz were *a*, you're living for the moment. You are the *spender* who is rather clueless. Your native habitat may be the mall or online cruising all the great sites. You may not have thought of yourself as dependent; in fact, you may think of yourself as totally independent, free as a bird. But someone has to pay for your wants, and it may not be you. You lack the planning drive for the future. You could even be a defiant spender; just defying him because it irritates him.

If most of your answers were *b*, you are still hanging on to the dependency on a man or partner. You are a *saver*. But you still may be trying to do the right thing. You will obviously get in less trouble than the clueless spender, but you may not be able to design the life you want.

If most of your answers were *c*, you show up as a financially independent woman. You have acquired the self-confidence to trust yourself financially and the motivation to go out and get what you need and want. You are taking charge of planning for your own future.

I obviously want you to end up financially independent, as the balanced *saver* and *spender*. That is clear. This exercise helps you to see where you have been and to make different choices moving forward into your new life.

Okay, I Know My Financial Personality, Now What?

I told you that this book was not going to be about the psychological side of divorce and money, but understanding your financial personality, and perhaps how you developed it from your past, is the first step to help you reshape your approach to earning, saving/investing, spending, and sharing going forward.

If you know that you are a spender, you probably know that you like whatever is "new." And new usually connotes expensive and not found on the bargain rack. It may be because you want to make a statement or keep up with the Joneses. You also may suffer from what some have deemed "affluenza,"[1] the combination of affluence and influenza. It could be defined

56   ～   Chapter 9

as a "painful, contagious, socially transmitted condition of overload, debt, anxiety, and waste, resulting from the dogged pursuit of more."

You can change this behavior, especially if you have become the *Joneses*. You may not care if you start to rack up debt, you will worry about that tomorrow. You may find that wealth may cloud your moral compass and lead to thinking that you are entitled to things because of your money.

You also may want to always pick up the check or buy lavish gifts. You may want to be known as "the good-time girl." Or you may feel that your friends are only there because you are always doling out money. You may want to explore why that is.

Oprah once told me that she felt that many of her friends and family were only being ingratiating to her because of what she gave them. She said that she always questioned that with any relationship, and it didn't make her feel good.

Savers are pretty much the opposite to spenders. They may turn off the TV or turn down the heat at every turn. They won't buy anything that is not on sale. They can have the reputation of being cheap. Extreme savers sometimes play the victim role. I'm not talking about someone who really can't afford something or splitting the tab for the meal, I'm talking about behavior that almost gets to be manipulative.

When the check comes at a restaurant, a saver may examine it and say, "I didn't have a drink and I just had a salad, I'll just pay for that." When typically, you all would just split the check, because you can all afford to do that.

This may be something that you need to seek professional help with, if your financial personality is something you want to change or modify. You may not be able to change your financial personality, but you may be able to acknowledge it and address how it has and is affecting your life. Whenever you manage money, it should involve self-awareness.

As Ayn Rand said, "Money is only a tool. It will take you wherever you wish, but it will not replace you as the driver. You need to decide if you are driving in the right direction, on the right road, or steering off the path that you want to travel."[2]

CHAPTER 10

~

Building Financial Security to Let You Sleep at Night

My goal is to educate you about the financial side of your gray divorce so that you don't wake up in the middle of the night in a cold sweat worrying about all the things that you still have to do. I want you to understand that it is never too late (or too early) to design and redesign your financial life. It's not easy, and that is why I am here to help, coach, and empower you to do it all yourself. You will stumble, but that's okay. As Colin Powell said, "A dream doesn't become a reality through magic; it takes sweat, determination and hard work."[1]

This is not easy. I more than understand that. But as Laurie Sennott said, "Every flower must grow through dirt."[2] Gray divorce issues for older couples are far more complex than the ones a young or newly married couple will face. You have been emotionally and financially intertwined for years and it's hard to disentangle that. And if you're not careful, your divorce can become a disaster!

Two major trends are profoundly impacting women. (I know I keep saying this, but it is something I want you to absorb.)

1. Women are living longer—longer than men.
2. Nearly half of marriages are likely to end in divorce, with rising rates among couples over fifty.

Inevitably eight out of ten women will be widows or divorcees. They all may not live alone, however, there are almost 10 million senior women versus 5 million senior men who live alone.[2]

I want you to really start a conversation with yourself; that is why I will continue to ask you questions that you will have to think about before

58 ～ Chapter 10

answering. This will help you to start to shape and reshape the life you are in now and the one you will be designing for the future.

Do you want to travel? Where do you want to live? Near the grandkids? What hobbies do you want to pursue? How about that exercise class or yoga retreat you have always wanted to pursue? And you will begin to look at tough later-in-life questions about long-term healthcare and beyond. Do you want to live with a group of friends and set up a "pod" of friends to share life? Do you want to live with your kids, and have you financially planned for that? The next step is to put a price-tag on each dream and lifestyle category.

The goal is to come out with a life plan, a *Money Map*, that needs to be funded. It will probably have to be pared down and revised, and revised . . . and revised, but this is what life is all about. Maybe instead of that expensive yoga retreat in India, you and your friends could take yoga classes together locally? You will come away empowered and energized with a workable plan that you are inspired to achieve.

Okay, you have decided to call it quits with your marriage in your twilight years—what do you have to know about the money side of your relationship and life on your own?

The biggest thing to consider is that your household income is most likely to go down, unless you are the major breadwinner. The most important thing now is to learn to budget.

A budget is a detailed plan for where and how you earn, save, spend, and share your money. You have already looked at some of the behaviors you have wanted to change when you reviewed your *Financial Sock Drawer* exercise. I'm counting on the fact that "Having a budget kept popping up." But before you can design the way forward, see where your spending habits have been. The reason most budgets don't work is that they are based upon your dream of what you would like it to look like, not what it is.

People often get to the end of their pay period, and they are out of money and just don't know where the money went. In fact, 50 percent of baby boomers and seniors live paycheck to paycheck.[3] You can't decide to cut back until you really know the impact of what you are shelling out each month on stuff you can modify or drop.

So, it's time to create your *No Magic Money Log*.

CHAPTER 11

~

No Magic Money Log

The goal of this exercise is to really track your spending, so you know what you have been doing. You can't decide where you are going until you know where you have been. If you are only using your debit card and your credit card for your spending needs, this is easy. But if you are using cash, you also need to figure that in as well.

You are going to track your daily spending. You can also go the old-fashioned way and write things down. However, you also need to look at your bank statements to see what bills were automatically deducted from your accounts.

When you look at your spending, you are also going to make a note as to whether the purchase or payment was a *Need* or a *Want*, and if it was a *Planned* or an *Impulse* purchase. Try not to have "other" categories. That doesn't help when you are trying to track your expenditures.

I call this the *No Magic Money Log*, because it has sort of a double meaning. First, it takes the mystery of where the money disappeared to; you spent it. It's not like your breath when you breathe out and don't know where it went because you can't see it. Money is tangible, your breath is not. And second, it reminds you that you're not going to get any money by magic. Roger Babson said it well, "More people should learn to tell their dollars where to go instead of asking them where they went."[1]

You know now that the divorce is in the works, the "butter is being passed," and the settlement will take place soon. It's time to figure out what you need. Really need.

Review your spending for a few months. If you are conscious of your spending, you are going to see how those lattes, at $5.00 a piece, add up to $50 a week, or even more terrifying, they could add up to $2,600 a year. That

59

60 ～ Chapter 11

could be the amount you wanted to spend going to see your grandkids. Or, your hydration method of buying bottled water could easily hit $1,000 a year, not to mention how this contributes to pollution.

Is it worth it to go out to lunch, when you could bring it to the office from home? Do you really use the gym membership? Can you bundle your streaming services and phone and save money each month? Have you been doling out money to your adult children who keep having financial problems? I'm not going to answer the questions, you must do that for yourself. You can decide what moves from the *Need* to the *Want* column or vice versa.

You now know what you have been spending, and how important each item is to your well-being and happiness. But the knowledge is not power. Your superpower will be to apply that knowledge. After this, you can look at building a real budget that you can embrace, for yourself. You will also need a serious budget for your divorce negotiations. Your lawyer should ask for this early on, so I want you to be prepared.

No Magic Money Log

Date:

Item Purchased:

Amount Spent:

Need or Want:

Planned or Impulse:

CHAPTER 12

~

A Budget Does Not Have to Be an Instrument of Torture

You may not know exactly what you will have or get until the divorce is finalized, but you need to think about your budget moving forward, so now is a good time to understand what yours could look like.

You don't want to end up like Ann did, in my earlier story. She was convinced that her alimony was sufficient to handle her spending. It wasn't. It's also not easy to go back and open the divorce case again to say that things are not working out well for you.

Your Monthly Budget

These are the elements of a monthly budget:

Step 1 – Income; Money In:
You will need to add up all the money you will receive. This should be created *AFTER TAXES*. Did I mention that this is net of taxes? It's the money you can really spend. This will probably come from multiple sources, such as Social Security, investment income, alimony, salary, pensions/retirement, and so on.

Step 2 – Expenses; Money Out:
Go back to your *No Magic Money Log* and decide what is realistic for your monthly expenses. The point here is to be *realistic*. You don't know exactly what your financial situation will be, but you want to go into divorce negotiations with a basic understanding of your expenses. You may not be able to afford to keep your current home, but you will have to live somewhere, and that will be an expense. You should also budget for emergencies, for instance.

62 ~ Chapter 12

Each month there will be a new surprise. It may be a leaky roof one month, or a tree that hits your car, another. You can only make sure that you have some emergency money put aside.

There are basic categories for expenses: rent/mortgage, utilities, phone and streaming services, transportation, debt repayment, food, clothing, healthcare, entertainment, gifts, and so on. List these from your *No Magic Money Log* and make sure that they are realistic. Making a fake budget will not help you or your lawyer when they are negotiating on your behalf.

We call some expenses *fixed costs* because they don't change much from one month to another, such as rent or mortgage, health insurance, health/ medication costs, debt repayment, a car lease, and so forth. Some are *variable costs* such as entertainment, utilities, food, travel, clothing, gifts, cable bill, personal care, and so on that can change or be adjusted as needed.

The little expenses can add up. This reminds me of the words of Benjamin Franklin when he said, "Beware of little expenses; a small leak will sink a great ship."[1]

Step 3 – Do the Math:

Subtract *Expenses* from your *Income* and hope that you have some income left. That is the ideal. If your expenses are greater than your income, you need to go back and reduce your expenses. It's easier to adjust expenses than to adjust income, because lots of income, like Social Security, is fixed. However, it may be time to consider a side hustle to increase your income, if need be. See if you can adjust some of your *Variable Expenses* first, like Entertainment. Understand that you may have to adjust *Fixed Expenses* and, for instance, buy a smaller house or rent a smaller apartment, or get a cheaper car.

After the final settlement is negotiated, you will need to track your expenses monthly. As you track your money, you will really know where it has gone, instead of wondering where it went. I promise that you will feel empowered now that you have control, if a big unplanned disaster does not come along. After the settlement is handed down, you will have to readjust your final budget, that we will discuss in Section 3.

A Budget Does Not Have to Be an Instrument of Torture ~ 63

Budget Chart

Money In:
Income (after-tax):

    Social Security = $_____

    Investment Income = $_____

    Alimony = $_____

    Salary = $_____

    Retirement = $_____

Total Income $_____

Money Out:
Fixed Expenses:

    Rent/Mortgage = $_____

    Transportation = $_____

    Health insurance = $_____

    Medication = $_____

Variable Expenses:

    Savings = $_____

    Entertainment = $_____

    Utilities = $_____

    Food = $_____

    Clothing = $_____

    Gifts = $_____

    TV/Phone = $_____

    Personal Care = $_____

Total Expenses $_____

After you complete the budgeting exercise, you should come out with a positive number.

Savings Will Save You

You don't need anyone else to tell you to "Pay yourself first." That payment to your savings will save you lots of future angst. I know that you may not have a lot of money to save. Even if you can only save a little each week, do it. Benjamin Franklin will be proud of you. "A penny saved is a penny earned."[2]

Put the Squeeze on Expenses

Yes, a *penny saved is indeed a penny earned*. Here are some money-saving ideas that can free up some money:

- *Car Insurance* – Looking for and changing car insurance companies is a hassle, and your insurance company knows that. That is why they feel they can increase your premiums each year. Go online and do an insurance search and see if you can save some money. It's worth it.
- *Homeowners Insurance* – Ditto for homeowners' insurance. Research some alternatives.
- *Life Insurance* – You may have gotten life insurance when the kids were little. That is exactly what it is for. But as you get older and your goals change and your kids are way out of college, it may not make sense to keep paying those premiums. Depending upon your policy, you may have built up a cash value. If you cancel the policy, that cash is yours. Call your insurance company to investigate. Also check to see if you are going to hit an age where the premiums become sky high. This is discussed in further detail.

Drip, Drip, Drip of Small Savings

You may have given this advice to your kids because you heard your mother's words ring in your ears every time you reached for your wallet. Regardless, even small savings can add up. That drip, drip, drip of water eventually made an ocean.

- *Make a real shopping list* based upon planning out your meals for the week. Each time you prepare a meal, make enough to freeze another meal. You will be happy when you have a great dinner and don't have to go out in the rain or snow to get food.

66 ～ Chapter 12

- *Skip the designer coffee* and get used to bringing your own from home. I know this sounds goofy, but buying just one cup of java each day can add up to almost $2,000 a year. That could be put toward a fun vacation, and you still can have your coffee.
- *Potluck it* with friends instead of going out. Each person can bring their favorite dish, or you can theme the dinners. For instance, for a book club one time, I was hosting the party and the cover of the book was orange, so I themed the book club around everyone bringing something that was orange.
- *Switch to Airbnbs* instead of hotels when you travel. Bring breakfast food and coffee, which will also save you some money.
- *Take a timeout* before you click to buy the purchase. I think at least a three-day waiting period is enough time to figure out how much you *need* or *want* that item. During one *Oprah* show, I recommended that the avid spender freeze her credit cards. This was during the days of shopping in person in malls. Freezing doesn't hurt the magnetic strip, but it does deter use. You can't put your block of ice in the microwave because that will melt and ruin your cards. You need to watch that block of ice melt and consider your purchase. It worked!
- *Set limits for gifts.* Set a dollar amount with your friends and family. Also, you can get creative and give nonmonetary gifts. If you have any talents, give a gift of knitting or cooking lessons, or helping to declutter a room, or even put those old photos in albums, even though no one has photos anymore! Or you can help your friend to clean out her sock drawer!
- *Really track your progress.* This will get to be just as exciting as tracking your steps per week. You can set up your goals and check in with yourself to see if you meet them.
- *Guilt-free spending is the endgame* on things you really want. Pick something you really want to save for. It could be a trip, a special night out with the family, helping with college for the kids, or adding to your investment account for your future. Whatever you decide, make sure that you celebrate your own success. And acknowledge what you have accomplished.

CHAPTER 13

~

"Wish I May, Wish I Might"

You are now going to build your own wish list. You need to focus on both fixed and variable expenses in your budget. The variable expenses are the ones that can be adjusted more easily, if you want. This is also where you are going to design all those things that you have always wanted to do that will bring you joy. Of course, you may know that a private retreat with the Dalai Lama may not be in the financial cards, but I work with my spiritualist, Rose-Marie Cappiello, who is a local friend. She is an awesome part of my spiritual journey and Lyndhurst, NJ, is closer than Tibet. You don't have to throw out your wish list because it does not satisfy all your exact dreams; adjust the dreams and your other variable expenses to accommodate both. Turning down the thermostat or getting a fan may allow for those Pickleball lessons!

Brooke Shields, who has great eyebrows, is quoted to having said, "Don't waste a minute not being happy. If one window closes, run to the next window—or break down the door."[1] Go, Brooke! You will now get to create your own wish list of the things you want to do and the life you want to live to make yourself happy. The trick is to start to figure out the price tags that go along with the wishes. You will also find that some of your greatest joys in life are FREE.

By the way, you can create a Vision Board, that contains all your wishes, and put that on the wall as a reminder. My dear friend Astera taught me to do this. She even had me put pictures next to my wishes to remind me of what I wanted to manifest. You will keep building your list of wishes and come at it from all different directions. It is a lifelong list, by the way. Circumstances will change and so will your list.

Also, it's a little morbid, but what would you like your obituary to be, reflecting who you were? "Loving Wife and Mother" only talks about who

68　～　Chapter 13

you were to others, not how you feel about yourself. I want mine to be "Neale was a Unicorn in a Field of Horses." My son rolled his eyes at that one. This should be part of your wishes, if you want.

Regarding your wish list, first ask yourself some of these questions to help you hone down what makes you happy. You get to create your own list, and really think about the moments that you enjoy the most and make you smile. Think about the situation as if money was no object. What would you keep or change about your life?

These are just some ideas to help you with the process.

Things that may make me happy:

- Traveling with friends/or alone.
- Hanging out with friends.
- Raising money for my favorite charities.
- Being with my family, kids, and grandkids.
- Making a Voodoo doll that looks exactly like my soon-to-be-ex.
- Raising capital for my next venture.
- Taking a nap.
- Doing yoga (or trying it with the goal of not limping).
- Reading a great book.
- Cleaning out my sock drawer.
- Opening a Bed & Breakfast at the shore.
- Learning to play the castanets in Spain.
- Volunteering in my community.
- Walking in the woods.
- Becoming a board member at some great companies.
- Planting a garden and tending to it.
- Raising goats and making goat cheese to sell.
- Going to theater/movies.
- Having a great meal.
- Cooking a fabulous meal for friends/family.
- Teaching my grandchildren to cook.
- Building a successful business that is truly innovative.
- Setting up my own charity.
- Writing my book.
- Finding a retirement village to live in.
- Taking salsa lessons.
- Learning a new language and practicing it in the actual country.
- Learning to play pickleball.

Your Wish List

After you have made up your own list, try to fill out the following graphic. (No, I do not have "learning to play the castanets" on my list; but I have wanted to learn to whistle with my fingers in my mouth to hail a cab. That would make me happy!)

You can now see if your "wish list" items can start to be incorporated into your budget. They may mostly fall into the *Variable Costs* section. You may have to adjust your price tags on your wish list, but that is okay.

Wish List Item   Estimated Cost – Adjusted Cost

CHAPTER 14

~

Wash That Man Right Out of Your Life

Think of this as a form of housecleaning. I'm putting this in this section of the book because this is the time to start doing these things. Okay, it's a really big list of incompletions that will make your life easier if completed. You are getting your ducks in a row.

Detanglement List

- Get extra copies of your divorce decree, when you have it. You will have to produce it for certain things you have to do, like applying to receive his Social Security benefits.
- Close your joint accounts, if you haven't already. This is just a reminder. Make sure he is off all your accounts. Remember, he can take money out unless two signatures are required.

Here are some accounts to close or change into your name alone:

- Bank, brokerage, credit card, and all investment accounts should only have your name on them. I'd be more comfortable if you just find a new bank. I'd hate a friendly teller who has always dealt with either you or your husband to "goof" at your expense.
- Take his name off your safety deposit box. Have him return his key. Get a new box and key.
- Notify Social Security in writing. This should have been covered in the divorce proceedings, but you could both receive benefits. Just check this.
- Get your car registration and title in your name.

72 ~ Chapter 14

- Notify the IRS that you are divorced. This may be done during the filing process. Consult your accountant.
- Change your insurance policies—health, life, homeowner's, disability—to make sure they have the current and correct information.
- Let the post office know that there is a name change.
- Notify your creditors/bills that the name is now yours. Also notify the billing offices of the ones that should only have his name on them. You don't want to be responsible for any of the bills that are his.
- If you are keeping the house, make sure that the title and mortgage are now in your name. Conversely, if he is keeping the house, make sure that your name is off the title and mortgage. Later on in the book I'll discuss mortgage refinancing: pros and cons as well as reverse mortgages.
- Notify your employer and make sure that your pension has the beneficiary changed if he is on it.
- Get a copy of your credit report and make sure that there are not any mistakes. If there are, correct them in writing.
- Make sure that you are now the owner of your life insurance policies and make sure that you take him off as a beneficiary. There can be a designation that is Transfer On Death (TOD) and Pay On Death (POD). Remember, these beneficiary designations may supersede what may have been left in your will. You will turn over in your grave if he gets any of these benefits that were overlooked.
- Make sure that you review and rewrite your will, trusts, health proxy, and living will. You will also have to change all medical directives, powers of attorney, and my guess is that you no longer want him to be the executor on your estate.

I'm a big believer in getting assistance with your money. You know I want you to find a financial advisor, if you haven't already, who can really help you go step by step to clean up the past and develop a plan to move forward. We will discuss how to find one in *Team-You.*

More Paperwork

This list is for your loved ones. You want to make sure that your kids or the folks who will be taking care of your wishes have access to all your documents. This is not as fun as taking salsa lessons, but is really important. I'll go through the list of documents needed and your wishes. This is your plan. As Eleanor Roosevelt said, "It takes as much energy to wish as it does to plan."[1] You need to convey your plans to your loved ones who will outlive you. Later in this book, I'll walk you through the conversations you should have with your kids.

List of Documents for Your Kids and Loved Ones

- Cemetery deed or proof of ownership
- Guest list for your funeral
- Copy of birth certificate
- Account statements: bank, brokerage, retirement: IRAs, 401(k)s, and so on. Where to find these documents.
- Names and numbers and emails of professionals in your life: financial advisors, bankers, lawyers, bookkeepers, accountants, and so on.
- Beneficiary designations: Life insurance, retirement accounts
- Deeds for real estate
- Safety deposit keys and location
- Will, trust agreements
- Health directives
- Living will
- Power of attorney
- Any other agreements you want your loved ones to have

Your Home

There are lots of different ways you can deal with the family home, but none are easy. They are not easy because your home is not just another asset to be assessed and sold; it's your home. You raised your kids there. You had lots of good times there. It's part of your history. You had neighbors and attachments to them, and the dry-cleaner guy knew not to put your clothes in plastic bags, and the local diner people who knew you didn't like carrots on your salad (even if your husband didn't know). It's hard to relocate.

Okay, I'll stop with the pulls on your heartstrings. This may have come up on your Incompletion List as things you could lose or gain in a divorce. Or maybe it will be a relief to downsize. No more shoveling snow or watching the gutters fill up with leaves in the fall. No more leaky pipes. No more headache.

You can make decisions here with your heart and your head. This should be covered in your Wish List. One way is for one spouse to buy out the other's interest. That means that you, in this case, will pay your husband an

74 ～ Chapter 14

agreed amount for you to continue to live in the house. This is all part of the art of the negotiation.

The buyout may require you, who is keeping the house, to get a new mortgage. If that is not an option, your husband may be willing to pay the mortgage for a period of time. Or, there may be a period of time where you can stay and then sell the home and later divvy up the proceeds. Again, this is all part of the negotiation.

You must decide the value to you of keeping the home and for how long. Yes, of course you should look at the fair market value of your home (the money part), but I also want you to look at what the value of the home is to you (the heart part).

Credit Reports

If keeping your home and remortgaging it in your own name, you will require good credit. You want to make sure that you keep your good credit standing or establish credit if you don't have it. Time to discuss FICO.

CHAPTER 15

FICO—More Than a Cute Name for a Dog

Your "D" in gym when you were in eighth grade may not follow you around, but your FICO score will. FICO stands for Fair Isaac Corporation, which is a data analytics company. There are three main credit bureaus—TransUnion, Experian, and Equifax—that report all your credit relationships into this data company. They are the "Big Brother" that is watching your financial moves. The information from every one of your relationships with any of your creditors is analyzed and a three-digit score is assigned to you. They determine your creditworthiness that is used whenever a lender, or creditor, or in many cases, an employer, wants to extend credit or a job.

There is a formula that the various credit companies use. Generally, they are looking for:

- *Your payment history*: This pertains to whether you paid your accounts on time. This means all debt and obligations, such as credit cards, mortgages, rent, student loans, car loans/lease payments, and so on. The credit agencies don't want you to have too many debt obligations versus your income, affecting your ability to pay your debt back and in a timely manner. They want to see that you are always responsible in paying your obligations on time. This accounts for about 35 percent of your FICO score.
- *Total amount of credit owed*: Having too much debt and unused credit card limits can hurt you. These agencies also don't want to see that you are maxing out your credit cards each month. This can be sometimes called your *utilization rate*. You know how it feels cool that all those credit card companies may reach out to you and make offers to get their cards? They say that you have been preapproved. Well, it's not

76 ~ Chapter 15

cool. All those cards have a credit limit, and that limit means that you could use all those cards and maybe get into financial trouble. This can account for about 30 percent of your FICO score.

- *Length of your credit history*: This is the length of time you had credit. The longer the better because it shows that lenders have trusted you. You have built up a sustained record of reliably paying your debt, no matter what. This accounts for about 15 percent of your FICO score.
- *New credit*: This is how often you have applied for and opened new accounts. If you have tried and been turned down for credit, this may be a sign of financial trouble. Each application and turn-down or acceptance is reported to the credit bureaus. Or, if you have all of a sudden gotten more cards or more debt, this may be a sign that you are getting into too much debt and may be headed for financial trouble. This accounts for about 10 percent of your FICO score.
- *Credit mix*: The credit bureaus want to see the mix of credit products you have, such as mortgages, credit cards, installment loans, and so forth. If everything, for instance, is put on your credit cards, it may mean that you didn't get another type of a loan that could be more appropriate. It may feel responsible to pay everything in cash and not have credit, but that is a big red flag for the credit bureaus. They assume that you could not get credit or that you want to fly under the radar. This accounts for about 10 percent of your FICO score.

FICO Score Ranges:
They generally range from 300 to 850:

- Very poor: 300–579
- Fair: 580–669
- Good: 670–739
- Very good: 740–799
- Excellent: 800–850

The average score in 2022 was 716.[1] The seventy-seven-plus Silent Generation, born between 1928 and 1945, had an average score of 760 and baby boomers, ages fifty-eight to seventy-six, had an average FICO score of 740.

Why Does My FICO Score Matter?

Your FICO score really matters. It matters if you have or want credit, are buying a home, or even if you are applying for a job or want to go into the military. If you want to stay in your home after your divorce, you may be applying for a mortgage. A low score will also cost you more in interest rates if you can even get credit. You need to know your score and you can get that for free. There are sites you can go to look at yours.

It just seems like a number, but it is a glimpse into how financially healthy and responsible you are. Think about how a lender looks at this. When you use credit, you are asking the issuer to lend you money that you promise to pay back later. They are trusting that you will pay that loan back. But if you don't, they just don't lose the interest on the loan that you didn't pay, they lose the rest of the balance on that loan, as well. That is a big risk for a lender.

Your FICO score gives creditors a glimpse into how you are handling money and if there may be a red flag showing that you are getting into financial trouble.

Years ago, I was working with military youth and in one of our meetings when we were discussing the importance of financial literacy, I learned something that disturbed me. I was told that military personnel can receive an "Other than Honorable Discharge" or "General Discharge" if they have messed up their credit. This is serious, because "Honorable" is the only discharge that doesn't have a negative impact on a veteran's benefits in the future.

It may be hard or impossible to get a job when the future employer sees this record. This kind of a discharge may make it harder for the veteran to get credit and it can hurt their credit score because they may not get any credit or pay more for it.

I went nuts when I heard this, until a general took me aside to straighten me out. He explained that if a soldier were captured, the enemy could perhaps compromise the POW with offering to pay their bad debts. I dismounted from my high-horse and could understand the impact that bad credit could have.

How to Improve Your Credit Score

It may feel like an arbitrary number that a bunch of credit bureaus tagged you with, that may govern when and if you can get credit. Who the hell are they to say or not say that you are responsible? They don't know that maybe you had joint accounts and your husband said that he would pay the bills and your credit cards, and didn't? Or that he took out a huge cash advance and that you now, in the divorce, find out that you both could be responsible for it? It's really hard. And unfair. But you will still have to deal with this and

78 ~ Chapter 15

try to fix it. This is the basis for your new and independent financial life. You now own it. As Abraham Lincoln said, "You cannot escape the responsibility of tomorrow by evading it today."[2]

So, if you are facing a gray divorce and don't have a great FICO score, there are many ways to improve it. It will take some time to do this, but it is worth it.

Here are some things to consider when trying to improve your credit score.

- *Review your statement for errors.* Mistakes are not unusual. The Fair Credit Act gives you the right to get information and to expect that that information is accurate and error-free. Don't just assume that the credit report is correct. In fact, the Federal Trade Commission (FTC) stated that they found that one in four people have an error on their credit report.

  The first step is to get the reports, which as stated before, you can download for free. Review them and see if you find mistakes. If there are mistakes, you can submit a dispute to each of the three credit reporting agencies. Make sure that you bug them to get their reports corrected. Mistakes can really mess up your FICO score. Four out of five consumers who filed disputes saw some modification in their credit report.[3] The FTC stated that approximately one in twenty consumers had a maximum score improvement of twenty-five points.

- *Don't miss a payment.* Pay all your bills on time every month. The credit bureaus track credit card payments, so make sure that these, and frankly all your debt, is paid on time. Set up a calendar schedule so that you pay a few days early. The high-FICO-scoring people never miss or are late on a payment. The credit reports will show nearly four years of payment history.

- *Don't max out cards.* It's important to charge money on your credit card every month, but make sure that the amount charged does not exceed 30 percent of your credit limit. This shows that you are not maxing out your balance, and therefore don't need all the available funds.

- *You only need two cards.* You really don't need more than two cards. Having more shows the credit rating services that you could get in trouble by maxing them out. Remember, each card carries a credit limit, and the agencies watch how much available credit you have.

- *Pay down balances on revolving credit accounts.* Try to make advance payments to reduce the maturity date for getting rid of that debt. The

FICO—More Than a Cute Name for a Dog　～　79

rating agencies like to see you pay debt before due dates, it shows that you have excess cash.

- *Limit the amount of credit* you are applying for. People don't realize that applying for new credit can work against them. Again, this is a red flag.

There is no exact timeline for improving your credit score. It all depends on how many negative marks you have on your credit, the types of negative marks, and your current credit score. Be patient and as you start to pay off accounts, small payments are better than missing payments. Amelia Earhart said, "The most difficult thing is the decision to act, the rest is merely tenacity."[4] You will need to heed her words and know that you are building your financial life; for you. Look at these ratios:

Credit Utilization Ratio

This shows the percentage of your total available credit that you are using. By lowering it you can help improve your credit score. A high score will reflect poorly on your credit score. Your credit utilization ratio will go up and down with payments and purchases. This is calculated by dividing your *current total credit card balance* by your *total credit limit*.

Credit Utilization =
Current Credit Card Total Balance / Total Credit Limit

For example, let's say you have four credit cards, and each have a credit limit of $2,500; therefore, your total credit limit is $10,000. Also, let's say you have a $1,500 balance on each card, or a total of current credit card balances of $6,000. You divide:

$6,000 / $10,000

Current Credit Card Balance / Total Credit Limit
$6,000 / $10,000 = 0.6 or 60%

This means that your credit utilization ratio is 60 percent.

Anything over a 30 percent credit utilization can potentially decrease your credit score. It's also important to understand that the 30 percent utilization applies to both your total debt and each account.

Debt-to-Income Ratio (DTI)

This is a personal financial measurement that compares the amount of debt you have to your income. Lenders use it to measure your ability to manage your debt payments and bills and even your mortgage. This also may be a signal, a red flag, when you have too much debt and may thwart your efforts to get approved for new credit. In theory, your DTI ratio does not directly affect your credit score. This is because the credit agencies do not know how

80 ∿ Chapter 15

much you earn, so they can't do this calculation. But the credit agencies do look at your credit utilization ratio, which compares all your credit card balances to the total amount of credit you have available. This means that the credit card companies may be nervous about whether you are racking up too many credit cards that each carry a credit limit. They feel that you may be headed for credit problems. Lenders don't want to extend credit to people who already have too much debt.

This is calculated by dividing your *total monthly debt payments* by your *total gross monthly income*. Debt includes any obligation that will take more than six to ten months to repay. That can include mortgage or rent payments, including property taxes and insurance, auto loans, student loans, credit card payments, personal loans, and even in-store credit lines for furniture or electronics.

Your *total gross monthly income* is before your employer takes out taxes and other deductions. You can find gross income listed on your pay stub. It also includes anything that you are required to list as income on your tax returns. That includes benefits like Social Security, pensions, alimony, and other payments you receive.

Debt-to-Income Ratio =
Total Monthly Debt Payments / Total Gross Monthly Income
Here is a simple worksheet to fill out to figure out this ratio:

Debt-to-Income Worksheet

Total Monthly Debt Payments:

Monthly Rent/Mortgage	$_____
Monthly Car Payments	$_____
Medical/Dental Bill Payments	$_____
Insurance Payments	$_____
Monthly Credit Card Payments	$_____
Appliance/Furniture Payments	$_____
Other Loan Payments	$_____
Total Monthly Debt Payments	$_____

Total Monthly Income:

Your Monthly Income	$_____
Alimony Received	$_____
Retirement Benefits	$_____
Social Security Benefits	$_____
Government Assistance	$_____
Other Monthly Income	$_____
Total Monthly Income	$_____

Let's look at a simple example:

Assume you pay $1,200 for your mortgage or rent, $400 for your car loan, and $400 for the rest of your debt, including credit cards, each month.

Debt = $1,200 + $400 + $400 = $2,000

Gross Income = $6,000 per month

DTI ratio = $2,000/$6,000 = .33 or 33 percent

What Is a Good DTI Ratio?

In 2019, the average American household had a DTI ratio of 9.69 percent.[5] Surprisingly, it dropped to a low of 8.69 percent in 2020, when we were knee-deep in the pandemic. (Remember, that this is the minimum debt payment due per month, not the total debt owed.) Most lenders want to see your debt-to-income ratio below 36 percent, with no more than 28 percent of that debt going toward servicing your mortgage.

Credit Card Debt Ratio

This is an easier ratio to use to measure credit worthiness. In general, you don't want your minimum credit card payments to exceed 10 percent of your net income. Net income is the amount of income you take home after taxes and other deductions, like Social Security. You use the net income for this ratio because that's the amount of income you will have available to spend on paying bills and other expenses.

When your credit card payments take up too much of your income, it makes it difficult to afford all the things you need to pay for each month, that you listed above.

Total Monthly Credit Card Payments / Total Net Monthly Income

Here is an example:

Let's say your total credit card payments are $500 a month and your take-home pay is $5,000. That is a good sign, because the agencies don't want this ratio to be more than 10 percent.

Total Monthly Credit Card Payments / Total Net Monthly Income

$500 / $5,000

To bring this down to real life and pay off $2,000 in credit card debt within thirty-six months, you need to pay $109 per month, assuming an APR of 18 percent. You would incur $608 in interest charges during that time.

How to Build Credit History

The trick to building credit is that you need credit to build a history. It's a catch-22 situation. How do you build good credit if you don't have credit?

Credit Cards

You need to establish your own credit, if you don't have any now. Apply for a credit card in your name only. If you get one, as mentioned above, use about 30 percent of the balance each month and pay it in full by the due date. The rating agencies don't want to see you max out the card each month, even if you are paying in full. You want to show the rating agencies that you are using credit responsibly. Even though credit card companies like you to carry balances because that is how they make money, the rating agencies want to see that you are using credit cards as a convenience and not as a substitute for not being able to pay monthly.

Also, as I mentioned, you don't need more than two credit cards. Having too many may send a signal to the rating agencies that you could use them all and potentially get in trouble. Remember, each card carries a credit limit, the amount you could charge.

If you can't get credit or have an extremely low FICO score, you may have to start out with a *secured credit card*.

Secured Credit Card

A secured credit card has a limit backed up by a cash deposit. These can be used to establish credit or for subprime borrowers who can't get credit. This means that you use a deposit as collateral against the card. The card looks like any other card and works the same, and no one will know that it is a secured card. The amount you put down in the cash deposit will become your credit card limit. If you do not pay back the balance, the bank will take your deposit to pay off your debt.

You can apply for a secured credit card in the same way that you would apply for a regular unsecured credit card. Nearly all the major credit card lenders offer them. Use the card and pay it back on time. It may take months or years to increase your FICO score. Your history with the card will be reported to the credit agencies. If you are responsible with this usage, this can help to improve your credit score. Be aware that secured credit cards typically have lower credit limits and higher fees.

The goal is to "graduate" to an unsecured card, which should happen as you build your positive credit history.

Loans

If you take out a personal loan, or a car loan, or even have student loan debt, and are paying on time, you can also build up a good credit rating. The credit agencies will measure how much debt you have against your income. They again want to make sure that you are not incurring more debt than you can handle.

As George Washington famously noted, "To contract new debts is not the way to pay old ones."[6] Building a good credit profile will make your money life easier, but you need to make sure that you are living within your means and not raking up too much debt.

CHAPTER 16

~

Put Together Team-You

This section is about amassing the proper team for you to move forward. Even if you are an attorney or another professional, you need your own team. You need advice because this is an emotional time, and it's hard to be dispassionate. I will explore the considerations for selecting either an attorney or a mediator, but first you will need to consult the following:

- A Financial Advisor

You need to examine and paint your whole financial picture. You should look in the rearview mirror to see where you and your husband have been, financially. But you also need advice as to how to look through the windshield to see where you are going and what your financial wellness will look like for the rest of your life.

I'll discuss my thirty-five-year relationship with Mitch and Ann, my financial advisors, and tell you why this type of trusted relationship is so important for your future. I'll also discuss why it's important for both members of the relationship to have had contact with the financial advisors. You can't change the past, but you can change the future if you couple again. (You can also add this to the list of "how to guide your adult children.")

- An Accountant

A regular accountant or CPA is important. They will work with your financial advisors to give advice on the settlement and tax implications and help to build the roadmap forward. They will aid in the creation of your tax returns that can get messy, especially if you have been filing as married and

86 ～ Chapter 16

now will be divvying up assets, income, and earnings and filing as a single person moving forward.

There are also accountants that specialize in being "valuation mavens." That means that they are experts in determining the fair market value of marital assets, including business interests, pensions, annuities, retiree health insurance benefits, and other valuations. This may be overkill. Ask your accountant if they have the expertise to advise you before you hire several accountants. I love my accounting team. Terry is my bookkeeper and works with Bob, my accountant. Again, I have found people I trust who have my back and are professionals in their fields.

Don't use your husband's accountant.

- A Forensic Accountant

One of the challenges with the divorce process is that one spouse may try to hide or has been hiding assets from the other. If things are messy and confusing financially, meaning that you may have no idea about your husband's assets, debts, expenses, and so on, and where the money may be hidden in real estate, or in overseas accounts, for instance, it may be time to hire a *forensic accountant.* They are accounting sleuths.

A forensic accountant can help to locate all the financial information that you need in order to get a clear picture of the total assets. If you have a strong suspicion, or you know that there are assets that your husband has not disclosed, you need to tell your lawyer and they will investigate it. Don't confront your spouse. These forensic experts do this digging and uncovering of assets for a living. Leave it to them.

- A Real Estate or Art/Antique and Collectible Appraiser

If your assets include art or collectibles, seek advice from professional appraisers. Your husband may get his own and eventually, after the wrangling, an average value may be decided upon.

Getting the right legal representation is key, which is why I have devoted a whole chapter to this. The lawyers handle the financial settlement with the aid from accountants and your financial advisors.

CHAPTER 17

~

How Do You Find Your Divorce Team?

My Grandma Jewel would have given you advice, when she was my weekly guest on my radio show. She did a segment called *Financial Tips from Grandma Jewel*. She was not a financial expert, but she was my grandma and my trusted life-adviser. If I asked Grandma how a person should find an accountant or a lawyer, she would say, "Ask the question to the women in the beauty parlor, of course." She is right. Ask trusted friends who don't have an agenda and start there. They will honestly discuss their experience.

Branch out in your search, if you dye your own hair and don't have an appointment in a salon in your immediate future, look on the Internet. It would be great if the divorce team has written some articles or blogs, so you can get a sense of their philosophy. Getting the "biggest gun in the field" is not necessarily the best way to go. They want to focus on the visible divorces where there are lots of assets. If you don't fit into the JLo or Angelina category, look for a more reasonable solution. You can consult friends, family, your financial advisors, your accountant, and obviously your hairdresser, but don't assume just because your friends love their accountant or lawyer means that you will.

Mediation vs. Your Own Lawyer— What Type of Divorce Is for You?

I will take you through the process of considering a mediator vs. an attorney. Basically, an attorney will work for each partner and represent them. So, your attorney is in your corner; your husband's is in his. It is more of an adversarial situation if there is a lawyer. But you will have a person just looking after you.

88 ～ Chapter 17

When you select a mediator, they work with both of you and do not take sides and do not give legal advice. Let's consider which may be best for your needs. For instance, if the divorce is amicable, a mediator may be more appropriate and cheaper.

You need to seek guidance. You both may not want to waste money on lawyers. It also takes more time to work through lawyers, where as a mediator may sit you both down together to hash things out. People often find mediation to be less stressful than a situation with lawyers, which is most likely to be contentious.

What Mediation Looks Like

Think of mediation as a tool that you both use together. It's not an "Us vs. Them," but rather, let's work this out as a team, if we can. *"If we can"* are the operative words here. You need to be able to clasp hands with your soon-to-become-ex and sing *Kumbaya*, or a mediator may not be for you.

The mediator has special training in negotiation and communication and is selected by you both or by a judge. The mediator will describe the process and what the hoped outcomes are. The mediator should assess the situation to advise you that this is a good course of action, or if they think it's best for you to each get your own attorney. You will see this pretty quickly. You can always start with a mediator, then switch to an attorney.

Warning: DON'T USE THE LAWYER or ACCOUNTANT or ANY PROFESSIONALS THAT YOUR SPOUSE IS USING.

Story: *Beware of Professional Tans*

When my friend was getting a divorce, she interviewed several high-powered lawyers. I was her advocate during these interviews. Frankly, the lawyers we met with were trying to take advantage of her. They knew there was lots of money, and they knew she was vulnerable. I'll call her Ruth. Ruth was very weak and stuck in the state-of-shock space and was constantly weeping. It was very sad, but I knew I had to be strong for her. I kept making her drink water because I was afraid that she could get dehydrated from crying.

I hated that she was going to all the high-powered lawyers. I finally put my two cents in and intervened and explained to her that we could find an attorney who could be her advocate, who didn't drive a brand-new Bentley, and who didn't have a professional tan in the middle of the winter.

I have also found other sound advice when picking a lawyer that I'll pass on to you. It is the lawyer's office. An office really tells a lot about the

How Do You Find Your Divorce Team?　～　89

person. If there is not a visible box of Kleenex on their desk . . . run. If there are inspirational posters around the room, read them carefully. If they have sayings like: "Difficult roads often lead to beautiful destinations" or "Storms draw something out of us that calm seas don't," . . . run. But if they have signs like: "I hope that you live a life you're proud of. If you find that you are not, I hope you have the strength to start over again; I'm here to help"[1] (Benjamin Button), or "I am not what happened to me. I am what I choose to become," (Carl Jung) . . . stay.[2]

I'm being facetious, but you want to know how your attorney is going to fight for you and protect you, if that is necessary. They don't need to coddle you; they need to respect you. You don't need a hug; you need a lawyer.

How to Select an Attorney

Finding the right attorney is important. They must have the training, experience, and empathy to match your circumstances and your personality. If you would not go to a yappy hairdresser, you should not go to a yappy lawyer either. This is not the time to just go to the first lawyer you Googled.

"Oops, I Did It Again"

Okay, I have been through three divorces; you'd think I'd have my crack team together. I didn't because circumstances had changed. With my third husband, I thought I was going to live out my life with him. I thought that he loved me unconditionally and respected me, and I felt the same way. Oops. I goofed. I ignored the real signs that our life was not OUR life, but rather all about him: his needs, his kids, and okay, I overlooked the signals: his drinking. Confession time. (Yes, I also see a pattern here.) I missed the signs of him being a narcissist, controlled by his kids.

My friend and financial advisor, Mitch, knew that I needed a great lawyer. I had a prenup, but that was not enough. My husband's lawyer, who refused to ever meet with me and my lawyer to discuss the prenup, had just presented me with his prenup. It was a trainwreck. It did provide for me after his eventual death, via a trust. The trust would have allowed me to continue to live in his apartment for my lifetime. That's the good news. The bad news is that the trust was not to be established until after his death and also after his estate went through probate. In simple terms, I was not protected and could not have afforded to carry his apartment, where we would be living together. The kid-sharks would have been circling in the water, waiting for me to move out before my trust kicked in.

Rather than fight, I decided to keep my other home and would just move there when he died and let his kids fight over his apartment. I'm financially

90　～　Chapter 17

independent and was going to keep it that way. We were not going to comingle anything, and I was good with that. I just thought that I'd like to continue to live in the apartment where we were to share our lives together and not be evicted.

Mitch introduced me to Pat Barbarito. She became my trusted lawyer during this whole process, and we are still friends today. I selected Pat, not only for her impressive credentials, but mostly because she "got it." She started to finish my sentences about how I wanted and needed representation. She didn't treat me like a child, but as a respected peer who needed advice. I asked Pat to give me some wisdom for my book pertaining to selecting a lawyer. She didn't have cute sayings on her wall, but she did have the box of Kleenex, which I used.

Pat told me, "Who you choose to represent you in a divorce is one of the most important decisions you will make as you enter this uncharted territory. You must select an attorney who is intelligent and financially sophisticated. However, the single most important quality I believe your divorce lawyer should have is emotional intelligence.

"Your attorney's ability to make decisions and develop a flexible strategy will ultimately result in a favorable outcome. EQ and sophistication are required to develop that strategy. Dissolving a marriage is emotionally complex. The ability to strategize, pivot, and understand your client, the soon to be ex-spouse, the adverse attorney, and all the players, as well as the dynamic of the marriage, is necessary. A marriage is not ended by simply imposing a clinical financial analysis."

Interview, Interview, Interview
I'll also keep saying that no matter how much pressure your spouse exudes, never use the same attorney. Conflict-of-interest rules prevent one attorney from representing you both. You can get around that by calling them a mediator, or saying that you have agreed. Don't. So, if he brings it up . . . just say, "No."

Remember, most attorneys specialize in one area of the law. You want one who specializes in divorces that take place later in life. There are lots of ways to find the right attorney.

- If you have a business attorney now, you can ask them, unless it's your husband's attorney.
- Ask other respected professionals you have in your life. They could be therapists, financial professionals, or counselors that may have heard of a great lawyer. I asked my trusted financial people, Mitch and Ann, and they referred me to Pat.

How Do You Find Your Divorce Team? ～ 91

- Referral services are available. Many local city and county bar associations operate these services. They are different from a directory because they will match you with an attorney. In a directory, the lawyers just pay for a listing.
- American Academy of Matrimonial Lawyers (AAML) is a resource you can use. There is a website with a directory of lawyers to check out.
- Friends and family are a great source to find a lawyer. Just be aware that your case may not be like the ones that came before you.

Not for nothing, most state bar associations keep records of lawyers who are licensed to practice in their state. They have search engines that can reveal the lawyer's record of any disciplinary actions that have been taken against an attorney.

Lawyer Checklist: Preparing for Your First Meeting

It seems like a lot of time to research your team, and it is, but it is important to interview professionals before you make a choice. Make sure that they don't roll their eyes when you ask such questions about:

- *Fees/retainers* – (My friend's fancy-tan Gucci-two-shoes-lawyer took his fee as a percentage of the assets. My response was, "Are you kidding? Run!") You want to pay an hourly fee. There most likely will be a retainer, as well. A retainer is a fee paid before any services have been performed. This protects the lawyer if you decide to skip out after they have done a lot of work. They will bill against the retainer and send you statements.
- *Their training and background.* How long have they been doing this?
- *Similar experience.* Have they handled other women who have similar backgrounds and gray divorces as yours?
- *Who handles your case?* Do you deal with them directly or their subordinates? What is the fee breakdown for subordinates?
- *Ask for references.* Call some up.
- *Take notes during the process* because all your lawyer meetings will start to blend together. Do not set your sights too low and settle for the first lawyer just because the process is too painful. This is the person who will have to be your advocate, who will have your back. Be diligent and listen to Benjamin Franklin, "Diligence is the mother of good luck."[3]

92 ～ Chapter 17

After you select the attorney and are preparing for the first meeting, make sure that you have lots of your ducks in order to maximize your time and minimize your bills. The clock will be ticking.

Basic Personal Information

Most of this list seems obvious, but it will help you to organize your information and present it to your lawyer.

- Your basic information/and your spouse's: full name, date of birth, Social Security numbers, cell phone numbers, email, and mailing addresses.
- Proof of residency. Usually, your driver's license and some utility bills.
- Wedding details: where and when.
- Health insurance details: who provides it and the coverage details.
- Name of spouse's divorce lawyer, if that is disclosed at this juncture.
- Information about your employer, if employed (even part-time and/or self-employed): name, address, and main phone number. Include all employers in the previous years and your salary.
- Length of employment: If you are self-employed, bring financial statements and any loan information. List any loans for your business. If you can, try to figure out a valuation.
- Information about your spouse's employer, if employed (even part-time, and/or self-employed): name, address, and main phone number. Your spouse's length of employment and his salary. Include all employers in the previous years. List any loans if he is self-employed. If you can, bring an evaluation of his business.

More Information to Bring

1. Any papers or correspondence you may have received that was sent from your husband or his attorney, even if he is filing or not.
2. A copy of your prenup, if you have one.
3. If you have compiled the list of assets and liabilities, bring that.
4. Try to outline your marriage. Date you were married, how many kids, whether you or he was married before, any kids from other marriages.
5. Names, birth dates, and Social Security numbers of not only your spouse, but your kids as well. And don't forget about children from previous marriages, for you both.
6. Name of marital therapist if you and your spouse have recently visited, with dates.
7. Addresses of all your properties.

How Do You Find Your Divorce Team? ～ 93

8. Major changes in health.
9. Marital problems: affairs, violence, or abuse.
10. Make your own list of questions for your lawyer. Include anything you can think of. For instance, cost, estimated time involved, time to resolution, how you get protected, how you can discover any other assets he has that you may not know about, or any other skeletons you may suspect.
11. Think about the best place to serve papers, if that is a goal. It could be at home, or at his work.
12. Information about previous marriages, for you both, including divorce decrees.
13. Details about child support from previous marriages, if applicable.
14. If there are temporary orders, bring them. You will be further down the road with this, if you started proceedings with another attorney. If you have, bring all the court documents.
15. List of properties you and your spouse owned prior to marriage and purchased during marriage.
16. Any inheritances or gifts.
17. Any trusts and their terms.
18. List the contents of any safety deposit boxes, if you know. List where they are and if they are joint, or not.

CHAPTER 18

~

Choosing the Right Financial Advisor

No matter your age, choosing the right financial advisor is a critical life decision that too often is either ignored completely, or considered decades later than it should.

Trust me, I know. Speaking as a member of the generation that preferred to walk on their frayed bell bottoms with flowers in our hair, we lived by the maxim, "Never trust anyone over 30." Many Baby Boomers haven't gotten the memo, fax, Post-it, text message, or telegram regarding long-term financial planning. "Sha-La-La, live for today" also translated into neither considering our future nor saving for it. In fact, a recent Bankrate.com study bears this out: 36 percent of adults lack retirement savings and as many as 14 percent of adults sixty-five and over have put away nothing.[1]

Furthermore, 26 percent of people between the ages of fifty to sixty-four haven't started to save for retirement. Come on, people. Who cares that bell bottoms are back. The flowers in your hair are wilted, and you will wilt on the vine if you don't take your future seriously. You need to consider the many decades we are *likely to live*. If you are a sixty-five-year-old woman today, you are expected to live until 86.6 years old.[2] And if you are healthy? Who knows how long.

This is all a long way of saying that you need to get serious about your financial future if you haven't already. Let's look at how to choose a financial advisor that has the IQ and EQ to deal with you and help design and manage your investing future.

Here's How

1. What Is a Financial Advisor?

They are professionals who will help you to design your financial life. There are all sorts of investment professionals with all sorts of designations, such as

96 ～ Chapter 18

investment professionals, tax professionals, wealth managers, financial consultants, financial planners, and so forth. There are even divorce financial advisors.

So, you have a lot of options. I prefer to have one from a mid to large firm because they have that muscle behind them, but it's your choice. I want my assets to matter to them. So, if the minimum their client is required to have is $10 million in assets and you have $1 million, they can't spend that much time with you.

You want a financial advisor with the knowledge and patience to treat you like a partner in your financial future. If they just want to tell you what to do . . . run. If they start out by selling you a product before knowing your needs and risk tolerance . . . run.

You want them to care and to understand your needs and wants, assist in determining your goals and set up an investment portfolio to achieve them, and help you to track your money-world moving forward.

2. Determine What the Money Is For

Before you walk into the office of a prospective financial advisor, ask yourself about your future needs and wants for your money. You want to think of a general design for your life. You will drilldown later.

If you're a Baby Boomer, like me, you're probably thinking about how you'll spend your retirement. I like the idea of spending my retirement years near my kids, grandkids, and friends, and being close to New York City so I can go to theaters and get into Columbia University. But I totally understand the snowbirds, who would rather spend their winter in Fort Lauderdale or Tucson. You'll likely need to figure out what this all could cost and there are plenty of online calculators and planning tools available to help you.

3. Consider Why You Need a Financial Advisor

Obviously, you know that you are knee-deep in *passing the butter*, but also think about what a financial advisor can be called upon to help you with:

- Creating a list of financial goals
- Setting up a workable budget
- Help in understanding investing and designing that plan
- Tax planning
- Charitable giving

4. Get to Know Your Financial Self

Are you the type of person looking for high risk/high reward assets? Remember there is no such thing as a free lunch. If the investment looks too good to be true, it probably is. And there will always be someone to sell you a get-rich-quick scheme. Are you more conservative, happy to invest your money in safer bonds and stocks that over time prove immune to major economic upswings and downswings? Your financial advisor should reflect those attitudes via their investment strategy designed for you.

5. Risk Tolerance

This is the level of risk any investor is willing to take. That means that you should decide what makes you comfortable. You have to gauge how much of the thrill of the *big wins* will balance against the possible tragedy of the *big losses*. I refer to this as the "cold sweat test." I don't want to wake up in the middle of the night in a cold sweat worrying about my investment decisions.

Also, as a senior, the time/value of money is not on your side. That means that you don't have a lot of time to make up any losses that you may have incurred when you take the big investment risks. Decide this for yourself, and your financial advisor should be coaching you through those decisions and setting up a portfolio that matches your risk tolerance. My advice is to go with a conservative portfolio that is balanced.

6. You're a Client, Not a Customer

Your financial advisor is a salesperson; however, they shouldn't high-pressure you into a decision you're not comfortable with. You want them to have your back. You want them to be consultative and offer advice, but you need to understand that the reality is they sell investments.

Ask friends and family for their recommendations and be wary of financial advisors who have had long careers elsewhere and are just starting out; they don't have the experience. Likewise, as stated before, if the advisor starts to sell you a product before they ask what the money will eventually be used for . . . leave.

7. The Best Things in Life Are (Not) Free

That was the running joke in the Beatles song "Money," but it's also a fact of life. Financial advisors advertise their services via several fee structures. Some are fee based where the client pays a monthly retainer. Others work off commissions. But many of those advisors use language that suggests their services are "free." For most clients, monthly fees are the preferred payment

98 ~ Chapter 18

structure. Commission-based structures incentivize greater risks taken by the advisor with *your money*. They should be transparent with their fee structure. There are lots of ways to invest:

- *Low cost* – Robo-advisors. These are digital solutions where you find a fin-tech company that offers investing options. You will answer some generic questions, such as age, risk-tolerance, goals, and so on, and then the computer algorithm will spit out a portfolio of investments for you. The fees may start as low as .25 percent of your balance. But remember, there is no one to talk to, you are flying alone. I'm in favor of real human interaction. This investing solution is great for your kids, but not really for you.
- *Medium cost* – There are online financial-planning services. They may have a minimum investing requirement of $25,000 or more to start out with; however, some have no minimum. They offer more than the robo-solution, so the fees are a little higher. Again, I want someone I can go to lunch with and discuss my future.
- *Higher cost* – Traditional financial advisors. They will meet you in person. They usually charge 1 percent of your assets per year and will probably indicate the minimum asset size they specialize in. I like these if you want specialized services and if your situation is complex. As I said, it's your money and your life. For me, it's important to have someone in my corner, and Mitch and Ann have been there with me for thirty-five years.

8. Verify Credentials and Ensure Goals Align
Verifying credentials means you are dealing with a certified financial planner (CFP) or others with financial credentials. You are interviewing and vetting these people. Doing so means they are required to adhere to Certified Financial Planning Board of Standards. But it's more than that. Ultimately, whomever you choose should demonstrate a genuine interest in your long-term financial goals. Often that may even mean selecting a professional who's in a similar stage of life as you. They have gray hair like yours and have been through many years of helping and coaching people.

9. Comfort Is Key
Credentials are important, but comfort is even more crucial to a successful relationship with your financial advisor. When I work with financial advisors, I often tell them that if they aren't invited to all the family parties, graduations, and weddings, they're probably not a trusted member of the family and

not doing their job. Choose a financial advisor the way you select a doctor, lawyer, and even hairdresser; seek out recommendations from trusted family members and friends. You also have to feel really comfortable telling them all of your *financial dirty laundry*, or they can't help you from collecting more. If you are not comfortable . . . keep interviewing.

It's time to know what you don't know, and there is no shame in that. I'm a financial expert and I still want financial advice I trust. I could do this alone, but why would I? I can also figure out how to do my own dry cleaning, but why would I when there are experts who can do it better? I seem to be quoting Benjamin Franklin a lot; but hey, he's Benjamin Franklin. "An investment in knowledge pays the best interest."[3]

CHAPTER 19

Get Your Money Act Together

Take a Deep Breath and Create Your To-Do List

Below is another list of information that will be needed for the divorce to proceed. I know that this is all tedious, but keep in mind, this will free you from the tedious life you are leaving and help you to grease the skids on *passing the butter* more quickly.

Income and Tax Documents
- Five years of federal and state tax returns for you and your spouse. If he doesn't hand over these documents freely, the courts will make him.
- Try to obtain statements that would include any income that may not show up on pay stubs. This may be more difficult to obtain, such as equity incentives, stock options, extraordinary income, accrued vacation, and cash tips; all are not shown on paystubs.
- You may have had a business together. I have not gone into detail in the book about that, but if you can, bring any financial statements and tax returns for the company even if you both or individually had an interest in it.

Real Estate Documents
- Marital home deed.
- Current appraisals or some market comparable values.
- List the mortgages (first, second, and home equity lines) against the property, or lines of credit affecting the property.
- Rental properties.
- Vacation properties and any timeshare interests.

101

102 ~ Chapter 19

Personal Property Information
- This one is not easy. Try to list your furniture and furnishings and what you think their current market value is.
- Jewelry, art, collectibles, wine, and so forth are also a challenge to value.
- Boats, trailers, motor homes, and so on.

Financial Information
- All your bank and investment accounts. Don't forget cash that you both may have in your home.
- All retirement accounts.
- Money owed to either of you.
- Life insurance policies, including disability and long-term health care insurance.
- Insurance, such as homeowners, car, other health insurance.
- Intellectual property that may have value, such as patents, trademarks, copyrights, licensing agreement, royalty agreements, and so on.
- All debt, including student loans, mortgages, auto, or money owed to private people.
- Tax debt that may be owed.

Estate-Planning Documents
- Wills plus living wills
- Any trust documents
- Powers of attorney
- Advance healthcare directives

Give Credit Where Credit Is Due

Start by taking charge of this part of your life. A divorce can be a financial as well as an emotional slap in the face. Your credit score can be affected, which I've discussed. You need to untangle everything in your life, including your money. Just because the judge has said that legally you are divorced, or about to be, you need to look at all that you had together and start the real break-up. Begin this process before the divorce, or you may have some troubling surprises, like he has raked up credit card debt that you both are liable for because it's a joint account. You are not a victim to all of this; you just need some guidance. Here is some:

1. Check up on Your Credit Report
You can get a free report each year from one of the three major credit bureaus: TransUnion, Equifax, or Experian. This report will allow you and

Get Your Money Act Together ⁓ 103

your soon-to-be ex-husband to see your full credit history and with this you can start to see what is yours, what is his, and what is joint.

2. Sign Up for a Credit-Monitoring Service
LifeLock has one. You will get notified if your spouse attempts to open credit cards and rack up debt jointly. If you see activity, report this to your lawyer immediately, and they may notify the court.

3. Open New Credit Cards in Your Name Only
You need to start building credit in your own name. It may be easier to get a card in your name while you are still married, so get on this.

4. Apply for a Secured Credit Card
If you can't get a credit card with your own credit, you should be able to get a secured credit card.

5. Close All Your Joint Accounts
Your goal is to build your own money life. Your credit report should tell you all of the accounts you both have. Make sure that you contact (email and keep the record) all of the lenders to have your joint accounts closed. You will discuss, with your lawyer, the amounts that go into yours and his. Remember to also remove your name from any accounts that list you as an authorized user as well.

6. Close Joint Investment Accounts
Again, work with your lawyers on this. You cannot just tell a financial institution to transfer the joint account into your name, obviously. Remember to also remove your name from any accounts that list you as an authorized user.

7. Pay Your Bills
This may seem obvious, but if you are not used to paying the bills, the task may feel daunting. You may be splitting the bills, for let's say, the house. Make sure he gives you his fair share of the money owed, if he is paying you and you pay the bank. Keep copious records of this. It's better that the bank knows that you each are paying them, although you are both on the mortgage and therefore both liable, individually for it to be paid in full. But the most important thing is to pay each bill on time. You do not want to miss any bills because this will negatively affect your credit score. Work with your lawyer to really decide who pays what bills and check in to make sure there is proof of payment. If you have the money, pay the bill, then go after him. Create a

104　～　Chapter 19

new budget based upon your individual capacity to pay bills. This may be an interim agreement, but it's important for your credit history.

8. Divide the Credit Card Debt

Debt is handled during a divorce according to the state you live in. If you live in a common-law state, which is most states, you are liable for your debts in your name and jointly liable for any debt that is in both of your names. In community-law states, like Texas and California, you will be held jointly responsible for all debt accrued during the marriage, even if it is in his name.

States/Countries Govern Marriage and Divorce

The question is: Can you file for divorce in a different state than where you and your spouse were married?[1] The short answer is, "Yes." But it may be more complicated than that. You can only file for divorce in the state and county that has jurisdiction to hear the case. You do not necessarily have to file in the state or county that issued your marriage license. The jurisdiction will depend on the location of both spouses and how long you both have lived there. This is a long answer. To get a divorce in the United States, you need to meet the requirements and laws in the state in which you now reside.

If you got married in a foreign country, most countries have reciprocity agreements with the US states. The important condition is that one of the spouses resides in the United States for at least a few months. Each state has different requirements, and you will have to figure those out with your attorney. If you are not a US citizen, it may be more complicated, but doable. Start with an attorney where you live.

Some places have weird laws[2] that you may have to deal with:

US State Laws
- In Maryland, people who are getting a divorce must swear in court that they have not spent the night with each other in the past year—and the kicker is that they need a witness to corroborate that.
- In Wichita, Kansas, a man's mistreatment of his mother-in-law cannot be used as grounds for divorce.
- In Truro, Massachusetts, a groom-to-be must prove himself "manly" by hunting and killing either six blackbirds or three crows.
- In Detroit, Michigan, it's illegal for a man to scowl at his wife on Sunday, and if he does, this is grounds for divorce.
- In Vermont, women need to get written permission from their husband to get false teeth.

Foreign Laws
(It's hard to check these laws, so just go with me.)

- In Hong Kong, if a woman discovers her husband is cheating on her, she can legally kill him and doesn't have to get a divorce. The catch is that she can only use her bare hands. But she can kill the mistress any way she wants.
- In Samoa, it's legal for a woman to divorce her husband if he forgets her birthday.
- The Philippines and the Vatican are the last countries in the world where divorce is not allowed.
- Supposedly, and I stress, supposedly, in Saudi Arabia, a woman can legally divorce her husband if he fails to bring her fresh coffee every morning. (Let's not discuss what happens to a woman who is caught cheating on her husband.)
- In Monaco, to be legally married, you must write a note announcing your marriage on a piece of paper and post it in the local town hall. The note has to remain there for ten days, but must include two Sundays. If couples do not comply, their marriage is not legal.

Okay, enough of this lunacy.

CHAPTER 20

~

Show Me the Money—
Some Things to Consider

Money Mistakes You Can Make in a Gray Divorce

- **Gray Divorce Money Mistake #1:** Holding onto your family house too long. It may be emotional, but it can also be a money pit.
- **Gray Divorce Money Mistake #2:** Not really having a clear handle on all the assets you and your husband have and their value.
- **Gray Divorce Money Mistake #3:** Health insurance considerations and costs now that you may not be on his plan.
- **Gray Divorce Money Mistake #4:** Not understanding Medicare and how it works.
- **Gray Divorce Money Mistake #5:** Not looking at the car lease for a luxury car and considering the ongoing costs of maintenance.
- **Gray Divorce Money Mistake #6:** Not really looking at what you share that you want to let go of and what you want to hold on to.
- **Gray Divorce Money Mistake #7:** Not considering college loans incurred before you got married.

Let's Look at the Gray Divorce Money Mistakes

Gray Divorce Money Mistake #1
Holding onto your family house too long. It may be emotional, but it can also be a money pit.

Your home can become the emotional pillar of your life. You decorated it so that Martha Stewart could walk in at any moment, and you would toast with her using your perfectly fluted champagne glasses that you saw on her

108 ～ Chapter 20

show. (Let's take a mental note that the last time she may have used those was when she was released from prison.)

Back to the moment. You raised your kids in this house. You hosted every soccer night. You had your family there for every holiday. I get it. It became part of your identity. You are not going to lose that, too. So, you dig in and do everything that you can do to keep your home . . . your old life.

I worked with a friend who did just that.

Story

Kanisha was a woman I met at one of my presentations. She explained that she was in the midst of her gray divorce and that her home was part of her soul, her being. "He will not take this away from me."

Her soon-to-be-ex, Jose, offered her a large settlement and could carry her if she sold the home and split the proceeds with him. I said that "Cash is King." She might be able to negotiate that number up and that was good.

She told me that I just didn't understand. This now-empty, nine-thousand-square-foot home, replete with a pool and tennis court, was part of her dream to be the new family retreat for her grandchildren and kids for every holiday and summers. She burst out in tears. I hugged her. Sometimes I know that I just have to let people go on their own journey. I lost touch with her until about a year later, when she reached out to me.

Kanisha's calm, level-headed lawyer also didn't think that the big house made sense. But frankly, he was condescending to her and treated her like a child. He just said that she didn't understand the costs of carrying a large home, because her husband had always handled the expenses.

Kanisha was hell-bent on hiring the lawyer who was going to dig in and get her the house. She found the creepy, expensive, overly tanned lawyer who did just that. She got the house, and a lower cash settlement.

She told me that in honor of "winning" the house, she threw a party to celebrate and went on with her new life. But things changed quickly. She really didn't understand how expensive it was to run the house. The utility bills were nuts and she had to hire people to take care of the pool and tennis court. She didn't play tennis and frankly the last people to play were her sons, who hadn't visited in over six months. One had moved to the Midwest and the other to the South. They spent most of their holidays at their spouses' relatives' homes and only popped in to visit Kanisha for a few days. She did love babysitting for the grandchildren, as her kids spent time visiting some of their old friends, but that was on rare occasions.

Kanisha began to know that the dream of the family-hub was not realistic, and it came at a huge cost. The roof needed to be fixed, one bathroom started to leak and had to be taken down to its studs to be fixed, the house needed painting, and so on. She was back in tears again.

The house was sucking all her money out of her investment account. She sobbed that she was not even sure that she could afford to visit the grandchildren now.

I, of course, did not do, "And I told you so." I just said, let's fix the problem now. I wanted her to sit down with her financial people to figure out how much it was going to cost to get the house in presentable shape to sell. Then, I dealt with the emotional part with Kanisha.

I asked her if the house was now a burden rather than a joy? Did it feel like a stone around her neck? I also told her how my kids and I dealt with the time it was necessary for me to sell the big house where my kids and I spent fun-filled times of laughter and growth with friends and family.

My son, Rhett, came up with a wonderful idea. It was almost like a ceremony. My daughter, son, and I walked around the old property to find a rock that was beautiful that was just lying on the path to the backyard. They then arranged for friends to call me to tell me stories of joy they experienced in our house. We shared the memories together. We told stories, laughed, cried, and then told our stone to absorb all the memories of the life in this house.

I know this sounds woo-woo. But it really highlighted the fact that the house was filled with memories, and it wasn't about the house. It was about the people and our lives. Memories go with you . . . utility bills do not have to.

The rock is still with me. It makes me smile. It warms my heart, and I'm grateful to my son for coming up with this idea.

Yes, I shared this with Kanisha. She first looked at me with skepticism. Here I was the objective money expert talking to her about filling a stone with memories.

About two months later, she reached out to me. She said she tried my crazy stone idea with her sons via Zoom. They loved the idea. I don't know if they loved it because it may have contributed to their mom putting the house on the market, or if they really bought into the "Memories Stone." It didn't matter.

Kanisha did sell the house and found a cute condo in the same town. She didn't want to move far from her familiar territory and friends, which was fine.

So, you can see that hanging on to the family house can be a big mistake in a gray divorce, or frankly in any divorce. When you get money, it's money. It doesn't come with a carrying cost, notwithstanding financial advisor fees, which are transparent. A home is a money-pit with hidden costs. You want to avoid any unknown carrying costs for assets in a divorce.

Gray Divorce Money Mistake #2
Not really having a clear handle on all the assets you and your husband have and their value.

110 ～ Chapter 20

The message is that two assets may appear to have the same market value but may not. The market value means the ability to sell those assets, their carrying costs, and taxes, and so forth. Therefore, these can greatly affect costs.

For instance, a thousand dollars in cash is different from a stock valued at one thousand dollars at the time of the divorce. Selling that stock may have a tax impact; using the cash will not. The profit made on a stock works like this: figure out the difference between the cost basis (what you paid) and the sale price. What is left is what is made or lost on that investment. It is either taxed as long-term or short-term capital gain, depending on whether the asset was held for under or over a year. The point is that investments are not the same as cash when you are divvying up assets.

Also, for instance, if you or your ex has a 401(k) or other workplace retirement accounts, be careful how you arrange the split. If you take money out of a 401(k) and then give it to your spouse, it is not worth the face value. There will be a 20 percent withholding on that. And if the account holder is younger than 59.5, a 10 percent penalty could apply for early withdrawal.

We talked about the family home, but also at the time of valuing that, you need at least two appraisals, and you need to determine the cost basis of that property. If you hold on to it, you will be responsible for paying the capital gains on any profit you make when you sell it. And the government doesn't let you take a loss if you sell it for less than its original purchase price. I found that out when I got hosed selling my huge family home.

Gray Divorce Money Mistake #3
Health insurance considerations and costs now that you may not be on his plan.

Gray divorce starts at age fifty for our purposes, so health insurance is a consideration if you are on the young side. Basically, if your spouse's health insurance policy covered you, you may now find yourself with a new hefty expense that you need to consider. Medicare will not kick in until age sixty-five.

Simply, there are three options: 1. If you are employed, your employer can cover you. 2. You can sign up for your state's healthcare under the Patient Protection and Affordable Care Act or ACA.[1] 3. You can continue your ex's existing coverage through COBRA for up to thirty-six months,[2] but the cost may be high.

Gray Divorce Money Mistake #4
Not understanding Medicare and how it works.

Just so you will be smart at your next cocktail party when you run out of things to talk about: Medicare was launched in 1965. President Harry Truman called for a national health insurance fund to be started in 1945, and he and First Lady Bess were the first recipients.[3] Today, it accounts for about 12 percent of the federal budget and 20 percent of all healthcare expenditures in the United States. As of 2022, 65 million Americans had coverage through Medicare.[4]

Who Is Eligible?
Medicare is available for seniors ages sixty-five and older and permanent US residents with qualifying disabilities and chronic medical conditions. These groups who have been in the United States for over five years and worked at least ten years paying Medicare taxes may qualify.

How Do You Enroll?
Initial enrollment begins three months before the first day of the month of your sixty-fifth birthday and ends four months after your birthday. Medicare open enrollment is available between October 15 and December 7 every year. You can enroll online or via phone. After you enroll, you will receive your Medicare benefits through the Centers for Medicare & Medicaid Services.

Can You Have an HSA (Health Savings Account) with Medicare?
No. If you are on Medicare, you are not eligible to contribute pretax to an HSA. But you can withdraw money from an existing HSA to cover Medicare costs.

What Does Medicare Cost?
If you qualify, you get Part A for free. For instance, the deductible for Part B in 2023 was $226 and the monthly premium would have been $164.90, and these only go higher depending on your income. Note, if you do not pay your premiums in a timely manner, your coverage can be taken away.

There are four parts to Medicare:

- **Part A** – Original Medicare: Inpatient hospital care, home health, nursing facilities, and hospice care.
- **Part B** – Original Medicare: Doctor visits, diagnostic and preventive care, lab test, and mental health.

112 ～ Chapter 20

- **Part C** – Private insurance option: Original Medicare coverage; dental and vision may be included.
- **Part D** – Private insurance option: Prescription drug coverage.

Original Medicare is the most common, which includes Part A and B. There is a deductible, which means that you pay the deductible before Medicare kicks in to start paying. Part A is typically paired with Medicare Part B, though there was an independent deductible of $1,600 in 2023. That must be paid before Medicare covers expenses.

Parts C and D are not included as part of Original Medicare, and you will not automatically be enrolled in these benefits. Private insurers can cover this, but you will have to find them and pay out of pocket for this. I recommend that you find a Medicare specialist—there are tons out there, who can discuss the different plans that private insurers offer. I have a policy. I'm healthy now, but who knows when I will have that skydiving accident and need extra coverage.

Gray Divorce Money Mistake #5
Not looking at the car lease for a luxury car and considering the ongoing maintenance.

A leased car can become an issue in your divorce. In most states, only marital property is divided in a divorce, and each spouse will keep their own separate assets. The judge or mediator will decide whether the vehicle belongs to one or both of you. It will matter whose name is on the vehicle's title.

The car leasing company will look to the person or persons who signed the lease and who is legally liable for the debt. Remember, the leasing company doesn't care that you are divorced; they are not bound by the divorce judgment.

If the car is leased, you will have to go back to the leasing company to explore your options. They may let you terminate the lease, which may include a termination fee, and/or paying off what's due, or give the car back with maybe some sort of compensation toward a new car purchase or lease.

I also want you to look at the costs to carry and maintain that luxury car and decide if it's worth it. You need to look at the mileage limitations and if that is going to fit into your current lifestyle. The average ten-year maintenance cost for a luxury car is about $12,000.[5] They also tend to take premium gas, notwithstanding electric vehicles. Luxury vehicles also cost more to insure and to repair.[6] Insurance premiums for luxury cars cost an average of 18 percent more than the cost of insuring a moderately priced sedan.

My point is that I'd like you to consider the cost/benefits of leasing or taking on the lease of a luxury car in your gray divorce.

Gray Divorce Money Mistake #6

Not really looking at what you share that you want to let go of and what you want to hold on to.

This is not easy. This was your life. You built memories. But it's time to examine what is important moving forward. That could be everything from a vacation home to a pet, to special art and furniture . . . anything you share. We are looking at all assets and debt. There will be lots of attention paid to assets and splitting them, but I want to look at some of the emotional assets (and real ones) that you may share. Examine what is important and what really isn't. Try not to hang on to the sentimental assets that remind you of the life that you are cleaning up and moving on from. There are psychological professionals to help you with that closure.

Gray Divorce Money Mistake #7

Not considering college loans incurred before you got married.

Generally, if you or your spouse took out student loans before you got married, those do not become shared debt or community property after marriage. That means that you are on the hook for your loans, as is he for his. The exception is if this was covered in the prenuptial agreement, then that would trump this.

CHAPTER 21

~

Initiating the Divorce

It's not pleasant and it's the only step you can take if mediation doesn't work out. The case will begin with the filing of a *pleading* that may be called a *petition*, a *complaint*, or a *request*. This will set out limited facts and tells the court what you are asking for—usually it will deal with property, assets, financial support, and so on. After the filing, the papers are delivered to the other spouse, who is expected to respond or answer within a set amount of time. Tensions could start to run higher now because when something is in writing and lawyers are involved, it suddenly becomes real.

"Remember the Alimony"

That was a saying from the famous Dr. Oscar Kruesi, the father of a dear friend, Kate Lincoln. Lots of Dr. Kruesi's female patients needed medical and psychological coaching through divorce, and he was there to help them put up a good fight until the end. This was one of his sayings that stuck in my mind that you can carry with you.

Alimony discussions are not easy. Women often don't like what can be *the fight*. I don't; I get it. But these negotiations will likely follow you for your life. As Carrie Fisher said, "Everything is negotiable. Whether or not the negotiation is easy is another thing."[1]

Alimony is almost always granted after long-term marriages, if there is a need. When you divorce in your younger years, usually "rehabilitative" alimony is granted that will supply support while the spouse gets back on their feet. However, if it's a long-term marriage, in many cases alimony is given for life. If it is a second marriage that is short term, alimony may fall in between the above

116 ⁓ Chapter 21

circumstances. I'll assume that because this is a gray divorce, that the children of the marriage are also starting to get gray; no child support is applicable.

Since you both are older, the person paying alimony is later in their career. This is good news because their compensation will be greater, but it also means that it can get complex. Know the total compensation and not just their base salary. Make sure all things are considered, including:

- *Retirement* money is usually cut in half. It doesn't matter if this is a no-fault or an at-fault divorce. Pension plans may be used to offset alimony, but make sure that you both are being advised on the tax implications.
- *The Family House* will become an asset that has to be valued and split. As mentioned before, make sure that if you opt to keep the house that you don't become house-poor. The mortgage debt is only part of this alimony consideration. The house needs to be maintained, taxes and utilities paid, and those costs may greatly eat into any monetary settlements.
- *Special Needs Children* may be living with you who need to be supported for their lifetime. The costs around that care have to be taken into account. Alimony may also have to cover a larger home to accommodate the adult child plus caregivers, medicine, food, extra services, and so forth.

Determining an Amount and Duration of Alimony

These are some of things that should be considered:

- Bonuses
- Restricted stock units
- Options
- Ownership stakes
- Executive compensation packages
- Car allowances
- Travel perks

So, when determining an amount of alimony in a long-term marriage, the *total* compensation a spouse receives needs to be considered, not just your husband's base salary (or yours).

Permanent Alimony
Permanent alimony is financial support paid from one party to another after the divorce. Unlike other types of alimony, permanent alimony is usually

Initiating the Divorce ~ 117

paid until one spouse dies. It was created at a time when it was typical for the man to be bringing home the bacon and the wife to be home raising the kids as a homemaker. This type of alimony is not applicable in many states today. The states are counting on the fact that women are more educated and in the workforce. Most states award the younger receiving spouse time and rehabilitative alimony to get back on their feet and to get a job if they have been raising the kids and out of the workforce. Rehabilitative alimony is great for younger women, but with gray divorce, a sixty-year-old woman may not be able to find a job to support herself; she may need permanent alimony.

There are no hard and fast rules on how permanent alimony is calculated. Common factors are your spouse's ability to pay, the length of the marriage, the ability for you to find employment, contributions to the marriage, your age, among other considerations. It typically would end if you remarried.

Story

This is about a woman, Joan, who married the heir to a famous family fortune at age thirty-five. She was the breadwinner because he spent most of his time on the golf course, and she later found out, was having an affair. He flitted from job to job because, frankly, he was biding his time until his trust fund kicked in. She had a high-powered job and supported them both and his money-spending habits.

She caught him cheating. And after throwing all the clothes and golf clubs she had bought him out of the apartment building window, she filed for divorce.

He hired a fancy family lawyer, and he was awarded alimony that she was to pay until his trust fund kicked in. It's a great story, culminating with her leaping to her feet in court declaring that she "Would rather use the alimony she had to pay him to hire a hit-man, before she would pay him a dime." The affair didn't seem to move the judge, who declared that "Her husband was used to being supported in the lifestyle she had provided and that he was entitled to have that continue."

Joan was held in contempt of court, but her attorney had the charges dropped. She did end up paying her ex alimony until he remarried.

The point was that Joan moved forward, really forward. She took one step at a time and became one of the highest-ranking women in the insurance world. Her gumption reminds me of the words of Martin Luther King Jr. when he said, "If you can't fly then run, if you can't run then walk, if you can't walk then crawl, but whatever you do you have to keep moving forward."[2]

CHAPTER 22

~

How Do You Legally Divvy-up Assets and Income?

This all varies from state to state. You can look this up online, but basically, in New Jersey, Illinois, Pennsylvania, New York, and thirty-seven other states, dividing a couple's marital assets and liabilities falls under the concept of equitable distribution.[1] While in California, Washington, and eight other states, the concepts of community property are applied.[2]

It feels like "equitable distribution"[3] should mean splitting things fifty-fifty, but actually, "it means 'fair' division," so it is not clear-cut, and the court or arbitrator will decide. "Community property is generally considered to be all property that the two parties acquired during the marriage or partnership and includes debts, physical property, financial instruments, and money. This means that community property includes bank accounts, retirement accounts, income, stocks, home equity, vehicles, furniture, mortgages, credit card debt, tax debt, and student loans. When two parties divorce in a community property state, all the property acquired during marriage will be divided evenly."[4]

Say you live in an equitable distribution state, you're sixty-three, got married at age thirty-six, and have a 401(k) that you've been contributing to since you were twenty-five. Do you really have the statements from the day you got married to know what its premarital value is? And let's say you both could have forked over money to help the other save in their plan. This could be impossible to prove.

Or, let's say you live in a community property state and have owned a baseball card collection from age ten, way before you were married, that has appreciated significantly over the years. You have been gifting baseball cards to your partner since you met. And worse yet, how do you figure out the appreciation over the original cost? Can you prove this is separate property

119

120 ～ Chapter 22

and shouldn't be included in the division of your marital assets and liabilities? It's important, because you could be giving away premarital property or separate assets your soon-to-be ex-spouse is not entitled to.

Fairness should be the theme, but it may not turn out that way. As Sue Monk Kidd said in her book *The Secret Life of Bees*, "Nothing is fair in this world. You might as well get that straight right now."[5]

A Hard Look at the Marital Assets Checklist

Do not just look to your attorney to do this. You are going to have to do the work and explore your financial life and how your divorce and money fits into it. Your attorney will ask you questions and give you checklists to help you list things, but maybe not all the right ones. You need to take control and be in control.

You should be prepared to:

- *Identify your assets*: That means create a detailed list of all your money, art, jewelry, and so forth. There are even things you may not have thought of, like credit card or frequent flier mile rewards programs, time-shares, or season tickets to games. I hate to mention it, but the family pets may also be an issue that has to be dealt with.
- *List your debt*: This includes credit cards, mortgages, car loans, college loans, the loan to Aunt Sarah, and so on. Debts are on the other side of the balance sheet from assets. The assets are the positive side and debt is the negative side. If your estate owes somebody money, or somebody owes you money, you need to be very clear about who owes what and to whom.
- *Marital or separate*: Your attorney can advise you on this. It gets murky because of when the assets and debt were acquired, but you need this spelled out.
- *Value*: You need to place values on your property. You may think that Grandma's dining room set is worth $2 million, but the outside appraisers may not share your thoughts. To avoid any disagreements, think about you each hiring agreed-upon outside professionals to assess things.
- *Divvy it up*: This gets tricky and may be emotional as you start to figure out who gets what. Decide what is most important to you to have. Also, you need to assess if "things" or "money" are going to be most important to you for your new life moving forward.

How Do You Legally Divvy-up Assets and Income ～ 121

Inheritances

Inheritance will muddy the waters. Typically, inheritances are considered separate property and are typically not subject to distribution; therefore, don't get equally split in a divorce. But it's not that simple. There could have been an inheritance during the marriage that was comingled into your marital assets for the benefit of both of you and your family. Marital assets and liabilities will have to be examined. You really need to know the amounts and when they were received. "Generally, inheritances are not subject to equitable distribution because, by law, inheritances are not considered marital property. Instead, inheritances are treated as separate property belonging to the person who received the inheritance, and therefore may not be divided between the parties in a divorce."[6] All said, inheritances can most certainly have a tremendous impact on your divorce settlement and finances.

For example, let's say the division of your assets and liabilities turns out to be fifty-fifty, with each of you receiving half of the retirement assets. But your spouse inherited a $500,000 lump sum from their now-deceased parents. So, was your distribution really fifty-fifty?

On one hand, the marital assets subject to distribution *were* split equally. But the reality is that your total asset pool is not fifty-fifty. And does income earned from investing that inheritance count toward a person's ability to pay or receive alimony?

As you can see, gray divorce issues for an older couple can get quite complex.

Also, assess the time value of your money and the settlement. How long will it take to get things settled and is the haggling worth it? How long will the support last is the basic question. Will you have to work? Will your lifestyle change? What kind of life will you enjoy? That is what this is all leading to.

Social Security

Social Security can add some security – Call up Social Security or go online to figure out your payments at different ages. The age at which you start collecting Social Security benefits makes a big difference in the size of your payment. You also have to think about how long you may live. Remember when you got your first paycheck and you saw a FICA tax (Federal Insurance Contributions Act)? Your first response may have been, "Who is FICA and what is he doing taking part of my paycheck?" Good question.

The reality is that the money you pay into FICA for your Social Security is not held in some account waiting for you when you retire. All those people working today and complaining about FICA are helping to pay your Social Security benefits.

122 ～ Chapter 22

You can start claiming benefits at age sixty-two, but your benefits will be smaller (forever) than if you wait to claim benefits at or beyond your full retirement age, which is based upon the year you were born. For every year that you hold off past your full retirement date until age seventy, your benefit will increase by as much as 8 percent. After age seventy, there are no more increases, so make sure you take your Social Security by your seventieth birthday.

The other good news is that each fall, there is a Cost of Living Adjustment (COLA). This means that your benefits will, in principle, go up as inflation increases.

You may have heard that when spouses in long-term marriages divorce, one party can collect Social Security from the other party's earnings, after a period of time. Again, it's not that simple. Be careful if you just assume that what you think you will receive in Social Security from your spouse can be deducted from your alimony. You may find out that you don't qualify to receive the other's benefits.

Check all of this with the Social Security Administration (SSA) when you're in negotiations on alimony. This is crucial if you're the one set to receive benefits. If you don't start to plan early on, you could be out of luck and so are your finances. It's crucial to understand your projected Social Security benefits so that you can incorporate them into your financial planning as you start to build your postdivorce budget. Start by obtaining a Social Security benefit statement.

Briefly, if your marriage lasted at least ten years, you could collect on your ex-spouse's benefits if:

- You are now unmarried
- You are age sixty-two or older
- Your ex-spouse is entitled to Social Security or disability benefits
- The benefit you will receive because of his Social Security is less than the benefit you would receive alone.[7]

If you meet all of these, you can first become entitled to receive full benefits when you reach full retirement age, even if your ex has not filed for his benefits, as long as you have been divorced for at least two continuous years. Full retirement age will vary on what year you were born, but in most cases, you must be sixty-two or older. At full retirement age, the highest benefit you can receive from his Social Security is 50 percent.

If your former spouse dies, divorced spouses may be eligible for survivor benefits, which have their own set of rules.[8]

How Do You Legally Divvy-up Assets and Income ~ 123

You can see that it is very important to speak to professionals in the Social Security office to navigate through all of this. Your financial advisors will also help you when you start to build your budget.

Life Insurance

Again, bring this up with the mediators/lawyers. But in many instances in a divorce where alimony or child support is to be paid, the person responsible may be required to carry a life insurance policy to cover those future payments in the event of their death.[9] You really want to look at this, because if for instance, you have been awarded permanent alimony (support until his death, or yours), you want to make sure that you are covered, forever, in case he dies. You will have to guess at your lifespan, but now that you don't have to put up with his snoring, figure that you will get enough sleep and live for a long time. This is all part of the negotiation.

Make sure that you are *the owner* of the policy, as well as the beneficiary, because the owner controls the policy and has the right to designate beneficiaries. If you are not in control, you may find out that his (her) new, perky beau is the designated beneficiary. Also make sure that he pays the premiums on the policy and gives you proof of that payment.

There are two main categories of life insurance:

- *Term Life Insurance* – It provides coverage for a specific period, typically between ten and thirty years. It is called "pure life insurance" because the benefit is purely life insurance and nothing more. Generally, these premiums are less expensive than permanent life insurance. You can apply at any age, but your rates will be higher as you get older, and obviously actuarially closer to death.
- *Permanent Insurance* – It is designed to provide death benefits with a wealth-building component. It builds cash because part of your premiums are invested and that cash value will grow tax-deferred over time. You can also borrow money against your cash value and even use them to pay premiums or surrender the policy to take out the cash. It is usually more expensive than term life insurance. There are two types of permanent life insurance:
  1. *Whole life insurance*, which provides a guaranteed death benefit for as long as you live because it won't expire if you keep up on premium payments. It will build the cash value, as discussed above.
  2. *Universal life insurance*, which provides permanent death benefits and cash value but allows you some flexibility in your premium payments. Your cash value and death benefits will fluctuate if you utilize this option.

124 ～ Chapter 22

Look Closely at the Premium Increases
Let's give a real-life example. Let's say now you're fifty-eight and you have been paying even premium payments for thirty years.

Well, guess what? As you age, the premium payments can skyrocket.

You need to get a new policy with a death benefit and duration to cover your alimony obligation. I just got my life insurance renewal today and it showed me that if I decide to renew my policy when I'm seventy-two, my annual premium will be $21,358 per year and increase from there.

$21,358!

I can hear your ex saying, "So you mean to tell me I not only have to pay alimony, but I also have to fork over copious amounts of cash to an insurance company?"

Yup.

I think that life insurance is a necessity for younger couples to make sure that there is protection for loved ones in the case of a death. Typically, as you age, it will become less of an issue. If you have it, keep it to cover final expenses, unless the premiums go sky-high. This should be part of your conversations with your financial planners and lawyers.

Long-Term Health Care Insurance
Chances are that as we age, we are going to need some help taking care of ourselves. Someone turning sixty-five today has almost a 70 percent chance of needing some type of long-term care services.[10] Women need care longer than men.

The question you may have is: "How are you going to pay for this?"

Long-Term Care (LTC) is a type of insurance that covers long-term health care needs and extra support that typically arise later in life when chronic conditions can raise their ugly heads. This is a type of insurance that will cover part or all your expenses when you may need extra home health care, or you may have to live in a nursing or care facility. It can cover having someone even come into your home to help with getting you dressed and bathed.

Here are some of the things to consider:

- LTC can pay for custodial care for people who cannot take care of all their needs on their own.
- It can pay for some of the benefits for care that Social Security and Medicare may not.
- LTC policies will not pay all expenses to cover in-house and nursing care costs.

How Do You Legally Divvy-up Assets and Income ⌒ 125

- Since it is a medically underwritten policy, you will have to have a medical examination to qualify. An underlying condition may make you ineligible for LTC.
- LTC is expensive. The younger you get it, the cheaper. You may be too old to obtain this, but it's worth a try if you are healthy. The majority of people with LTC buy it in their mid-fifties to mid-sixties.

You need to really have this as part of your divorce negotiations to see if these costs can be covered.

Pension Plans and Retirement Accounts

While many companies are moving away from pension plans in favor of 401(k)s, state and local governments still offer pension plans to their employees. So, if your spouse is a teacher, firefighter, police officer, or government official, chances are they have a pension. And it's probably quite substantial.

Now that you're divorcing, how do you divide such an asset? It's not like there's money sitting in an account as with an IRA or 401(k).

A pension is a promise made by an employer to provide an employee a monthly payment (typically) until they pass away. Notice nowhere in the pension docs does it say, *"provide an employee's ex-spouse a monthly payment."* When women previously said, in the UBS study, "that they were confident about their financial future," many were saying that because they were counting on their spouse's pension.

Retirement money is usually cut in half. But your lawyer must examine the benefits and include them in some way into the settlement. They must project the money that will be received in the future. It doesn't matter if this is a no-fault or an at-fault divorce. Pension plans may be used to offset alimony, but make sure that you both are being advised of the tax implications.

Terms You Will Need to Understand When Looking at Pensions/Retirement Plans

Gobblety Gook: (I'll define the terms.) For corporate pension plans, it's a bit more straightforward.

- Do a *Present Value (PV)* calculation. (What are the future payments valued at today?)

126 ～ Chapter 22

- Determine the *Coverture Fraction*. (This is a tool used by an appraiser to separate the portion of the benefits that were during the marriage from the portion that were not.)
- Get a *Qualified Domestic Relations Order (QDRO)*. It creates or recognizes the existence of an alternative payee, and the right to receive all or a portion of the benefits payable with respect to a participant under a retirement plan. A separate interest can be created, and the pension benefit shared between the parties.

(I just took a deep breath because that was a mouthful.)

When it comes to government pensions, it's not nearly as straightforward. If your spouse was a civil servant, plans are a thing of the past. Typically, a pension is considered a joint account or marital property,[11] and should be divided in a divorce. Remember, this is not automatic and unless specified, the employer will not just split the funds. Government pension plans are even more complicated than company pension plans.

As mentioned, 401(k)s,[12] 403(b)s, IRAs, or pensions become part of the marital asset calculation. The first step, even before you speak to your advisors, is to research the plans' rules to understand the options and value.

Why is this important? Your retirement plan and your husband's retirement plan may be the largest assets in your divorce, so you need to focus on them. Your lawyer may have mentioned getting a QDRO. I briefly described it above. What is that, again? It's a *qualified domestic relations order*, which is a special court order that grants a person a right to a portion of the retirement benefits of your former spouse. QDROs are typically prepared during the divorce, but they can be filed even years after the divorce. It is an important consideration because federal law says that a retirement benefit can only be divided between former spouses if there is a QDRO.

Tax Considerations

Divorce has lots of tax consequences, and you need to consult an accountant so that you understand the ramifications. You want to know the "net" amount you must live on each year. Tax laws on alimony have changed. If your divorce was finalized on or after January 2019, the person paying the alimony will pay the taxes on this and the person receiving alimony will *not* pay any taxes on this income.[13]

Your accountant also needs to be consulted about the tax consequences of distributing retirement funds. They will differ depending upon what plan you have. I'm not going to go into this now because I will put you to sleep.

How Do You Legally Divvy-up Assets and Income ⌐ 127

Just make sure this is on your "To Do List" because it is an issue, and I don't want you to have any surprises later.

I'm not going to deal with possible family businesses you and your spouse may be involved in together. That is a whole separate book! That is hard to unravel or stay raveled as Bill and Melinda have decided to do regarding the Bill & Melinda Gates Foundation. It's not easy.

In some states, divorcing parents are *required* to pay for their children's college education through child support. Yet, if you remain married, there is no such requirement of you.

It's true!

Maybe you're one of the fortunate few who've managed to put away enough to fund your children's college education(s). But if you're not, your retirement may be further away than you'd like it to be.

As you just learned, gray divorce issues for older couples are far more complex than the ones a young or newly married couple face.

This can all be taxing

Yes, if your "combined income" is too high, Uncle Sam can tax your Social Security. Combined income is the sum of your adjusted gross income, non-taxable interest, and one-half of your Social Security. According to the SSA, you may owe taxes on up to as much as 85 percent of your benefits if your combined income is high enough. Remember the accountant who was part of your divorce team? Time to have them help with your taxes!

If your only income in retirement will be from Social Security, you probably won't have to worry about paying income taxes; I didn't mean to scare you.

Are You Staying Together Because You Are Terrified to Lose Health Insurance?

Unfortunately, this happens to many couples. You may feel that you are being held hostage when facing being dropped from his healthcare coverage. Gray divorce starts at age fifty, which is far away from Medicare kicking in at age sixty-five. The most important thing is to bring this up to your team and make sure that you have a plan to move forward.

State law may come into play. For example, in some states, it is illegal for a spouse to drop the other person from their healthcare coverage while a divorce is in progress. Other states view legal separation the same as divorce and the spouse may be dropped from the policy.

128 ～ Chapter 22

In all cases following a divorce, an employer will no longer cover a spouse under an employee's healthcare plan. Federal law dictates that health insurance ends as soon as you are divorced. However, a spouse does have rights under COBRA (Consolidated Omnibus Budget Reconciliation Act).[14] COBRA premiums are expensive and can hold you over until you look for other coverage. You can also investigate the Affordable Care Act (ACA)[15] and private/individual health insurance plans for coverage.

My message is that you need health insurance, and you should be asking for this to be built into the divorce budget and settlement moving forward. You may have to adjust deductibles, lower premiums, or look at more reasonably priced plans that may choose doctors in or out of network for you.

Health insurance brokers help you navigate a complex ecosystem of insurance companies. Brokers serve as an intermediary between you, as the consumer, and the carrier, the insurance company. They can give you options and explain the terms and coverage. They are paid a commission from the insurance company, and not by you.

Alternatively, health insurance agents represent a single insurance company and may be pushing you toward their company's products, whereas brokers represent you, the consumer.

You know how to select your financial team; apply the same techniques here to interview and feel comfortable with your insurance broker/agent choices and eventually your decisions.

I know this all seems complicated and daunting. I'm only suggesting that you approach this as a business deal, even though it may feel as if you are drinking from a fire hose. You have faced way more challenging issues, and there are lots of professionals to help you through this process. Don't give up if this is what you want. You don't have to resign yourself to a life of compromise with a person whom you no longer know or love . . . and just remember the bright side: you don't have to go out and buy that lingerie just to keep the fake flames blazing!

Think of what Winston Churchill said, as the Nazis were bombing London, "If you are going through hell, keep going."[16]

SECTION 3

YOUR FINANCIAL LIFE AFTER GRAY DIVORCE

CHAPTER 23

~

Choose Your New Butter Dish

You are going to go through a period that is like the process of *ecdysis*. What the hell is that? It's when a snake sheds its skin. It is stressful for the snake. But they come out of the process of growing new skin so they can face the world again by being new and healthy. Okay, I'll stop with the metaphor of shedding your skin with your gray divorce, but doesn't it sort of feel that way? You come to the world with a fresh start to make new choices.

Your Choice

Speaking of creating new skin, my good friend Kim DeYoung, as it happens, has developed a method to help you examine that new skin. She is also the daughter of my corporate lawyer and protector, Eric Martins. Eric presented me with my ninety-two-page prenup before my second marriage. He saved my skin . . . big time.

Kim has spent the last decade coaching people around the topic of "Choice." In her book *The Book of Choice: Mapping the Life You Want by Understanding the Life You Have*, she gives her readers a roadmap of how to determine their choices—past and present—and how those impact their lives.

I bring this up because, when Kim read my manuscript, she commented that my book shows that "Our personal money stories are a combination of how we have internalized our family's money beliefs coupled with our own experiences making, spending, and saving money. We then have the choice about whether we perpetuate these stories. How do we let go of messages we deem unhealthy, and shift our language and belief system to one that is more aligned with our present-day values? Your book is a necessary part of how

132   ～   Chapter 23

choices affect us and how your readers will be empowered to examine those choices and to perhaps make different ones moving forward."

It's a great time for you to take a deep breath and pat yourself on the back. You are now going to move forward and make some new choices. You have *passed the butter.* You have shed your old skin. You are designing your new butter dish. You have just made a clearing . . . a real clearing in your life, for your life. And I know it was all hard. It may not be apparent, but there are all sorts of things that you can now do, because you are making new choices. As Joan Rivers said, "Listen, I wish I could tell you it gets better. But it doesn't get better. You get better."[1]

You will start to see life differently. Some of the new changes will be minute, and you may not notice them. But they will build up to create a new way you look at the world. It would be fun to even write a list of the small things. These choices should make you smile, as some of these are quirky funny things that you can do because you don't have that guy in your life, your house, or your bed anymore.

Things I Can Now Do That I Don't Have to Worry About

My checklist looked like this:

- I can watch any channel on the TV without hearing him sigh or tell me that the game was on.
- I don't have to hear him ask me what restaurant I wanted to go to, only to hear him say, "Really? But I don't like that place. Don't you want to go to (my favorite restaurant)?" ("Why did you ask?")
- I don't have to shave my legs if I don't want to.
- I can plan a trip to a place I have always wanted to go.
- I can see the grandchildren alone without having to also worry about entertaining him.
- I don't have to panic when I notice a three-inch hair that has grown out of my chin overnight worrying that he may have seen it.
- I can binge-watch my favorite girl-shows without worrying about his comments.
- I can let the cats sleep in my bed.
- I don't have to leave my bed to sleep in another room because his snoring is shaking the rafters. Speaking of snoring, I don't have to hear that his snoring is *my problem* because his friends' wives never complain.

Choose Your New Butter Dish ⟋ 133

I didn't include any financial stuff on this list, because I've always felt comfortable with that part of my life and didn't turn those reins over to any man. In my last marriage, we kept everything very separate, which was weird to me, but we were older, and I was fine with that. (Did I mention how his kids were in his wallet and resented me? No problems here! He supported them. In fact, one didn't work as a fifty-year-old. The other one fake-worked. I didn't see the writing on the wall, so I really understand how we can all get blindsided.)

Your checklist may include some of mine, but yours may also include some money issues:

- I can now know exactly where I stand financially.
- I can manage my investments and understand all of them.
- I don't have to wonder what "Don't worry, you are taken care of" means.
- I can decide how much I can spend and how I want to spend it.
- I can save for what I want and is important to me.
- I can no longer feel stupid about money.
- I don't have anyone telling me, "That purchase was ridiculous, why did you buy that?"
- And yes, you can now sleep horizontally across the bed if you want!

You need to look at your financial life after your divorce in a very methodical way. Some are housekeeping issues, and some are strategic issues. Think of this time in your life as *disinheriting* your spouse. Many of these items should have been done already, but if not, this is a gentle reminder. I know we all hate these types of tasks; I do. It may even feel so final, so scary that the divorce is now *really* real. But you will enjoy a sense of accomplishment as you get on top of these things. Think of the sage words of Eleanor Roosevelt, "Do one thing every day that scares you."[2]

CHAPTER 24

'Til Debt Do We Part—The
Golden Years Are Tarnishing

Without appearing overly dramatic, we are in a crisis. A real one. "In the past decade, there's been a steep increase in debt among households headed by someone age 75 and older," according to reporting by CNBC.[1] If you are sixty-five to seventy-four years of age, according to SmartAsset, you have average debt of approximately $108,700.[2] In fact, MarketWatch reports that "Seniors have more household debt now than they did during the financial crisis."[3]

The good news is that you are living longer than ever before; therefore, you have more time to pay off the debt. The bad news is that many seniors are economically insecure—living at or below 25 percent of the federal poverty level (FPL), which is $29,425 per year for a single person, and they may never be able to pay off the debt. These older adults struggle with rising housing and health care bills, inadequate nutrition, lack of access to transportation, diminished savings, and job loss," according to the National Council on Aging (NCOA).[4]

The United States of Aging Survey for Low- & Moderate-Income findings posed this: "The ultimate question is: Are we as individuals and communities ready to address the challenges of an aging population?"[5] My answer is: NO.

How Serious Is This?

According to the National Council on Aging, "1 in 3 older adults is economically insecure."

> Low- and moderate-income older adults are very vulnerable, and even small reductions in income or benefits could be devastating to their health and economic well-being and their confidence level in receiving needed services.

136 ～ Chapter 24

Nearly half (46 percent) of low- and moderate-income seniors are not confident that their income will be sufficient to meet their monthly expenses over the next five to 10 years, compared to 16 percent of seniors with incomes over $30,000. Sixteen percent report that they have no financial plan for retirement whatsoever.

Four in 10 (41 percent) low- and moderate-income seniors are not confident that they are aware of all the benefits and programs that can help them, compared to 25 percent of seniors with incomes over $30,000.[6]

The median retirement savings for all workers is $97,000, which has caused over half of these workers planning to work in retirement.[7] We know that women have found themselves behind the eight-ball, with one-third having no retirement strategy at all. Women's average total retirement savings in the United States is just $57,000, whereas men's average total retirement savings is $118,000.

Now let's look at the debt that is owed.

Debt You May Not Have Considered

There is obvious debt that you, your financial team, and legal team will deal with, such as: mortgages, car loans, college debt for your kids, but there may be older debt to consider:

College Loans before You Got Married

Generally, as mentioned in the *Money Mistakes*, if you or your spouse took out student loans before you got married, those do not become shared debt or community property after marriage. That means that you are on the hook for your loans, and he is for his. The exception is if this was covered in the prenup, then that would trump this.

College Loans after You Got Married

If the student loan debt was incurred after you got married, the division of that can get stickier. If you both signed the loan, it may be considered marital debt. If one of you borrowed the money and it's in one name, it may not be considered marital debt. Look at the promissory note to make sure.

Understand that if you cosigned a loan for your spouse, the lender does not care if you got a divorce, you are still responsible for this. The only way to remove yourself as the cosigner is to see if the lender offers a cosigner release. Usually, if they even allow it, it's because the new main borrower has qualified to take on the loan by themselves.

If the lender doesn't offer this release, your spouse or you can refinance the loan without each other. The divorce decree should state how this debt will be handled. Remember, the lender must bless this.

Loans to Friends and Family
These will have to be disclosed and negotiated as part of the settlement. Is the debt to your friends and family yours or his? That will play a factor. You also may have invested in family or friends' businesses and that can become an asset that also has to be valued and dealt with in a settlement.

Joint Consolidation Loan Separation Act[8]
In 2022, Congress passed a new act that lets borrowers divide spousal consolidation loans into separate loans. This allows the loan to be split proportionally to how much you originally owed as an individual. You will retain the same amount you had back then with this new loan moving forward. This is now in effect, and again, your lawyer will walk you through this.

Medical Debt
Thirty-four percent of Americans have increased their credit card debt to pay off medical bills.[9] You can consolidate your medical debt and you can negotiate with the hospitals and other caregivers. There are services that can help to resolve some of your medical debt, as well. Your lawyers and his will determine who owes what amounts of this debt in your divorce.

What Can Be Done?
The National Council on Aging (NCOA)[10] and others direct seniors to programs that will help them economically.
Some of these include:

- *Medical Costs*: NCOA will help individuals to learn how to navigate the Medicare system to get help with understanding various options available under different plans, plus finding discounts on prescription drugs that help to cover other costs relating to dental and hearing programs. These discount cards and programs are available to everyone.
- *Medicare Savings Programs*: This will help qualifying low-income and disabled individuals to pay their Medicare premiums and associated costs.
- *Food*: NCOA can connect qualifying seniors with the Supplemental Nutrition Assistance Program (SNAP) where they can find food and

138 ～ Chapter 24

nutritional advice available in their specific location.[11] Seniors Farmers Market Nutrition Program (SFMNP) provides low-income seniors with coupon booklets that can be used at local farmers markets and food stands.[12]

- *Medicaid*: This is a joint federal and state program that provides health care benefits to low-income and disabled people.
- *Prescription Drug Assistance Programs* (PAPs): Most pharmaceutical companies offer patient assistance programs that will help low-income folks to get access to prescription drugs.[13]
- *IRS Help*: Higher deductions and tax credits are offered for lower earning populations by the IRS. You can refer to IRS Publications 524[14] and 502[15] for more details.
- *Rental Relief*: There is rental assistance for low-income families from several US Department of Housing and Urban Development (HUD) programs.[16]
- *Shop Once a Week*: Make your shopping list complete and stick to it. This will help you to limit impulse buying. You can get your friends to split some of the big-box purchases like paper products as well and this will save money on the goods and on transportation.
- *Everything Is Negotiable*: If you have any debt outstanding, which could include credit card, student loan, or mortgage debt, you can call the bank and try to negotiate lower rates.
- *Hit the Library*: You don't have to buy books or load your readable device. These costs add up, but your library will offer them for free.
- *Turn Down the Heat*: You can turn off the heat in unused rooms and get a programmable thermostat to make sure the heat is turned down while you are sleeping.
- *Dump Your House Phone*: There is no need to have a house phone if you have a cell phone.
- *Play the Age-Card*: Many places offer senior discounts; ask wherever you are.

Student Loan Debt

If you think that student loan debt is just for the young; think again. In 2020, people aged sixty-two and over owed $107 billion in federal student loans.[17] Many older borrowers are helping to finance their children's and grandchildren's college education.

Older people are also taking out retirement savings to help their grandchildren pay for college. In fact, seniors are the fastest-growing cohort of student debt borrowers.[18] Baby Boomers have the highest average monthly payment of any of the generations, at $722 a month in 2020, based upon an average balance of $75,000.[19] This means that if you, as a senior, are unable to pay off the student loan debt, your Social Security income can be garnished by the government. There was a moratorium during the pandemic, but that is over. Up to 15 percent of your benefits can be withheld to repay student loan debt. However, there are some stipulations. Garnishment for student loan defaults can't leave you with less than $750 in Social Security benefits a month.[20]

You know how I feel about the burgeoning student loan debt that seniors are taking on for their kids and grandkids. They can take out the loans and have a long time to pay them back. You can't take out loans for your retirement.

The point is that this is real debt that has to be considered in your divorce.

Problems with Some Solutions

Dump the Debt – You don't want to drag that ball-and-chain of debt into your golden years . . . if you can avoid it. Pundits say that no more than 28 percent of your pretax income should go to servicing home debt (principal, interest, taxes, and insurance). And no more than 36 percent of your pretax income should go to *all* debt (home debt, credit card, student loan debt, and auto loans). You should also think about not adding any more debt. If you charge something, make sure that you can pay for it when the bills come in.

The Debt Dig-Out after Divorce

There are several strategies you can use to get a handle on your debt, short of moving to the Bahamas and not answering your emails or phone. You can take out a debt-consolidation loan, take out a reverse mortgage, or you could even borrow from friends or family. (Okay, I just think you threw up in your mouth at the thought of borrowing money from your friends or family.) Keep breathing.

Consider a Debt-Consolidation Loan

If you feel that you can't get your head above water with your debt, you can research a debt-consolidation loan. Basically, it is a loan that does just what its name suggests; it consolidates all your debt into one, more manageable loan, hopefully at a lower interest rate.

140 ～ Chapter 24

Debt-Consolidation Loans

The typical rates on debt consolidation loans can be all over the map, depending upon how good or poor your credit score is. Rates can range from 6 percent to 36 percent. Obviously, the better your credit score, the lower the rate. So, make sure that you check out the rates before you get too deep into this process. Your goal is to both consolidate your loans and to reduce your average interest rates.

For instance, let's say you have a total of $15,000 in credit card debt with an APR of 20 percent. You monthly payment is $450. You would pay off the loan in a little over four years, costing you about $7,000 in interest. If you consolidated your loans at, let's say a 10 percent rate, you would save over $3,000 in interest charges.

You can search online to find and compare lenders, their rates, and terms, and to see if you will qualify. There are also calculators to help you see your savings. It also makes sense to start with your current bank after you get a picture of the landscape from the options you have discovered from your internet search. Many debt-consolidation loans are based upon the bank taking out a first or second mortgage on your home.

You may feel that the lender would discriminate against you because you are a senior. But legally they can't. The Federal Trade Commission (FTC) protects elderly people against discrimination from getting a home loan or any kind of credit based upon their age. This is because of the Equal Credit Opportunity Act, a federal law that protects borrowers against any bias due to age, race, color, religion, national origin, sex, marital status, or even those who get public assistance.[21]

You must consider what is best for you. If your home is paid off, and you have an income from a job or investments or alimony, you may want to consider this. Remember, any options will be dependent upon your income and credit history. Be aware that even looking to a debt-consolidation loan may negatively affect your credit score. But not paying your debts will obviously hurt you more.

If you and your financial "Team-You" decide that this is a viable option to consolidate your debt, you must think about how long you want the maturity to be. It may seem ridiculous to ask for a thirty-year mortgage if you are seventy-five years old. But the whole point is to lower your monthly financial nut. The loan, if it remains outstanding, would eventually be paid out of the sale of your home after your death. The scary part is that if you do get into further financial trouble and miss payments, the lender could foreclose on the mortgage and possibly take your home.

CHAPTER 25

⁓

Refinancing Your Mortgage

I'll be honest, refinancing your home as a senior, and a single senior to boot, can be challenging. There is no age limit for a mortgage or a refinancing, but the banks will take a hard look at the risks. The Equal Credit Opportunity Act, as noted above, gives seniors rights. In deference to the banks, as with any mortgage, they want to make sure that you can pay their loan back. So, if your retirement income is not sufficient to carry the loan and your other obligations, this may be a nonstarter.

Rate-and-Term Refinance

When interest rates drop, this is a good thing for seniors to consider. Basically, the lender doesn't give you the option to take cash out of our home, but rather replace your existing mortgage with one that carries a lower rate. Rates have moved up, but when they drop again, this may be something to consider.

How to qualify:

- *Equity in your home* – Lenders may require you to have at least 20 percent equity in your home to qualify for the refinance.
- *Credit score* – You will have to have a good credit score. The bank may tell you what they require; there is no universal number.
- *Debt-to-Income Ratio* – Your DTI, as discussed, measures what percentage of your gross monthly income goes toward repaying debt. The requirements will vary depending upon the lender, but typically, you will need a DTI of 43 percent or lower to refinance.

142 ～ Chapter 25

- *Appraisal* – A lender will require an appraisal to figure out your home's market value, meaning if it were sold today, what could you get. This is their collateral on the loan, and if your home's value has gone down significantly, you may not be eligible to refinance.

Here Are Some Pros and Cons

Pros

- *Lower interest rate.*
- *Reduction of your monthly payment* if you stretch out the maturity date, with the bank's permission.
- *Fixed rate*, if the bank lets you. It's always better to have a fixed rate. If rates go up with an Adjustable-Rate Mortgage (ARM), you are caught with increased costs.

Cons

- *Fees* can be steep, as you will have to pay for new closing costs, including an attorney. They could range from 2 percent to 5 percent of the loan amount.
- *More interest in the long term* will be paid if you lengthen the life of the loan, even though your monthly payment may go down.

I like this idea for you in a low-interest environment, or even in a raising interest rate market. You don't know how high rates can go, and at least you have locked in your fixed costs. Run the numbers and examine the costs and what you are gaining.

It's also interesting to note here, that often, single women borrowers (of all ages), are charged higher mortgage rates than single men. And paradoxically, women are less likely to default on their mortgages compared with men.[1]

CHAPTER 26

Reverse Mortgages

We see lots of old cowboy models touting the benefits of reverse mortgages for seniors. They lean into the camera and say, "Trust me." You need to ask yourself, what does an old male model know about reverse mortgages? The only answer is, "Nothing."

What Is a Reverse Mortgage?[1]

A reverse mortgage is a financial vehicle that allows seniors to tap into their home's equity. That means that it is a loan based upon the current value, or equity in your home, minus any mortgages or debt that may still be on it. Unlike a conventional mortgage where you pay your lender, in this case, the lender pays you a monthly payment, or a lump sum. You don't repay the loan until you sell your home, move, or die. Your balance on the loan is then deducted from the proceeds of the sale, and you or your heirs will get the money that is left over.

There is no fixed equity requirement to create a reverse mortgage. All the limits are set by the individual lenders. However, if you are using a government-backed reverse mortgage, homeowners are prohibited from borrowing up to the appraised value or the FHA max of $765,000. Your lender will explain all the terms and conditions.

To figure out how much you should consider borrowing, fill out this simple worksheet and take it to your financial advisors so together you can discuss the best way forward:

143

144 ～ Chapter 26

How Much Money Do I Need to Borrow?

EXISTING LOANS:

Credit Card Debt = $_____
Personal Loans = $_____
Retirement Account Loans = $_____
Mortgages = $_____
Other Loans = $_____

Existing Loan Balance $_____

PAST DUE BILLS:

Mortgage/Rent = $_____
(including taxes and insurance)
Utility Bills = $_____
Health Care Insurance = $_____
Auto Insurance = $_____
Life Insurance = $_____
Medical Bills = $_____
Streaming/Phone = $_____
Other Bills = $_____

Total Past Due Balance $_____

The pros of a reverse mortgage are:

- It can supplement your income.
- It can help you pay off debt.
- No payments are due until you sell, move, or die.

The cons of a reverse mortgage are:

- You can lose some home equity.
- Your heirs may inherit less money.
- You must cover property taxes, homeowners' insurance, and any association fees.
- If you don't live in the house as your primary residence, the loan will become due.

CHAPTER 27

~

"The Bag Lady Syndrome"—How to Leave Your Shopping Cart Behind

Many women have feared that after their divorce they will be reduced to a "bag lady status." It is said that this is a term first coined in the 1970s to describe feelings that some middle-aged women have that they will wind up homeless and carrying around their possessions in a shopping cart.

Women still are more uncomfortable handling money than men. As mentioned before, the UBS study found that 58 percent of women still let their husbands lead the way on long-term investment and financial-planning decisions.[1] Why? "Many women think men know more about investing and planning finances." Eighty-two percent said, "I think my spouse knows more than I do."

It may have nothing to do with reality; it may just be a strong feeling. You know the feeling I mean. That you're never quite secure. That somewhere out there, where you least expect it, there is a door, and on the other side of that door is an elevator shaft. It's the fear of free fall, with no one to catch you, nothing to grab onto, until you hit the bottom.

By the way, I'm not just blaming men for this situation. Many women have opted out of getting involved with family money issues. "You handle the money, sweetie, I'm so bad with money." This is not that uncommon. There are many reasons why women have abdicated these responsibilities. Some are because they were told as young girls that money issues are to be handled by men, and they bought into that damaging stereotype. Many women just wanted to deal with other tasks, like the home and kids. Others were just not interested and didn't care. Or, others felt that they lacked the necessary financial education or the ability to understand what seemed like daunting tasks around paying bills, investing money, and following their financial professionals. This added up to a lack of confidence and many women were thrilled when their husbands stepped in to take the reins.

147

148 ~ Chapter 27

Often, women were not necessarily victims to this. They supported the men who handled their money and were satisfied with the explanation of "Don't worry your pretty little head, you are taken care of." This doesn't work in real life, and it certainly doesn't work in a divorce.

How to Stop the Money FOG

Fear, *Obligation*, and *Guilt* can block a woman's view of her money-life. It's important to look at these feelings to end them. I'll show that, the more a woman takes charge of her financial life, the better she can do at combating these negative feelings. The "bag lady syndrome" doesn't have to happen. Knowledge is power. Every bit of new financial awareness you gain is a hand reaching out to catch you. Every old stereotype you smash is a ladder you can grab hold of to stop your fall and start climbing back up.

Stop It!

Stepping away from taking charge of your financial life is not just reserved for the middle-class. In fact, according to Quartz at Work, "Wealthy millennial women are more likely to defer to their husbands on investing."[2] Women will get involved in managing the day-to-day expenses, but step aside when it comes to the long term. No wonder they feel insecure and expect to end up schlepping around all their possessions in a shopping cart. Have you turned over your power?

If you are turning your power over to men and playing Scarlett O'Hara when it comes to money and you'd "Rather worry about that tomorrow," then, yes, you should worry about what happens to you and invest in a shopping cart now.

I'm not sure why men don't really suffer from this, but then again, men don't ask for directions, even if they are lost. (This reminds me of a bad joke: "Why does it take millions of sperm to fertilize one egg? Because men will never ask for directions.")

One in three people ages fifty-five to sixty-four revealed in a GoBankingRates survey that they have "concerns about the state of their financial lives."[3] The survey also found that almost one in three women over sixty-five years old were most worried about their finances in 2019. You don't have to be one of those women. You have to just commit to some of this advice:

- Don't be afraid of the jargon.
- Ask questions.

- Know the money side of your life: now.
- After you get involved with your money and take charge of it, you will see that:
  - o it's not so hard.
  - o you feel really empowered.

Financial Stress Is Alive but Not So Well

We all deal with stress. We are humans, stress is part of our lives. At our house we often marvel at pets who seem so content to just sleep and eat and sit in the sun or play with a ball. I've wondered what that life would be like. Then, I snap myself out of that fantasy of having someone provide for my every need, including rubbing my tummy while I purr.

I'm back, and so are the stressors in my life. For many people financial stress floats to the top of the list. In fact, in the American Psychological Association's (APA) "Stress in America Survey 2022," findings showed that 65 percent of Americans had stress due to money issues. That is the highest figure recorded in more than six years.[4]

The National Library of Medicine, National Center for Biotechnology Information reported that financial stress could be linked to depression.[5] One interesting note is that they found this association between financial stress and depression in high-income and low- and middle-income countries. We sometimes delude ourselves into thinking that the rich don't worry about money. It looks like everyone worries about money.

Being stressed affects every other part of our lives. It lingers and bubbles up all the time. It can cause arguments with loved ones and friends, missed work, or lack of focus; it can affect our health and our well-being; it can keep us up at night. Wichita State University conducted a survey of older adults, "Financial Stress: How Older Adults' Health Is Affected."[6] They found that there was a strong correlation between one's financial stress levels and their physical and mental health, and went on to say that it was important for older adults to manage their stress levels by managing their debt levels.

The scary part is that when you have debt, the interest clock is always ticking, and interest is always mounting up. You can't hide from that, and it grows just like your stress levels do. There is a Yiddish Proverb that notes: "Interest on debts grows without rain." It's scary, but true, so this must be faced and dealt with.

150 ～ Chapter 27

Getting Your Act Together

It's not easy to do the work to really know where you are so you have a clear picture of where you want to go and how to get there. One major stressor is credit card debt. Now that you are building your new financial life, let's explore some of the warning signs that may let you know that you could be stepping into troubled waters and want to stop that behavior and find a life raft.

Take this short quiz that may help you to see if you are headed toward a debt disaster.

AM I DROWNING IN CREDIT CARD DEBT?

Answer True or False

I have at least 4 credit cards.	TRUE	FALSE
Debts were causing arguments at home.	TRUE	FALSE
I'm good at juggling my bills. I often find a way to pay them with a credit card.	TRUE	FALSE
I've thought about getting a consolidation loan to pay off my credit card debt.	TRUE	FALSE
I hid the credit card bills from my partner.	TRUE	FALSE
I have maxed out my credit cards.	TRUE	FALSE
I can't cover an emergency of $500.	TRUE	FALSE
Creditors have called to discuss late payments.	TRUE	FALSE
I can only pay the minimum on my credit cards.	TRUE	FALSE
I don't know how much credit card debt is too much.	TRUE	FALSE
I have used cash advances on one card to pay another.	TRUE	FALSE
I've used some of my savings to pay the minimum on my credit cards.	TRUE	FALSE
I've hidden purchases from my partner.	TRUE	FALSE
I've borrowed money from friends or family to make ends meet.	TRUE	FALSE

"The Bag Lady Syndrome"—How to Leave Your Shopping Cart Behind ~ 151

Score:

You know the answer to this. If any of these pop up for you, you may have a problem with growing debt. You want to get on top of this as soon as possible. But for now, you may be asking what a healthy relationship to credit card debt should look like. Remember the words of Ogden Nash, "Some debts are fun when you are acquiring them, but none are fun when you set about retiring them."[7]

It is also generally accepted that you should never spend more than 10 percent of your take-home income toward credit card debt. So, for example, if you take home $4,000 a month, you should not charge more than $400 a month. If you carry a balance, try to pay it off within six months.

Misery Loves Company

If you have credit card debt, you are not alone. The average household's credit card balance is $9,200.[8] But how much is too much? Experts at WalletHub have done an analysis of how much households can carry and still hang in there. The number they have come up with is $8,428.[9] This means that if you have this amount in credit card debt, you will be required to pay a minimum monthly payment of about $206.20, assuming an APR of 18 percent. This also means that you would have to bring home at least $2,062 per month if you are doing the 10 percent rule. But know that if you paid that fixed payment every month, it would take over five years to eliminate that debt. You also would be paying $4,442 in interest charges.

With inflation increasing, basic products like food, housing, and utilities are going up and putting more pressure on you if you are on a fixed income. Many seniors have sold their homes and are renters. More than six in ten renters are over the age of sixty-five and they felt the squeeze of increases in rental properties.[10] It doesn't look like rental prices will start falling soon, either. (I do discuss how it's great to sell your home to cut expenses, and it is; I just want you to be aware of the costs of renting a place may not serve your purposes of cutting costs.)

Retirees now outspend their annual incomes by more than $4,000, according to the Bureau of Labor Statistics.[11] It's been challenging for many seniors to tackle the bills that are mounting.[12] Many seniors have no choice but to take out their credit cards to bridge this gap.

Let's see if you can reduce some of that debt:

152 ~ Chapter 27

Tips to Deal with How to Get Credit
Card Debt Under Control

- Tip #1: Get your bills in order and know what you owe, interest rates, and to whom. Also, have a tally of your monthly expenses. If you have had any emergencies, like health-related problems, have a list of those unusual expenses, as well.
- Tip #2: Pick up the phone and tell your credit card company that you are having trouble paying your credit card debt and why. You may have medical or prescription drug bills, you may be paying off other debt, or costs of living are outstripping your income. Be honest. Remember, they will pull up your statement to corroborate your predicament. If they see lots of charges for restaurants, travel, and entertainment, they will not be very sympathetic.

But if your story is real, they will probably work with you to give you some relief by lowering rates, cutting the debt, or stretching out the payments. It's worth a shot. Make sure that you take the name of the person with whom you have spoken and make sure that they send you the "new agreement" in an email, which you will print for your files.

Here are some questions to ask your credit card company:

1. Do they have a forbearance program, and if so, will you qualify?
2. Can they lower the amount due each month by stretching out the payments and maturity?
3. Can they reduce the interest rate?
4. You don't want to default; do they have any other suggestions?

- Tip #3: Seek help from a certified credit counselor to assist you to get a handle on your debt. They will help you to determine how much you can afford to pay each month. If you are uncomfortable calling your credit card companies, the credit counselor often will supply this service for you. They may also collect a monthly payment from you and pay all your creditors. This helps you to juggle all the payments and try to figure out which bills to pay.

It's time to make some choices.

CHAPTER 28

~

Never Own Anything Bigger Than Your Hat

Let's circle back to "The Bag Lady Syndrome," because it is a real stressor for so many women. One way to combat "The Bag Lady Syndrome" is to get rid of it all. I wrote an article about this for *Forbes*, years ago.[1]

Retirement means downsizing. Being a divorced senior means downsizing. You know that, but you may look forward to it mostly with trepidation. You've gotten used to the empty nest. You're no longer bursting into tears in the middle of the supermarket because it suddenly hits you that you don't have to figure out how to plan a meal that will satisfy the vegetarian, and the one who won't eat anything that's orange, and the one who only wants hot dogs for every meal, and the one who insists on ketchup instead of spaghetti sauce.

So, your nest is empty. But it's still a big nest, with big heating bills and electric bills and repair bills and rooms you haven't even walked into in the past year.

And still, it's hard to give it up. We've spent the first two-thirds of our lives accumulating. Accumulating furniture. Accumulating art. Accumulating books and records and CDs and knickknacks and Hummel figurines and cars and boats and cottages by the lake. Accumulating lovers and spouses, children and grandchildren, friends and coworkers and partners. It's mostly all been rewarding, and it's all given you valuable life lessons. And now, you have just cast off your partner, who used to be an important person in your life. It's both sad and a relief. He may have been the center of your universe. The one you built your life around. Every step you took may have been choreographed around his needs. That just became your habit.

And it's a hard habit to stop. *But to everything there is a season: turn, turn, turn. A time to cast away stones, and a time to gather stones together.* And as we

153

154 ~ Chapter 28

move through retirement age, which may well be as much as one-third of your total life span, it's time to cast away stones.

Or, to quote from another vinyl LP that's gathering dust on your shelves, *freedom's just another word for nothing left to lose*. But more to the point: nothing left to lose is another word for *freedom*. Freedom to travel. To see those far-flung grandchildren, and those places on the map you've always wanted to visit. Freedom to make your time your own. Freedom to speak and be heard. Freedom to handle your own destiny.

So, here's the goal that many people subscribe to. Don't own anything. Okay, this is a little drastic, but go with me.

Too much to ask? What about those place settings Aunt Helen left you in her will, that the kids will *not* want some day? That book you read on the beach during a wonderful summer of 1983, which is part of all of the other thousand books that you have schlepped from one home to another? That Janis Joplin record on vinyl? You say that you just listened to it . . . well, five years ago? But you might listen to it again.

Can you start to identify with the story about the little boy who cut off his dog's tail an inch at a time, so it wouldn't hurt so much?

Don't own anything. Rip off the Band-Aid.

Sell the house. That not only adds a nice sum to your nest egg, but it also cuts down your expenses like you wouldn't believe. (Add up the ways your house drains the old coffers, and you'll start to believe it. And we haven't even gotten to property taxes yet.) And don't buy another one. Rent. If you don't own it, you can move. Renting is expensive today, but if the appliance breaks, or the roof leaks, it's not your pocketbook that gets slammed again. Remember, nothing left to lose is another word for freedom.

The car? Everyone needs a car. But maybe not as much as you think. How often do you use it? If you live in that quaint farmhouse in the country, you might use it every day, but you're not buying another house, remember? If you live in a city, you scarcely need it at all. Even in a small town, if you can walk or bicycle to shopping, you might not need it more than once a week. True, a bicycle is bigger than your hat, but not that much bigger, and it will keep you in shape. If you do absolutely need a car, do you really need a fancy car? And with today's car-sharing companies like Zipcar, access to a vehicle can be pretty easy and not all that costly.

Access. Take a tip from your grandchildren's lifestyle. The millennial generation has learned that ownership isn't necessary if you have access. The collection of original Beatles recordings on vinyl? The CDs in all those CD towers that you had to have? The stereo system, with wall-mounted speakers and subwoofers? You're a dinosaur. With your cell phone, and a tiny compact Bluetooth speaker system, you can access Spotify or Apple Music for ten dollars a month and listen to virtually any piece of music you can think of. Or you can access Pandora or Slacker for free and listen to their playlists of any genre you can think of. All those books, going back to your high school days? You can pack ten times as many, and more, into a Kindle. With a Kindle app on your cell phone, you can go even smaller.

The stuff you're saving to leave to your kids? The silverware, the furniture, the artwork? Give it to them now. If they don't want it now, they're not likely to want it later.

Noth'in ain't worth noth'in, but it's free. And *noth'in don't cost noth'in,* neither, which means more money in your pocket for more choices.

Try this hat on for size!

CHAPTER 29

Time to Get Off Your Assets and Learn to Vision Your New Life

I've spoken to lots of women who say they wished they had done things differently when it came to money issues. In fact, when you look at the UBS study,[1] *more than half* of all the women they interviewed said . . .

- They wished they had been more involved in long-term financial decisions;
- Don't consider themselves very knowledgeable about investing;
- They didn't have to think about the consequences around long-term financial decisions because it was too far off to be relevant;
- They discovered financial surprises during their divorce;
- They would have done fewer household chores to find more time for finances; and
- If they remarry, they will take a more active role in their money life.

I'm not *burning my bra* while singing, "I am woman, hear me roar"; I'm being practical and hopefully, empowering. You may have just come out of a relationship where you were dependent upon him. You may have gotten dumped. Or you could be the dumper. Or you may have come out of a relationship where you were the breadwinner. Or again, your relationship may have been economically equal. Regardless of whatever relationship you came out of, you want to only design your financial life as a single woman. That's great. If someone comes into your life again, and you want to tie the knot again, refer to the prenuptial section. Read it carefully.

The real truth is that your happiness is up to you. Happiness is an *inside* job. It's not someone else's responsibility, it's yours.

158 ⌢ Chapter 29

Caution: People Will Start to Tell You What You Should Do

It's your life. You get to design it. You get to choose. I have been here to only help you to have a template for that design. There is a *Visioning Model* that I have created, originally for young people to envision their future and now for you, to do the same.

It is a wonderful exercise of exploration. You can do it over and over again. Be bold with your design. Remember the words of Nelson Mandela, "There is no passion to be found playing small—in settling for a life that is less than the one you are capable of living."[2]

How to Vision Your New Life

Life Goals

It is not easy to reimagine your life. In fact, you may, rightfully so, even resent having to do it. Or, you may have initiated the divorce and feel exhilarated about redesigning your life. It's time to dream and imagine all sorts of possibilities so that they can be manifested. As Gloria Steinem said, "Without leaps of imagination or dreaming, we lose the excitement of possibilities. Dreaming, after all, is a form of planning."[3]

VISION YOUR LIFE

Create a <u>VISION</u> of life after your gray divorce.

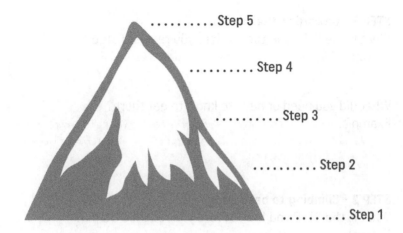

ASK THESE QUESTIONS AND FILL IN THE ANSWERS.

STEP 5 – Stand at the top of the mountain.
How do you imagine your new life? Think about five years in the future. Write down all of your thoughts and dreams, plus what you will need to know to make that step happen.

What does your new vision look like?
Example: I'm living in a small townhouse and don't have the headaches or expenses of keeping the family home.

What did you need to get there?
Example: Sell the family house.

STEP 4 - Reaching the peak
What is the STEP you took before you reached your vision?
Example: Find my new home.

160 ⁓ Chapter 29

What did you need or have to know to get there?
Example: Calculate one-time closing costs plus ongoing mortgage payments and carrying costs.

STEP 3 - Onward to the summit
What is the STEP you took before you reached Step 4?
Example: Get a real estate agent and qualify for a mortgage.

What did you need or have to know to get there?
Example: Go online and search for comparables for selling my home. Decide where I want to live. Check my credit score and report. (Make plans to fix it, if necessary.)

STEP 2 - Climbing to base camp
What is the STEP you took before you reached Step 3?
Example: How much can I afford for a new home?

What did you need or have to know to get there?
Example: Meet with your financial planner or accountant to calculate my budget. What is my income and my allocation of living expenses? What is the equity in my current home?

STEP 1 - Making the approach
What is the STEP you took before you reached Step 2?
Example: Downsize by moving to a smaller home.

NOW...

Turn the STEPS around from 1 to 5 and complete your action plan below. See STEP 1 for an example.

HOW DID YOU GET HERE?

STEP 1: Downsize by moving to a smaller home.

STEP 2: How much can I afford for a new home?

STEP 3: Get a real estate agent and qualify for a mortgage.

STEP 4: Find my new home.

STEP 5: I'm living in a small townhouse and don't have the headaches or expenses of keeping the family home.

WHAT DID YOU NEED TO KNOW?

Make my new life a priority.

Meet with your financial planner or accountant to calculate my budget. What is my income and my allocation of living expenses? What is the equity in my current home?

Go online and search for comparables for selling my home. Decide where I want to live. Check my credit score and report. (Make plans to fix it, if necessary.)

Calculate one-time closing costs plus ongoing mortgage payments and carrying costs.

Sell the family house.

It's time for you to be bold; really bold. You have found your voice and you can now listen to your head and your heart. Your *life* is yours and your *dreams* are yours and your *plan* is yours. Abraham Lincoln said it well, "The best way to predict the future is to create it."[4]

CHAPTER 30

~

Financial Goals—Why Die on the Vine When You Can Replant?

I will help you to breakdown *your* financial goals and understand *your* budget that will match *your* goals. You will have to make trade-offs, but you get to decide what those are. Many people put this off or stall out with a life design. But now is the time to look at your life and what you want it to look like, within your budget.

Mapping Your Goals

The great part of this is that you get to design your own financial future. Generally, your goals will probably fall into broad categories.

- *I can be financially independent.* (Meaning that you don't have to rely upon anyone else for support.)
- *I can take charge of my financial life.* (Meaning that you oversee your finances; designing a budget, paying bills, working with financial people or investing for yourself.)
- *I'm not financially independent.* (Meaning that you may have to rely upon others, like friends and family, for support.)

Take this quiz to help you decide what you want.

Your Choices

Which statements resonate with you:

1. *I want to have enough money to pay for myself until I die.*
2. *I have enough money to pay for myself until I die.*

163

164 ∿ Chapter 30

3. *I will not have enough money until I die.*
4. *I must come up with ideas to cut expenses.*
5. *I will investigate living with friends and sharing expenses.*
6. *I would like to live with one of my children.*
7. *I need to think about selling my house and downsizing.*
8. *I will have enough for private health care.*
9. *I will have to rely on Medicare for my care.*
10. *I want to stay in my home as long as I can.*
11. *I should look into buying long-term health care insurance.*

What Does Financial Independence Look Like?

Which statements resonate with you:

1. *I can create a plan to figure out what I need to live now and in the future.*
2. *I need help putting a financial plan together.*
3. *I can learn what I need to know to pay bills, invest money, pay down debt, and anything else that comes up.*
4. *I can find trusted financial professionals to help me.*
5. *I put my wishes in writing.*
6. *I have made a list of the financial things I want to learn.*
7. *I can track my monthly budget.*
8. *I don't need help.*
9. *I need help.*
10. *I have set up a charitable giving plan.*

I Can Have the *Talks* with My Family and Loved Ones

You should communicate what you are doing, your goals, and your plans for how things will be handled when and if you can't live independently; your plans for when you are gone; inheritance; funerals . . . all the tough conversations.

Which statements are true for you:

1. *I have spoken to my kids about my financial situation.*
2. *I have shown them where all of the important documents are.*
3. *I have introduced them to my financial people.*

Financial Goals—Why Die on the Vine When You Can Replant? ~ 165

4. *I have designated a financial power of attorney to manage my finances and informed my kids.*
5. *I have discussed my financial wishes.*
6. *Different kids may be treated differently, financially. I have explained that to my kids.*
7. *If I can't afford to live currently, I have discussed this and asked for help.*
8. *If I can't afford long-term health care, I have discussed this and alternatives, like in-home nursing care or a nursing home.*
9. *I have discussed what would happen if I need a family member to supply care. Is there money to pay them?*
10. *I have told my kids about the charities that are important to me.*

Your Money Map

You are now ready to create your *Money Map* based upon all the work that you have done thus far. You have looked back via your *No Magic Money Log* and really seen how you had been spending money. You have designed your wish lists for your new life without your ex, you have visioned what it will look like, and you have worked with your professionals to see how you can fund all of this. You have culled your garden of any of the deadwood that does not serve you and you know the life you can now create within your means.

Your *Money Map* is just that. It is a chronological roadmap or blueprint for your life based upon your wishes and your ability to see them come to fruition. It can be a real map that you can draw on poster board and put on your wall, which will highlight your new goals and how you will get there. Or it can be just an outline you create on your laptop. It will deal with the things you want to do. I'm asking you to also put an estimated cost next to the item, if you can, just to keep you on track and to let you adjust other money you may need or want to spend. This may inspire you to ditch your old budget, if you so choose. You will set your goals, and the month and year you hope to achieve them.

Some items will recur on a regular basis, like checking in quarterly with your financial advisor.

Chapter 30

MONEY MAP

Date	Event
● September 2025	Sign-up for Pickleball lessons. Cost = $_____
● September 2025	Find a masseuse for after Pickleball. Cost = $_____
● September 2025	Check-in with my financial advisor to review my portfolio.
● October 2025	Start looking for a new and smaller place to live in my town. Budget for new place $_____
● January 2026	Find the new place to live. Speak to my friend who is a real estate agent.
● January 2026	Check-in with my accountant and bookkeeper to make sure they have what they need to prepare my taxes.
● January 2026	Check out year-end sales for next year's holiday gifts. Gift Budget $_____
● February 2026	Check-in with my financial advisor to review my portfolio.
● March 2026	Plan summer trip to see the grandkids. Trip Budget $_____

Keep this going for as long as you want. You can set milestones way in the future, if you want. Make sure that you keep this as a living document that you refer to and update. Life will always get in the way, but stand strong and try to deal with the curve balls, change your map, and get back on your road.

CHAPTER 31

⌇

Women Beat Men at Investing

You can now shed the old paradigm that *women are not as good with money as men*. Why? Because it's true. Fidelity Investments conducted a survey and found that women outperformed men when it came to generating a better return on their investments.[1]

The survey found that:

- *Women earn higher returns*: The Fidelity client data found that "on average, women performed better than men when it comes to investing by 0.4%." That seems like a slim margin, but think of 0.4 percent over twenty years; it starts to make a difference.
- *Women save more*: When Fidelity looked at workplace retirement accounts, women saved an annual average of 9 percent of their paychecks, as compared to 8.6 percent for males. The same held true for accounts outside of work, like brokerage accounts and IRAs. Women added an average of 12.4 percent to their account balance, compared to 11.6 percent for men.

  Let's look at the numbers: Let's assume a 6 percent annual rate of return. Let's say that you both start working at age twenty-two with a salary of $50,000 each. By the time you are sixty-seven, the potential difference for women over men is $276,170.
- *Women have skills they don't recognize*: Women were found to build their financial plans with purpose. In other words, they looked at the life goals they wanted for themselves and their family.
- *Women are more likely to take on less risk*. I call this the "cold sweat test" that I discussed before. The Fidelity study showed this. Men tended to invest in equities more heavily than women. Women were more

168 ∼ Chapter 31

conscious of being diversified and making sure that the money would be there when they needed it.

- *Women are not impressed with the high-flying broker* who brags that they got a 40 percent return on a hot stock for their clients. She knows that if there is a winner, there is also a loser. Women feel more comfortable following the words of Paul Samuelson, when he said, "Investing should be more like watching paint dry or watching grass grow. If you want excitement, take $800 and go to Las Vegas."[2]
- *Take a deep breath:* The Fidelity study found that men are 35 percent more likely to make trades than women. Women are more patient and don't react emotionally to the market swings.
- *Education:* The research showed that among professional women, over 90 percent wanted to learn more about financial planning. It was found that "for many this stems from a need to play 'catch up,' with a majority reporting a lack of opportunity to learn financial skills earlier in life. . . . Overall, only nine percent of women said their education through high school left them well prepared to manage personal finances as an adult."

But here it is: The study also showed that women still feel uncomfortable about their abilities with money: "a mere nine percent of women thought they would outperform men." This insecurity was found "Regardless of education levels, personal or professional achievements, many women still have doubts about their ability to invest effectively. In fact, when asked what financial skills they wished they learned earlier, the number one answer was 'how to invest and make the most of my money.'"

The Big Deal about Investing

The big deal is that when you put your money under your mattress, it still may be there in twenty years when you need it, but it hasn't grown in value. When an investment earns interest, your initial investment (principal) earns money, but as that money grows, so does the accumulated interest and you earn on that, too. The more compounding periods, like six months versus one year, the greater your compound interest will be. So, the result is that you generate interest on interest, which is called *compound interest.*

I have given the following example to young kids in some of my books:

"Would you rather have a job that pays you $50,000 for the month or one that starts you at a penny and doubles it every day for thirty-one days?"

The kids all scoff and say that they would, of course, rather have the job that pays $50,000 a month.

Women Beat Men at Investing ～ 169

Let's unpack this concept. The original penny turned into two cents the first day, then four the second day, and then on the fourth turned into eight, and so on. If you keep going for thirty-one days, you will end up with $21,474,836!

Time Is Your Friend (or Your Kid's)

The big rub with the *miracle of compounding* is that the more time you have, the more of a miracle it is. I know this book is about gray divorce, so if you haven't started to save, this part of the book should be given to your kids and grandkids. To make the conversation with them more poignant, tell them that the earlier they start, the sooner they will become a millionaire.

For instance: Assume a 7.64 percent annualized rate of return (which is reasonable because long-term stock investments have averaged approximately 10 percent over a long period of time) on a well-balanced portfolio.

The goal is to reach a $1 million by age sixty-five.

If you started at age twenty-five and invested $342 a month, or $4,242 yearly, you would have $1 million by age sixty-five.

If you waited until you were age thirty-five, you would have to invest $759 a month, or $9,428 yearly to become a millionaire at age sixty-five.

If you started at age fifty, you would have to invest $3,051 a month, or $37,874 a year to cash out at a million by age sixty-five.

More good news for your grandchildren. If there is a one-time $100,000 investment, at the same 7.64 percent average annual return, that will grow to almost $2 million in forty years; just sayin'.

Now think about this in reverse and how compound interest on your credit cards or mortgage can work against you. Many cards compound interest daily. Let's look at that. Let's say you have a balance of $1,000 on your card that is charging a whopping 29.9 percent APR, but is compounded daily. It looks like you would pay $299 in interest, and the $1,000 in principal, right? Nope. Because of the daily compounding, that is $1,353.95. I won't bore you with more examples of how much you will pay for a car loan or a mortgage.

You get the point. That is the big deal about compound interest and why Albert Einstein said, "Compound interest is the eighth wonder of the world. He who understands it, earns it . . . he who doesn't . . . pays it."[3]

CHAPTER 32

~

Financial Wellness Later in Life

There is a joke that is between a financial advisor and her client. Financial advisor: "Do you have your financial affairs in order?" Client: "Yes, I do. I have all my bills lined up in order of delinquencies." This is not my goal with you.

You have come a long way on this journey. You need to design a real budget based upon your goals. We will explore:

- How to Live Below Your Means with Joy
- Getting a Handle on Debt
- Setting up a Realistic Budget
- Creating an Emergency Fund
- Setting up Some Guilt-Free Spending on Perks
- Your Charitable Giving and Volunteering
- Investing Made Easy

Take this simple quiz to test your investment knowledge.

172 ~ Chapter 32

THE ONLY INVESTMENT QUIZ YOU'LL EVER NEED... *SORT OF*

1. **Leverage is:**
   a. The gearshift in a sports car.
   b. The method the Egyptians used to move those humongous rocks to build the pyramids.
   c. Debt.

2. **Stock is:**
   a. A base for soup.
   b. Large animals that Super Woman herds together and drives north to free them from the slaughterhouse.
   c. Part ownership in a corporation.

3. **Face Value is:**
   a. How you feel after an expensive facial.
   b. When you stand out on the sidewalk and stare directly at a diamond necklace in the window of your favorite jewelry store.
   c. The value, usually of a bond, when it comes out or when it matures.

4. **A Prospectus is:**
   a. A date found on Tinder.
   b. An old man with a white beard who wanders around the mountains leading a burro and looking for gold.
   c. A document explaining things about a company or mutual fund, for instance, when they offer securities for sale.

5. **A Mutual Fund is:**
   a. A party in a hot tub.
   b. Two people splitting the check at lunch.
   c. A company that invests money.

6. Dollar-cost Averaging is:
a. Spending an extra fifty dollars on something you don't need to get a free item you don't want.
b. Ten friends splitting the tab at lunch—one of them only had a salad and water.
c. Investing a fixed amount in stock or other investments regularly.

7. Diversification is:
a. When two people get together to write a poem.
b. Kim Kardashian's shoe closet.
c. An investing principle that encourages you to buy different types of investments.

8. A Bond is:
a. How you feel after eating too many bananas and rice.
b. When your friend shares your political views.
c. Debt issued by a company or government.

9. Laddering is:
a. What firefighters use if a kitten is stuck in a tree.
b. A big run in your panty hose.
c. A way to stagger the maturities of bonds or CDs.

10. A Load is:
a. A pile of rocks.
b. What you expect to find when you change your grandchild's diaper.
c. A fee charged when you buy or sell certain investments like, mutual funds.

174　〜　Chapter 32

Results:

Obviously, c is the correct answer to all the questions, and I hope this made you smile. Back to the serious stuff . . .

Have Confidence

There are simple steps to start budgeting and investing. You may be uncomfortable with the feeling of "Not Knowing Enough." In fact, 30 percent of women say they don't know enough to start investing.[1] Your financial advisors should be making you feel comfortable, but here are some tips. You should be on a real budget by now and your financial advisors should be looking over your shoulder to help you build regular investing into that.

I'll start by explaining the jargon and show you that investing is about buying what you know, stepping away from the news, and making sure that you stay the course.

Here are the things and terms you need to know that will give you self-confidence:

- *Assets* – Any item that has value. Your home is an asset and so is your engagement ring.
- *Liabilities* – Money that you owe to other people. Your mortgage and credit cards are liabilities.
- *Compound interest* – A method of calculating interest where your money keeps earning on the principal and the interest you have already earned.
- *FICO score* – A three-digit score given to you by the three rating agencies. It's based upon your credit history. The scores range from a low of 300 to a high of 850. Typically, the higher the score, the more access you will have to credit at lower rates.
- *Net worth* – You add up all of your assets (cash, savings, home, jewelry, and so on), and subtract all of your debt (mortgage, credit card, car loans, and so on) from that; whatever is left over is your net worth (your assets minus your debt).
- *Asset allocation* – A mixture of the financial stocks, bonds, mutual funds, and other investments that you own. It's important because your asset allocation should reflect your risk tolerance, or what you are comfortable investing in.
- *Risk tolerance* – A cold-sweat test reflecting the risk you are willing to take in your investments. If you wake up in the middle of the night feeling that your investments are too risky, you will understand

Financial Wellness Later in Life ～ 175

your *risk tolerance*. In that case, reduce the risk in your portfolio of investments.

- *Capital gains* – The profit you get when you sell an asset for more than you paid. Capital gains are taxed at a lower rate than regular income.
- *Appreciation* – An increase in the value of an asset over time. Stocks can appreciate, and so can real estate or other assets. Your perfect Barbie doll or motorcycle can appreciate over time as well.
- *Defined-contribution plan* – A type of investment vehicle, like a 401(k). It allows the employee to contribute in a tax-advantaged way. The money goes into the account before you pay taxes. The goal is to use it for retirement.
- *Defined-benefit plan* – An employer pays you a certain amount periodically once you retire. A pension is a defined-benefit plan.
- *Annuity* – An investment offered by an insurance company that guarantees a certain payout in the future. This type of investment may make sense if you are older and have maxed out your 401(k) or other retirement accounts. An annuity can give you a steady source of income in the future.
- *Diversification* – A method of investing based upon the theory of "Don't put all of your eggs in one basket." Typically, if you buy a variety of stocks and investments, it is considered less risky than if you bought one stock, for instance, and the company failed and disappeared, along with your investment.
- *Dividends* – When a company does well, they sometimes share some of their earnings with the people who bought their stock.
- *Yield* – The earnings your investment returns to you. It includes interest and dividends. It is expressed as a percentage.
- *Equity* – Is what is left over from subtracting the debt you used to buy an asset. For instance, let's say you bought a home for $500,000 and have a $300,000 mortgage. Your equity in that home is $200,000.
- *Escrow* – An account that is set up to make sure that you pay what is owed in the future. Property taxes usually have an escrow account that you pay into. Your lawyer will set this up for you at your bank.
- *Estate planning* – You want to get your money life all set up before you die; that is estate planning. You may do such things as create a will, designate a power of attorney, look at your life insurance policies, and so forth.
- *Fee-only financial planner* - A financial planner who makes money by charging a fee and who does not receive commissions on buying and selling stock.

176 ~ Chapter 32

- *Roth IRA* – A savings plan that lets you contribute after you pay taxes on that money. The money is then taken by you in retirement and you don't have to pay taxes on it again. A Roth IRA retirement plan is set up by you and is not offered by your employer.
- *Rollover* – The process of moving the funds in a retirement account, like a 401(k) into another retirement account; often another 401(k). This usually happens when you get a new job. Moving the money keeps you from incurring taxes.
- *Liquidity* – A term that describes how quickly and easily you can pull cash out of an asset. A checking account is liquid, but your home is illiquid. You should always have some emergency money in your bank so you can get it out easily. You decide how much.
- *Living will* – This is a legal document that explains what medical measures you want to be taken if you are unable to discuss your medical care wishes. It will instruct your loved ones about what you want and don't want to be done.
- *Power of attorney (POA)* (legal decisions) or *health proxy* (health decisions) – You can designate a trusted adult child, friend, or lawyer and allow them to make major decisions, like financial and medical, on your behalf if you can't.
- *Premium* – The amount you pay, usually monthly, for your insurance policy. Make sure that you are the owner of the policy, because only the owner can change the beneficiary.
- *Beneficiary* – The person who will receive your money or assets, usually when you die.
- *Trust* – A legal instrument that allows it to hold and/or manage assets for another person, called a beneficiary.

What You Shouldn't Do

Of course, your goal is to retire with as little debt as possible, but if you find yourself in debt, don't panic, because panic may cause you to do imprudent things. For instance, stay away from payday lenders who may offer you a quick fix.

- *Payday loans* are short-term cash loans that are based upon your personal check that the lenders hold for future deposit. They initially look like a way to get over a cash shortage, but you will have to pay finance charges and the loans are really short.
- *Don't take on more debt*. I know you want to help your grandchildren with their college expenses, but taking on their debt can really add to

Financial Wellness Later in Life ～ 177

your financial problems. There is no demographic group that is adding educational student loan debt faster than seniors. This is primarily due to the fact that older Americans are taking out loans to help their kids and grandkids go to college.[2] The Consumer Financial Protection Bureau (CFPB) indicates that 57 percent of all those who cosigned student loans were aged fifty-five and older.

I know these are your loved ones, but remember, unpaid student loan debt can be deducted from your Social Security each month. Please understand that your kids and grandkids can borrow on their own for college; you can't borrow for retirement.

A 2019 Congressional Research Service report found that the percentage of elderly households—those led by people sixty-five plus—with any type of debt increased from 38 percent in 1989 to 61 percent in 2016.[3] That amount jumped from about $7,500 to more than $31,000. Also, the percentage of households led by someone age sixty-five to seventy-four who has credit card debt increased 41 percent in 2019 from 27 percent in 1989.[4]

CHAPTER 33

~

Before the Plunge—Prenups

All marriages are on the decline; in fact, over the last fifty years, they have declined by 60 percent.[1] Our new generations do not value tying the knot the way we Boomers have. We may be holding on to the notion that marriage is the cornerstone of our American way of life, providing some sort of stability, while our offspring may view this tradition as downright archaic. In a recent survey, almost half of our kids say that mental health is more important than marriage.[2]

Money issues always seem to crop up and influence decisions. The survey showed that 20 percent of Americans feel that financial stability was the primary purpose for marriage, with nearly two in three married couples reporting improved finances after marriage.

"Boomers are 75% more likely than Gen X, 168% more likely than millennials, and 394% more likely than Gen Z to say nothing is more important than marriage," the same survey shows. That is why if marriage is important to you, and you are considering it again, you need to go into it with your money issues in order. It's time to discuss prenups.

This info on prenups could go in several places in this book. I chose to put it here, because as you design your new life, love and remarriage may be in the cards. This info is for you and also so that you can spread your wisdom to your kids or grandkids if they are thinking about marriage. I hope you learn along with your offspring. It's important to understand if and when you or your adult children should create a prenup. Also, it should be noted that even with what may be considered an "airtight" prenup, you or your spouse may be able to contest it in a divorce.

180 ∽ Chapter 33

Remarriages are more likely to end in divorce,[3] so think about a prenup for your next marriage. In it you can deal with a lot of these monetary issues before emotions are running at a fevered pitch. There may be adult children on both sides to consider; other assets, and lots of other issues to think about. Seek professional advice from your lawyers, accountants, and financial advisors. Your wills need to be adjusted to reflect your new circumstances as well.

With my second marriage, I felt it was fine to marry without a prenup. I was in the frame of mind, "I love and trust him." Oops. Fortunately, my friend and lawyer, Eric Martins (Kim DeYoung's father), was smarter than I. He didn't like or trust this guy. He was right. My career was booming—I was actually on *Oprah* two days before my wedding—and Eric showed up at my fiancé's office with a ninety-three-page prenup. Can you say, "Eric *really* didn't trust this guy?" Basically, Eric forced him to sign it. He did. Luckily for me.

About two months after the wedding, I caught my husband with another woman. (Okay, the real story is that my eighty-seven-year-old Grandma Jewel figured out he was cheating on me. It's a great story, but you will have to wait for my next book.) My prenup became my settlement for the divorce. Thank you, Eric!

The moral of the story? Get a prenup when there is an income disparity and find a lawyer like Eric in your life.

Don't Let Tying the Knot Tie You in Knots: Your Prenup

A prenuptial agreement is just a private agreement between you and your partner-to-be. It basically lays out the financial side of your marriage and divorce (if there is one). You want it to be a fair agreement that is clear and understandable. You are planning for the worst, sort of like an insurance policy that can be in place for something that you never want to happen. This is the time to come clean with each other about all of your income, assets, and liabilities, because the process of writing a prenup will force those conversations. This is really the most important part. Of course, memorializing it legally gives you protection in the divorce, which the sweet words of love fail to do.

There is a misconception floating out there that prenups overwhelmingly favor men. In the olden days, when men typically were the ones

Before the Plunge—Prenups ～ 181

bringing home the bacon, they had more income and assets than women and yes, the prenup could protect the man. Obviously, the woman could argue that point in the divorce, but it seemed that men were protecting their assets.

Today, the income disparity is not as great as women have come into their own, but it is still alive and well. The process of getting a prenup should be a natural conversation and does not have to be compared to cutting off your arm without anesthesia. Think of it as a means to really discuss your life moving forward. Statistics do say that about half of marriages will end in divorce, so this is just a way to communicate in that event. And as noted earlier, second and third marriages fail at higher rates. A prenup does not have to be based upon distrust.

You Cancelled the Romance

Many couples avoid this tough conversation. It seems valid to ask, "Why are we discussing the end of our marriage, when we should be discussing our wedding?" and "Here we are discussing how we fell in love, and the prenup is asking us to play this picture backward." The point is that this discussion should not be the tinder to start a fire. And frankly if it is, you may want to examine who you are getting in bed with. Is this a loving relationship where you both want to fairly protect each other, or not? Why are there secrets?

The prenup will dispassionately outline property rights and financial arrangements that you mutually agreed upon in the event of a divorce. You both basically agree to a contract for yourselves that deals with assets, income, inheritance, and other money matters. If you don't have a prenup, your state law will control how your property is viewed and divided. That means that your grandma's brooch that you inherited could end up in his pile of assets and you may see his new squeeze wearing it, which will cause your grandma to roll over in her grave. I'm being snarky, but a prenup will deal with a lot of these issues. The prenup can help to protect those valuable assets that you want to stay in your family.

Think of a prenup as strengthening the marriage, not tearing it apart. You want to protect family assets and, in many cases, shield your kids from prior marriages. If you have children from a previous marriage, you may want to protect their interests in your assets and property that you bring into this new marriage.

182 ～ Chapter 33

When Do You Need a Prenup?

As far as I'm concerned, if you are thinking of whether you need a prenup, you probably need one. Think of it this way. You may be perfectly healthy now and are not planning on getting sick, but chances are at some point, you may. Do you think you need health insurance?

If you come into the marriage totally on the same economic footing as young people without much in the way of assets, then you probably don't need one. But if you do have assets and an income disparity, you need one. If you have kids, or he does or if you want to take time off to have them and step out of work for a while, you need one. If you are going to be left an inheritance, you need one. You also need one because life can change dramatically. You may be on equal economic footing now, but things can change for the better or worse. In any case, you need one.

Prenups can also provide debt protection. Some people get married with tremendous debt. The prenup can clarify that the debt will remain separate in a divorce and be the responsibility of the spouse who incurred it. Debt incurred during the marriage can also be handled.

"I Do" Can Equal "I Due"

Another situation may arise when you are coming clean with each other during the prenup conversations about debt obligations. If one partner has huge debt, or let's say something like a gambling problem, filing joint tax returns may be a mistake.

When you file a joint income tax return with your spouse, the law says that you are both jointly and severally responsible for the entire tax liability.[4] In plain language, if one of you has tax debt, the IRS can come after you both, unequally, to collect that . . . forever. There is a big misconception that taxes created during marriage will disappear after a separation, divorce, or death. There is no forgiveness of a federal tax debt in divorce. You are wrong if you think that the IRS will just split the tax debt, with each of you responsible for your portion. It's not true. Tax debt remains joint debt forever. Even if one spouse agrees to pay his/her share, and if they don't, the IRS can pursue the other spouse.

There is no forgiveness of a federal tax debt even at death. It does not simply disappear. The tax debt is now the responsibility of the descendants, and the IRS may go after the estate. If the taxpayers filed jointly,

Before the Plunge—Prenups ～ 183

you are basically on the hook forever, even if he/she is not around or declared bankruptcy.

What Does a Prenup Cost?

The price will depend upon the state where you reside and how complex your economic situation. There are do-it-yourself prenups as well. That is a great way to start, but have it finalized by a lawyer to make sure that you have a valid contract. Each state has complex laws, and you don't want to find out that your prenup is null and void at the time of a divorce when it's too late. Each of you should have your own lawyer.

If it is simple, and you did your homework beforehand, the legal cost could be under $1,000.

Oops, I Forgot to Tell Her

This story does not deal with a prenup, it deals with not *coming clean* with your spouse before you get married. I'm putting it here because I want to stress that full disclosure of your financial situation is not only part of the process of creating a prenup, but it should be the basis of your marriage moving forward.

Oprah had me doing her money shows in the 1990s. She wanted me to do a show based upon my information pertaining to how we all have distinct financial personalities. She loved my Financial Personality Quiz that you have already taken. The point is that basically we are either savers or spenders and we need to know how your financial personality affects the relationship. We were going to show how couples can start to communicate about money, even if they never have.

For this one, her producers found a cute, young couple in their twenties who were from the Midwest and had a young child. They came in for prerecording and then I was to prep them for the show. They brought their young daughter along. A friend was sitting close by offstage and holding their two-year-old baby girl.

I'll call them Muffin and Biff. Muffin was a perky housewife who loved to decorate their home for every holiday and buy lots of gifts for everyone. She sometimes hid the bills when they came in, because she was afraid Biff would get angry. Muffin was a spender. Biff was a saver. Biff paid the bills. Muffin had no idea

184 ～ Chapter 33

how much Biff earned or really what they could afford to spend. She really didn't know if she was being extravagant or not.

Biff would sometimes find the bills stuffed in a drawer and discover that they were past due and understandably get angry. He really didn't buy into the decorating and felt that spending $5,000 a year on stuffed Santas and life-sized ceramic bunnies were not necessities. He did complain to Muffin; however, he admitted that he loved the way the house looked and always brought his friends over to see Muffin's decorations. So there were mixed messages being sent to Muffin.

The point of the show was going to be how this couple was going to compromise on their budget and to make sure that they really communicated about all things financial. I hoped that Biff would understand that he treated Muffin like a child, and frankly, Muffin was acting like one.

Biff was going to tell Muffin what he earned and explain their budget. He was actually going to build their budget on air, so the audience could see how this can be done together. He was going to explain his income, debt, and the monthly obligations. The big reveal, I hoped, was to agree to let Muffin have money each month to buy chachkas, guilt-free, so she no longer felt compelled to hide bills. She could be empowered with her budget and not feel like she had to ask Biff for every penny, or worse yet, hide bills from him.

I was doing B-Roll. That is when you do a taped interview that will be edited and later pieced into the show. I was excited about it because they both were going to be honest and come together as a couple to show how this can be done in a loving relationship built on trust.

I had a big easel with a large pad of paper so Biff could write down the basics of the budget. It would later be chyroned for air. (That means that it would be superimposed over a TV video image. You see these charts on TV all the time.)

This was looking great; I was so happy. This was a perfect exercise for couples to visualize how to build a budget, even if the wife was not involved in the money side of their life. The audience could see how to come clean with the person they are married to. And Biff's budget was going to allow for Muffin to have some money to spend. Not the $5,000, but some number.

Then all hell broke loose.

Biff stopped speaking. In fact, Biff looked like he had stopped breathing. He said there was some more debt that he had to pay each month. I joyfully asked him to write that down. He looked at the ground and then at his wife. I sort of thought that he was going to reveal that he bought an expensive lawn mower and didn't tell Muffin what it really cost. Or that he was secretly saving for a vacation for them to take and wanted to surprise her. But it was worse.

Surprise her, he did.

None of us . . . really none of us were expecting this reveal.

Before the Plunge—Prenups $\sim$ 185

*He stammered and took the marker and wrote down the words Baby Bob
on the paper. He then started shaking and blurted out; "When I was sixteen,
I had a child with my girlfriend. I pay her $100 a week for our child to help sup-
port him."*

*We all froze. My camera man whispered, "Oh, shit," because he saw the horrified
look on Muffin's face. Obviously, she didn't know.*

*She burst into tears, sniffling, "You have a baby? That you never told me about?
Baby Bob?"*

*Biff had turned ashen gray by now and said, "I didn't want you to know that
I was paying money to Christa for Baby Bob." (And now the producer whispered,
"Bad answer.")*

*Biff was frozen on stage and didn't go to Muffin whose sobs turned into moans
of horror.*

*I went to Muffin, but she ran out of the room, grabbing her baby from her friend.
The friend was also a deer caught in the headlights. Muffin was screaming that she
was going to throw herself off the roof.*

*We sent security after her and we all followed. We found her trying to open a
door to the roof. I had so many emotions swirling through me. I was devastated
for Muffin and obviously terrified that she was going to hurt herself and maybe
the baby.*

*Muffin needed some time to recover. I am not trained in these things, and I
asked her if she had someone to call, or maybe a therapist. She said she wanted to
call her mom and mom had a therapist. She called her mom, and her mom took
over.*

*The next day, I explained to Oprah that the segment did not really go as
planned. In fact, even writing about it now sends shivers down my spine. Obviously, we had to find another couple and I'd do a little more homework before
we had the cameras rolling. I was really so sorry for all of the grief this couple
experienced.*

*Here is the weirdest part. After about a week, I got a call from both Biff and
Muffin, and they said that they still wanted to come on the show. They had told all
their friends that they were going to be on Oprah. It was a dream of theirs. Muffin
had calmed down and Biff had come clean about the whole situation, monetary and
otherwise.*

*They both said that if I hadn't encouraged Biff to do a budget, Muffin may never
have known about Baby Bob. Etcetera, etcetera.*

*We redid the budget and kept it simple. No mention of any obligations outside
of the plain vanilla ones were ever mentioned. Baby Bob was not a line item. The
producer and technical crew were as relieved as I was, but still in shock.*

Muffin and Biff's Budget - 1994

CATEGORY	MONTHLY TOTALS	ANNUAL TOTALS
Income		
Net income After Taxes	$3,917	$47,000
Savings	$300	$3,600
Expenses		
Rent	$1,000	$12,000
Utilities & Mobile Phone	$225	$2,700
Car Loan	$230	$2,760
Clothing	$200	$2,400
Medical, Life, Homeowners, and Car Insurance Premiums	$420	$5,040
Food & Misc. Expenses (not including Muffin's spending)	$250	$3,000
Credit Card/Student Debt	$300	$3,600
	$2,625	$31,500

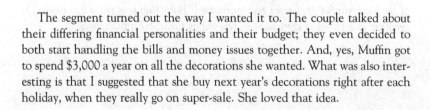

The segment turned out the way I wanted it to. The couple talked about their differing financial personalities and their budget; they even decided to both start handling the bills and money issues together. And, yes, Muffin got to spend $3,000 a year on all the decorations she wanted. What was also interesting is that I suggested that she buy next year's decorations right after each holiday, when they really go on super-sale. She loved that idea.

Before the Plunge—Prenups ～ 187

The moral of the story? Besides doing my homework to see if there are any landmines, the real money discussions are important to have before you say, "I do," whether or not you have a prenup.

Prenup Topics You Should be Prepared to Discuss

You should come armed (bad turn of phrase) to discuss:

- Savings and investments—know where the money is and basically, how much it is earning
- Your debt—college loans, credit card debt, tax liabilities, and any other debt owed to any others
- Your budget and spending habits
- Working versus being home with the kids (Remember, this prenup section is something you will share with your children or grandchildren who are embarking on marriage as well.)
- Property you own
- Inheritances you now have and any you think will be there in the future, including trust funds

By the way, there is something called a postnup as well. A postnup is an agreement that is created after the marriage and is still between the two spouses. It also outlines their financial and property rights in the event of a divorce. The real difference with that of a prenup is that you are already married. It should be noted that not all states will enforce a postnup.

When Should You Get a Prenup?

My advice is, by the third date! No, seriously, I'm in favor of them, because they force the tough money talks many people avoid. You should start the money conversations early on in your relationship. If you are comfortable enough to get naked in front of each other, you should be equally as comfortable discussing your college debt.

You should create and sign your prenup way before the wedding . . . like three to six months before. If you wait until you are putting on your veil, the agreement can be challenged later assuming the premise that it was signed under duress. If you sign it way before the wedding, you are assured, hopefully, that both parties had plenty of time to review it. Your situation, and that of your kids, is going to be unique, but think about having a prenup if either of you:

188   ～   Chapter 33

- Owns a business or will take over a business; family or otherwise
- Is wealthier than the other
- Is going to inherit wealth
- Earns a lot more than the other
- Has property
- Has dependents who may or will need support
- Has children from a prior relationship
- Has income disparity
- Has savings and investment accounts
- Has retirement accounts
- Has jewelry or collectibles
- Owns cars

Avoid the Big Prenup Marriage Money Mistakes

Prenup Marriage Money Mistake #1

Avoiding the Money Talk – Yes, you love each other, or you would not be getting married. Avoiding the "money talk" because it is not romantic and smacks of not trusting each other is just being naïve. I'll make it stronger; it's being stupid not to have it. Frankly, money conversations should be taking place throughout your relationship. If they are not, try to do some soul searching to find out why. And as I said, don't wait until the day before the wedding to start with this conversation.

Prenup Marriage Money Mistake #2

Using the Same Lawyer – Of course you trust each other, or again, you would not be getting married. If I'm going into business with you, I trust you. But I will not use the same lawyer as you. So, don't use the same lawyer for the prenup.

Prenup Marriage Money Mistake #3

Causing Drama and Tears – Don't get so emotional that you end up screaming or in tears. You may want to use a financial advisor, who is neutral, to go through some of the issues. They will act as sort of a mediator, because they should be impartial. You both should find that person; don't just use your financial person or his. If you're young, your parents' financial advisor may be a good choice for yours. They need to be impartial.

Prenup Marriage Money Mistake #4

Skipping the Talk – Don't run out of gumption and just decide to end the discussion and acquiesce to what the stronger partner wants. This will set the

Before the Plunge—Prenups ~ 189

stage for other disagreements down the road. If you want to have a financial voice in your relationship, now is a good time to find it. It's perfectly fine to say that you want to take the document and think about it.

Love Hurts: Epic Celeb Prenups

These are some examples of prenups from the ultra-wealthy and famous people.[5] Prenups can also include some nonmonetary clauses as well. Some of these are *eye-rollers*.

- Beyoncé and Jay-Z

Their prenup says that Beyoncé will get $5 million for every baby she has. She will also get $1 million for every year they are married if they get divorced. She clearly doesn't need the money.

- Tiger Woods and Elin Nordegren

Their prenup said that she was going to be left $20 million, which was signed before Tiger cheated on her. However, once he cheated on her, they renegotiated the prenup and she settled for $110 million. Now, this is interesting. During the negotiations, Woods offered Nordegren $200 million if she would take him back. Nope, she didn't and had to scrape by on just $110 million.

- Mark Zuckerberg and Priscilla Chan

Their prenup is not about money. Theirs has a lifestyle clause. If they get divorced, Chan gets one hundred minutes of alone time with Zuckerberg and one date night per week, without either going on Facebook during that time.

- Stephen Spielberg and Amy Irving

This is an example of following the advice to *get a lawyer*. Romance got the best of Spielberg when he was courting Irving. He penned their prenup on a cocktail napkin. But the napkin didn't hold up in court and the judge awarded Irving $100 million.[6]

- Queen Elizabeth II and Prince Philip

Their arrangement can sort of be called a prenup because these were the terms agreed to prior to their marriage. The monarchy worried that Prince

190 ～ Chapter 33

Philip would not be accepted considering his Danish, Greek, and German roots.[7] In 1947, he was "made" to renounce his Danish and Greek royal titles and he also had to be baptized by and become a member of the Church of England before the marriage.[8] He also had to change his last name from a German-sounding name of Schleswig-Holstein-Sonderburg-Glucksburg to Mountbatten, an anglicized version of his mother's surname, Battenberg. (It actually makes sense to me; just think of how hard it would have been to monogram towels.)

- Prince Harry and Meghan Markle

Supposedly, but I can't verify it, Prince Harry didn't want a prenup, but Queen Elizabeth insisted on one.[9] The story goes that when they were signing their final paperwork at St. George's Church and about to sign the marriage registry, they also were required by the Queen to sign a prenup. Meghan will not receive any crown jewels, and if they didn't have kids, she would get nothing at all.

Basic Elements of a Prenup
If there is bickering, this can start to undermine any relationship. Misunderstandings can grow and we know that money issues are one of the leading causes for a divorce. This advice is for you and for you to give your kids, if they are approaching a marriage or even a long-term relationship.

You should consult a lawyer who will give you advice. You need to know the laws of your state as well. Think of the prenup as not only protection, but also as a real conversation starter to think about the financial part of your relationship. I keep repeating this because it is so important.

Here are some of the basics to consider in any prenup:

- *Premarital assets and debt*
   Many couples come into a relationship with assets (money, property, jewelry, and so on) and also with debt (student loan, credit card, mortgages, car loans, and so forth). You need to decide how you are going to handle these if there is a split up. You may have family heirlooms that your family expects to stay in the family. It's also a great conversation starter to have about how preexisting debt will be handled within the marriage. Are you both going to pay the others debt off?
   One example of things to consider is student loan debt, because it may be big. You can stipulate, for instance, that if you (or he) are using

Before the Plunge—Prenups ⁓ 191

their income to pay off this debt, or frankly any debt, the other person should make you whole in a divorce.

- *Children from previous marriages*

You need to think about how these kids will be dealt with in a divorce. Think about dependent and emancipated kids. You can't really agree on future child custody or child support, but it's a great topic to discuss. You may not be able to put firm numbers by these items, but at least you will have the conversation if you have not already had it. Do the kids inherit money? Jointly, from you both? Separately? Suppose you have kids from this marriage; are all kids dealt with equally? Again, all issues that should be addressed.

- *Marital assets and debts*

These are assets and debt that you acquired during your marriage. One of you may be starting a business and rack up debt. Are you both going to own the business? Are you both going to assume the debt? By the way, be careful when you sign joint tax returns. You are jointly and separately liable for the taxes owed. The IRS is not sympathetic to "I didn't know I'd owe *his* taxes." If you sign a joint return, those are his and your taxes. If he can't pay, the IRS will go after you.

- *Marital financial responsibilities*

You can memorialize who is expected to pay bills, file tax returns, how bank and investment accounts will be handled, how you will save for retirement, how you both will spend money or get credit, and so on. Are accounts joint? Are there some separate accounts? If one of you is not working, for instance, you can specify that the working partner will put a certain amount of money into an account (jointly or otherwise), each month. How much insurance will be purchased? Will there be long-term health care policies?

- *Work*

You can discuss how you will handle a situation where a job may require a transfer to another state. How will you handle that? Will there be a stay-at-home parent? Discuss how monthly expenses will be handled.

- *Property division*

This can be real property, or businesses, or pensions. You need to decide who gets what in a divorce.

- *Protection of your estate planning*

You both need wills and living wills to outline your wishes. Are you buying funeral plots? A prenup can help all assets from being lumped together, as I have said. But it can also limit the inheritance of a

192 ～ Chapter 33

spouse. Think about a situation where there are kids from a previous marriage. If your spouse who fathered those kids dies before you and he doesn't have a will, you could inherit the assets. When you die, the kids of your dead husband may not get anything. This highlights why you need to sit down with professionals who can walk you through all the scenarios.

The Tough Conversation: How to Talk about Getting a Prenup

This conversation is for you if you decide to get married again, and also it can be used as advice for your kids who may be considering marriage.

I know that many of you consider this and other money issues as taboo. "If I love him, I trust him, and he loves me, why would I ever think that he would hurt me in a divorce?" I can't tell you how many times I've heard those words. These words sting. They sting for all involved. Life changes and so do people. Yes, you both were in love at one point, but unfortunately, things can change, and they do. Life and love can turn against you to the point that you may not even recognize the man sitting across from you. Things may come out of both of your mouths that you could never imagine possible.

I'm not a psychologist, and I told you that I was going to deal with the money side of divorce and help to empower you to take charge of that and to design your way forward. I will stay in that wheelhouse. But I want you to know that I appreciate that this is not a walk in the park and that these conversations can be hard.

With all of that said, I feel that you and your kids who are considering marriage need to have them with prospective spouses.

Here are some tips:

- Ducks in a Row

Speak to a matrimonial lawyer before you have the discussion with your to-be mate. The reason is that you want to make sure that you know all of the points you will need to discuss. The word "prenup" scares some people, and you want to be clear on the important points before you start the conversation.

- Don't Put This Off

It's hard to imagine being in the romantic setting, cuddling, when one of you turns to the other and says, "I think it's time to discuss a prenup." If you

Before the Plunge—Prenups 193

are younger, I have couples ease into the discussion to say that "My parents are concerned and they feel strongly that they want me to have a prenup. There are family assets . . . family heirlooms . . ." whatever.

Start by saying that you love him and you know he loves you, and that you both want to protect each other in the future, no matter what. A divorce is unthinkable, but they happen. This is a good time to tell a story about a friend, or your parents, or someone who thought they were in love and protected and weren't in a divorce. Explain that this process will give you both a chance to really understand each other's finances and desires if something does not work out. I like calling a prenup "Marriage Insurance." It's actually "Divorce Insurance." (My friend Kelly and I wanted to start a company to cover divorces . . . but that's another story.)

You can also say that you want to remain friends for life and a prenup can iron out some problems that may cause irreparable damage to a relationship in a divorce.

- Before You or He Gets Down on One Knee

Start the prenup process as soon as you know there is going to be serious marriage-talk. You may be asking him to marry you; I don't care. It's just that this conversation gets harder and harder the longer you wait.

Use the information you have garnered from your attorney to give real reasons why the prenup is important. Don't use a PowerPoint presentation and overwhelm him. Say that it was suggested that you investigate getting a prenup and you wanted to talk to a lawyer to see if that was suggested and what it should contain. Ask him his opinion; just don't make demands. You don't want him to feel blindsided, which he may. Let him think about it all before the next conversation.

Explain that the prenup is protecting both of you and if applicable, your future and present kids. If the marriage does end, you want to reduce the arguments and recrimination as much as possible.

- "Tip-Toe through the Tulips"

Don't be heavy-handed, but suggest that he can go online to research prenups and how they are important and what they should contain. Stress that the most important thing is that you both will come clean on all your income, investments, assets, and debt, and that is a really good thing. You want your marriage to be open and transparent for you both. You want both of you to handle all aspects of the "business part" of your life, as well as all of the emotional and physical parts.

194   ~   Chapter 33

- Lawyer Up

Say that it is important for him to have his own lawyer, and that's great because she may suggest some things that your lawyer did not.

A prenup can be changed at any time, as long as both parties agree to the changes. It can also time out, which should signal that it's time to revise the agreement. So this should give him some relief and not make him have to think of every eventuality that may affect the prenup in the future.

Remember, just like life insurance, a prenup is that insurance for the future. It doesn't doom your marriage; it should cause peace of mind. Find that together.

CHAPTER 34

Giving Is Part of Living

Charitable giving and volunteering are near and dear to my heart and has been a part of my life, forever. I know that I can make a difference, but I also know what giving does for me. I get energy from it, and it feeds my soul. I love what Victor Hugo said, "As the purse is emptied, the heart is filled."[1]

I raised my kids saying, "We are not here to just take up space." Yes, they rolled their eyes, but they also live their lives by giving back. In fact, my son Rhett is a social entrepreneur and has created the first blockchain organic cotton coalition that has organized twenty-five thousand organic cotton-growing families in India to give them a sustainable way of life. My daughter Kyel is also an entrepreneur in the tech wellness space. Okay, enough about being a proud mom.

Giving is just a part of all my teachings. In fact, my allowance system for kids includes 10 percent for charity, which just becomes a kid's natural part of handling money. I also give families the ability to teach their values around giving and volunteering.

I'm sure that philanthropy is also a part of your life, as well. I'm *preaching to the choir*. In fact, 72 percent of Baby Boomers give to charity, donating an annual average of $1,212. They are also most likely to make recurring donations on a regular basis as compared to the other generations. What's interesting is that 30 percent of donors age seventy-five and older said in a survey that they have given online, which means that they give 25 percent more frequently than younger generations.[2] I feel it is important to stay connected and make giving part of your life. It keeps us humble and thankful for what we have. It also adds to our self-worth. It keeps us human. It is frankly a vital part of living if you want a happy life. Anne Frank said, "No one has ever become poor by giving."[3]

196 ～ Chapter 34

There are also tax benefits for charitable giving. They change and are different depending upon the type of asset you are giving; money or property, and so on, so check these with your accountant. The organization to which you are donating must prove that they serve charitable purposes, and they must qualify for tax-exempt status as determined by the IRS. They are usually such organizations as religious, literary, or educational institutions, those that prevent cruelty to animals or children, veteran's groups, others who support certain medical conditions and diseases, and so on. You can now only claim a charitable contribution deduction up to 60% of your Adjusted Gross Income (AGI).

Fifty-eight percent of Baby Boomers attend fundraising events, and 71 percent volunteer locally.[4] But note, that if you attend one of those $500-a-plate charitable dinners, you cannot deduct the full $500 on your taxes. You can deduct the cost minus the value of the dinner. Usually, the deductible amount is noted on your ticket, or the charity will send you a note or email. Again, this is something to be reviewed with your accountant.

Interesting Ways to Donate

- **Charitable Remainder Trust** – A charitable remainder trust is a financial vehicle that gives you the benefit of supporting your charitable goals while still generating some income from the underlying assets that support the gifts.[5] These are designed to be tax-exempt and irrevocable and reduce taxable income for you.

You set them up by making a donation (by the trustor) that legally then provides a tax donation. They will give income to the trustor or other named beneficiaries that are not charities (like your kids) and after a designated time period (that you indicate), the remainder of the trust will go to the charities you have named.

- **Donor-Advised Fund (DAF)** – A DAF is an account where you can deposit assets for donation to a charity over time. You, as the donor will get a tax deduction. There will be a sponsoring organization behind this that will manage the account. Technically, you as the donor will have to choose IRS-recognized charitable organizations, and the sponsoring organization will donate according to your wishes.

You can claim a tax deduction in the year you contribute the assets rather than the year the money goes to the charity. Some people like DAFs because

Giving Is Part of Living ～ 197

they can provide anonymity by withholding your identity if you don't want your name known or don't want to be solicited for future donations.

- **Qualified Charitable Distribution (QCD)** – A QCD is a nontaxable distribution made directly by the trustee of an IRA to an eligible charitable organization.[6] Making a QCD can benefit the taxpayer by reducing your taxable income while you are supporting your charity.

When you are meeting with your financial advisors and legal *Team-You*, and you are also considering your estate planning, consider a bequest in your will to set many of these vehicles up for your charitable giving.

Keep the words of Winston Churchill in mind, "We make a living by what we get, but we make a life by what we give."[7]

CHAPTER 35

~

Retirees, "Let the Force Be with You" (and Your Grandchildren)

Albert Einstein is credited with saying that compound interest is "the most powerful force in the universe."[1] I would add that education combined with the miracle of compounding may be the real power we are seeking. Who can have this superpower? Baby Boomers.

TV personalities, bloggers, and almost everyone else yells at us because we apparently didn't get the message about saving for our future. Ok, we hear you. We may have blown it for ourselves, but it is not too late for us to do something *now* to protect our most precious asset: our grandchildren.

Even though the savings/investing stats are depressing, Baby Boomers are in the midst of the largest transfer of wealth that this nation has ever experienced. Folks like the Center on Wealth and Philanthropy out of Boston College originally estimated the transfer to be $41 trillion dollars. Now the estimate has climbed to $59 trillion.[2]

I'm not hung up on the exact amount; I'm fascinated about its significance and what this means to Boomers and their children and grandchildren. The huge numbers make us think that this is about money. I want you to consider that your legacy is not only about money, it's about more than money. Isn't the gift you want to pass on to the next generation, resulting from your hard work, really about who you are . . . about your values?

Let's first talk about the money part and how you can act on Einstein's words and make the *miracle of compounding* work for your loved ones. Your grandchildren have time on their side. Do the simple math. If you have a one-year-old grandchild and you invest $50,000 for that child and earn simple yearly compounded interest at 6 percent, when that child is sixty-five, they'll have over $2 million. Now raise the interest rate to 8 percent annually and the number jumps to over $6.8 million. I know we are not considering

200 ~ Chapter 35

inflation and the future Consumer Price Index (CPI), but the point is that today's investing allows Einstein's theory to take real shape. The other part of the miracle involves your connection with your grandchildren. Your legacy is about the values and life skills you want to pass on to your grandkids. They actually want to hang out with you. They think you are cool. Take advantage of them wanting to listen to you.

Of course, you are worried that your kids or grandkids may take their inheritance and indulge in sex, drugs, and rock 'n' roll and may try to perfect the recipe for the next original designer martini. You lower the risk of that by talking about and showing your offspring what money can and can't do. You don't want them to ever confuse net worth with self-worth. Talk about the responsibility that goes along with your money. It didn't just happen . . . you earned it.

I raised my kids with my allowance system, which teaches "Earning, Saving, Spending, and Sharing."[3] The sharing part hopefully teaches that the act of giving is one that expects nothing in return, but as a mom, you never know if the lessons are being absorbed. I wasn't sure that I could teach that giving doesn't need an award or any recognition. It is simply giving.

This story still brings tears to my eyes. My son, Rhett, was five years old. My kids both earned their allowance and could spend 30 percent of it each week on what I called *Quick Cash*. That was instant gratification. They had done chores and had to budget their money into 10 percent *Charity*, 30 percent *Quick Cash*, 30 percent *Medium Term-Saving* (to pick something to save for), and 30 percent *Long-Term Saving*.

My goal was to give my kids freedom to choose their weekly *Quick Cash* to buy something fun, on impulse and to teach that when your *Quick Cash* is gone, it's gone.

We were living in New York City at the time. Rhett wanted to take his hard-earned *Quick Cash* to the local corner bodega to buy Tootsie Rolls. (I was liberal on his sugar intake; my bad.)

I hung out at the back of the store watching him count out his penny Tootsie Rolls and count his change over and over again. That is all part of the process. He then cupped his bounty and strolled to stand in line at the cash register. He didn't realize it, but there was a homeless woman in front of him with a cup of change and an orange.

She dumped her change on the counter and the cashier counted it out. He said she was short money and couldn't buy the orange, which cost thirty-three cents. Rhett was watching and listening to all of this. As the woman was scraping up her change back into her cup and turning around to put the orange back, he quipped, "Hi, I'm Rhett and I'd like to buy you that orange."

She got embarrassed and looked away. He said, "No, it's ok, this is my Quick Cash and I get to spend it any way I want. I just have to start all over again counting out my money."

This time, she looked flustered, as did everyone else in the store. There was silence as all eyes fell on this little kid. Again, she resisted. He became more insistent, "I work for a living, and this is my Quick Cash, and this is how it works. I want to buy this orange for you, because someday if I don't have money, someone else will use their Quick Cash to buy me food. Didn't you read my mother's book?"

Evidently, she had not. Her eyes were wide as she handed Rhett the orange. He set down his Tootsie Rolls and began to figure out his change, taking into account the orange.

Every mother flashed looks at me as I started to cry. There were lots of sniffles.

He concluded the transaction and the cashier handled over the orange to the woman and Rhett strolled back to me. I started to gush, "I'm so proud of you, that was amazing."

He held his ground and said, "Didn't you read your book? This is what you have taught us. These are the rules. You are not supposed to be proud of me when I do what I'm supposed to do, you are supposed to be proud of me when I do something really great."

Out of the mouth of babes. Yes, if you raise them with your values, they will live those values.

Pay It Forward

Get your grandkids involved in the charities and philanthropic activities that are near and dear to you. Tell them what you think is important . . . is it education, the arts, travel, religion, helping others? Show them. If your passion is building homes with Habitat for Humanity, take them along domestically or internationally to help build a home. I've travelled with my kids for years to all sorts of places, from Borneo to Papua New Guinea to Madagascar. Every trip includes a charitable element, which is either prearranged or set up via our local guide. We have planted trees, read to homeless children, and donated clothes and food to local charities, among other things. I allowed my kids to be empowered to make a difference, and the added benefit was that these experiences reduced the times I had to say, "You don't know how lucky you are." This all hopefully may reduce the risk of your money going to buy the Ferrari as soon as your funeral is over.

202 ～ Chapter 35

Also, talk to your grandchildren about how you earned the money. Take them to your office or explain what you do or did. Tell them the stories about the "good 'ole days." Show them the products you inspired or manufactured or moved. This education connects them with the reality of how the money came to be. This opens the door to address your intentions around the inheritance, and the meetings you all should have with financial advisors. Conversations with family members around money are emotional. Demystify them and make them normal. I feel strongly that you must make sure that all family members understand your wishes prior to the wealth transfer.

By the way, the most expensive way to give away wealth is to die with it. You can't take it with you. David Rockefeller, former Chairman of The Chase Manhattan Bank, summed it up with great aplomb. I was lucky enough to know David well. It was 2004 and I was hitting him up for a jacket quote for my recent book. We were talking about passing wealth onto the next generation and David said, "You'll never see a hearse with a luggage rack."

CHAPTER 36

~

When Your Kids Are Concerned, Can You Step Away from Your Wallet?

We are parents, and we always will be. Our kids know that we have always been there to kiss their boo-boos when they fell off their bikes or bail them out when they scraped the car fender bringing it into the garage when they first got their license, and maybe reaching into your retirement funds if they needed it later in life.

If you are doing this, or still doing this, you are not alone. Nearly one in three parents have made significant financial sacrifices to help their adult kids. Bankrate.com reported that parents are stepping up to help their adult children when they are having financial problems.[1] The problem is that many older adult parents are sacrificing their own savings to bail out their kids.

Also, 41 percent of parents have an adult child currently living with them. These offspring living back home are called the Boomerang Generation;[2] however, according to a Thrivent survey, 75 percent of parents are not even discussing money management with these adult kids, and worse yet, 80 percent aren't setting financial expectations with these kids.[3]

"Over two-thirds (68 percent) of parents of adult children have made or are currently making a financial sacrifice to help their kids financially."[4] Parents say they sacrificed retirement savings (43 percent), emergency savings (51 percent), paying down their own debt (49 percent), or reaching a financial milestone (55 percent).

This is not just affecting higher socioeconomic families. The Bankrate study also noted that more lower-income households are sacrificing emergency savings to help their adult kids out: "58% of households with a yearly income under $50,000 have made financial sacrifices to help their adult children, compared to 46% of those households with a yearly income of $100,000 or more."

204   ～   Chapter 36

This is a big dilemma for many divorced moms. Even though most Baby Boomers report that their adult kids should be paying their own bills by age twenty, they have still been there to pick up the pieces.

If you know that you have been doing this, it's time for four things to happen:

1. This should be brought up in the divorce discussions, to see if and how you both will contribute.
2. Have the tough talk with your kids to see if it's time for them to stop putting their hands out for help. If this is temporary, try to work out a time frame.
3. Share your new superpower of building and sticking to a budget, and maybe downsizing to make this happen. Tell your kids that you can be their guide to really start to build a life that they can fund.
4. It may sound harsh, but you may want to consider your "help" as a loan to be paid off by your kids when they are back on their feet.

You want to try to set boundaries without feeling guilty. Guilt is a tough one, I know. But your help may be keeping them from achieving the self-reliance that they may seek. There is an old saying, "Those for whom you do the most, wind up resenting you the worst." Help them to write their own life plan. Show them the *Visioning* exercise in this book. Make sure that it is *not* your life plan for them, but something they own and want to achieve. They will need to take the initiative to find the path to achieve their goals on their own. You may see them stumble and fall, but let them do that on their own.

Of course, you will always be there for your kids. They are your kids. Setting expectations is healthy. It will avoid any future resentment from both you and the kids. You are actually helping them to become independent. I think the words of Calvin Coolidge nailed it, "There is no dignity so impressive, and no one independence quite so important, as living within your means."[5]

CHAPTER 37

Adult Children Returning to the Empty Nest

You may not have to worry about empty-nest syndrome. The pandemic has exacerbated this situation. In fact, "A majority of young adults in the U.S. live with their parents for the first time since the Great Depression."[1] It's also interesting to note that a Pew Research Center Survey found that many Americans think that this is bad for society.[2] Also, interestingly, more young men, 36 percent, were likely than young women, 30 percent, to live in their parents' home.

Our young adults are coping with rising student debt and housing costs, and multigenerational living is increasing.[3] These financial issues have forced them back home. This trend is more pronounced among young adults without a college degree.

A mom is the first one to want to bail out the kids. It doesn't matter the age of your kids; they are your kids forever. I get that. But you also need to have open and honest conversations about their financial situation and yours. We want to be the first ones they call upon for help. We also feel obligated to help our kids in need. But you also want your adult kids to be adults and learn to stand on their own two feet.

Setup a Lease with Your Adult Children

I will walk you through some techniques to deal with adult kids returning to the nest. These are tough conversations, but are necessary. If you are proactive about expectations and responsibilities, you will avoid a blow-up that could damage your relationship.

If your grown offspring (temporarily) fails at the American Dream and must choose between going from friend to friend or living in your home, we

206 ～ Chapter 37

are parents and grandparents first, and the door is always open. In today's world, it's better to just think of our young adults as *free-range kids*.

You are trying to avoid the situation where you just become *Hotel Mom* that comes replete with room service and gas in the car. Having grown children at home can now be a great time to teach or reinforce some of your imparted wisdom. You gave them roots, and you gave them wings. You love them and you want them to be able to fly, so now it's time for *the talk*.

Why the Lease?

I'm not being harsh; it's your house. It's just that without a real understanding, misunderstandings can take place, and those can lead to tough times for all of you. Expectations need to be explicitly discussed and memorialized. When I say "memorialized," I mean written down in a lease. You do not need a lawyer to draw up a lease; you are a family held together by love and trust. But this should be taken seriously, and all parties have a voice. The agreement actually will help your offspring to be established as an adult with certain responsibilities.

The lease discussion should start at the point when your young adult has decided to wait before leaving home, or before they move in. It is much harder to break old habits after your child has taken up residency. Don't wait for the first blow-up, if you can. If you have waited, then just say that you read this book that recommended that we draw up a lease.

Remember, in this case, you are the landlord and the child is the tenant. While you want to relate to your offspring as an adult, you do have certain prerogatives that your child does not. By the way, you may have financially been counting on being an empty-nester, and having boarders is expensive.

Worksheet for Soon-to-Be Parental Landlords

You need to first ask yourself these questions to establish what you feel is fair to request of your child. Take your financial circumstances into account. If you know before the divorce that this is the case, build extra joint support into your divorce decree.

The above questions do not constitute a quiz. There are no right or wrong answers; in fact, these may not even be the right questions. You may want to discuss whether or not your offspring can have overnight guests, or if they can smoke in or around your home, or if they need to let you know if they are coming home late, so you don't have to worry. These are only things to think about so that you can take the next step to have *the talk* with your kids.

The next step is to have the conversation. You will frame this around the fact that you love them unconditionally, but that these things need to be memorialized so that there are clear understandings. Allow your kids to bring up other issues that are also on their minds that need to be addressed.

Now just write out *the lease*. If the term is bothersome, call it *an agreement*. As always, you are willing to compromise. For instance, if your offspring is willing to take on the responsibility of car maintenance, they can have the privilege of parking their vehicle in the garage. They may have children, and those responsibilities also have to be addressed.

Enjoy your time with your adult children and view this as a gift. The lease will make things run more smoothly. This is a great time to coach them through some of the financial lessons that they may not have garnered as kids. They will feel good about contributing to your multigenerational household; it's empowering for them to feel needed, as well. I love the words of Abigail Van Buren when she said, "If you want your children to turn out well, spend twice as much time with them, and half as much money."[4]

SAMPLE LEASE WORKSHEET

1. Should your adult child pay rent? Yes _____ No _____

2. How much rent should your adult child pay?
   (You should try to calculate the extra utility, food, car, and other expenses.)
   If employed, $_____
   If unemployed, $_____

3. Should the lease be for a specific period?
   Yes _____ No _____

4. How will you divide utilities? (Go bill by bill and be specific.)

5. What household chores are the responsibility of your adult child? (Be specific and include indoor and outdoor duties.)

6. Is your adult child allowed to use your car? Who pays for gas, maintenance, and insurance?

7. Is your adult child allowed to have pets? Who takes care of them and who pays for those expenses?

8. May your adult child eat your groceries, or do they have to shop on their own? Who makes the food list? Who buys the food and other non-food items?

9. Who prepares the meals, and is there a schedule?

10. Does your adult child need assistance in visioning their life goals, setting up a budget, reducing debt, etc.?

CHAPTER 38

~

The End or New Beginning?

Most of our existence is spent on the treadmill of daily life, which may even feel like it is the gap in between the momentous events. Some of those momentous events will leave your cheeks cramping from having to hold back your laughter, and some will leave your cheeks burning from your streaming tears. Your divorce is a momentous event.

You certainly didn't go into marriage all those years ago thinking that you would need a book about gray divorce. In fact, when you got married that was not even a term. But here you are, for better or worse. This situation demands courage and perseverance. It would have been a lot easier to just stay and to do nothing about it. But you didn't. You took the step into your next momentous moment. You may be questioning this step and even feel that your very self-worth has come under question and assault.

Your self-worth can now be defined by how you are able to take charge, navigate the pain, and free yourself from the shackles of your old life. I love the image of Michelangelo's sculpture "Slaves" in Florence. It was explained to me that Michelangelo felt that he had finished the sculptures, even though you could only see a hand or foot peeking out of the stone. He felt that he had freed the slave from the rock that encased him and that the slave would have to do the rest of the work to release themselves from the stone.

This book has hopefully started to chisel your release from the relationship that has bound you, and given you tools to fully break free to sculpt your new life. You need not define yourself by your circumstances, but by how you deal with what life has thrown your way. You will now be the leading actress in the scenes of your life's play, when perhaps before you were just a supporting actress.

210   ~   Chapter 38

Or, I hope you have come into this situation with joy and are looking forward to the next chapter . . . and the next chapter after that . . .

I'm so glad that I could assist you with the money journey that you are taking, or about to take. You can now start to say that you have both the confidence and competence to deal with this. The biggest thing to remember is that as long as you are alive, you can grow, learn, and change. Whatever your past may have dealt you, you have the fortitude to sculpt your new future.

Never lose track of what your true goal is: self-reliance. Henry David Thoreau popularized the idea almost two hundred years ago, and the concept worked its way so firmly into the fabric of American thinking that it has never once become obsolete or irrelevant. Self-reliance has been my overarching theme in all my books and teachings. It is the ultimate empowerment—to design, make decisions, and live the financial life you want.

While Thoreau connected self-reliance (in part) with the ability to "grow" and consume all one's own food on a sustainable basis, he encouraged people to design and grow their own nourishment. I relate self-reliance to the ability to design, grow, and reap nourishment from one's own financial life.

I look forward to hearing about your new, beautiful, and nurturing financial garden!

Notes

Preface

1. Sylvia Smith, "5 Potential Signs of Miserable Husband Syndrome & How to Deal," Marriage.com, December 12, 2023, https://www.marriage.com/advice/relationship/miserable-husband-syndrome/.

2. Angelou, Maya. Letter to my daughter. New York, NY: Random House, 2008.

3. Tolle, Eckhart. The power of now: A guide to spiritual enlightenment. Novato, CA: New World Library, 2001.

4. Holly Ellyatt, "Arguing with Your Partner over Covid? You're Not Alone, with the Pandemic Straining Many Relationships," CNBC, January 21, 2022, https://www.cnbc.com/2022/01/21/covid-has-put-pressures-and-strains-on-relationships.html.

5. Claire Ewing-Nelson, "All of the Jobs Lost in December Were Women's Jobs," National Women's Law Center, January 2021, https://nwlc.org/wp-content/uploads/2021/01/December-Jobs-Day.pdf.

6. John C. Bluedorn, Francesca Caselli, Niels-Jakob H. Hansen, Ippei Shibata, and Marina Mendes Tavares, "Gender and Employment in the COVID-19 Recession: Evidence on 'She-Cessions,'" International Monetary Fund, March 31, 2021, https://www.imf.org/en/Publications/WP/Issues/2021/03/31/Gender-and-Employment-in-the-COVID-19-Recession-Evidence-on-She-cessions-50316.

7. Emily Field, Alexis Krivkovich, Sandra Kügele, Nicole Robinson, and Lareina Yee, "Women in the Workplace 2023," McKinsey & Company, October 5, 2023, https://www.mckinsey.com/featured-insights/diversity-and-inclusion/women-in-the-workplace.

212 ～ Notes

8. "Is Divorce Seasonal? UW Research Shows Biannual Spike in Divorce Filings," University of Washington, August 21, 2016, https://www.washington.edu/news/2016/08/21/is-divorce-seasonal-uw-research-shows-biannual-spike-in-divorce-filings/.

9. Jo Craven McGinty, "The Divorce Rate Is at a 40-Year Low, Unless You're 55 or Older," *Wall Street Journal*, June 21, 2019, https://www.wsj.com/articles/the-divorce-rate-is-at-a-40-year-low-unless-youre-55-or-older-11561116601.

10. Susan L. Brown and I-Fen Lin, "Gray Divorce: A Growing Risk Regardless of Class or Education," Council on Contemporary Families, 2024, https://sites.utexas.edu/contemporaryfamilies/2014/10/08/growing-risk-brief-report/.

11. "Provisional Number of Marriages and Marriage Rate: United States, 2000–2021," Centers of Disease Control and Prevention, 2021.

12. Erica Pandey, "America the Single," Axios, February 25, 2023, https://www.axios.com/2023/02/25/marriage-declining-single-dating-taxes-relationships.

13. Darragh McManus, "How You Can Cope with Competitive Marriage Syndrome," *Irish Independent*, April 11, 2014, https://www.independent.ie/lifestyle/how-you-can-cope-with-competitive-marriage-syndrome-30175393.html.

14. "When Women Earn More than Their Husbands," The University of Chicago Booth School of Business, February 18, 2013, the University of Chicago, https://www.chicagobooth.edu/media-relations-and-communications/press-releases/when-women-earn-more-than-their-husbands.

15. Aimee Picchi, "More Women Are Now Outearning Their Husbands—And Emotions Can Be Big," *USA Today*, March 3, 2020, https://www.usatoday.com/story/money/2020/03/03/gender-wage-gap-more-women-out-earning-husbands/4933666002/.

16. Rebecca Coffey, "Have We Discovered a Prime Reason Why Some Men Cheat?," *Psychology Today*, June 1, 2015, https://www.psychologytoday.com/us/blog/the-bejeezus-out-me/201506/have-we-discovered-prime-reason-why-some-men-cheat.

17. A. Novotney, "In Brief: Snapshots of Some of the Latest Peer-Reviewed Research within Psychology and Related Fields," *Monitor on Psychology* 44, no. 10, November 1, 2013, https://www.apa.org/monitor/2013/11/inbrief.

18. Obama, Michelle. Becoming. New York, NY: Crown, 2021.

19. Health Research Funding, "26 Surprising Statistics on Cheating Spouses," HRF, January 6, 2015, https://healthresearchfunding.org/26-surprising-statistics-cheating-spouses/.

20. Ari Tuckman, "Will a Partner Who Cheated Cheat Again?," *Psychology Today*, February 28, 2021, https://www.psychologytoday.com/us/blog/sex-matters/202102/will-partner-who-cheated-cheat-again.

21. Parks, Rosa, Gregory J. Reed, and Deforia Lane. Quiet strength: The faith, the hope, and the heart of a woman who changed a nation. Grand Rapids, MI: Zondervan Audio Pages, 1994.

Notes ~ 213

22. Pablo Picasso Quotes. BrainyQuote.com, BrainyMedia Inc, 2024. https://www.brainyquote.com/quotes/pablo_picasso_120939, accessed September 2, 2024.

23. Pete Carroll Quotes. BrainyQuote.com, BrainyMedia Inc, 2024. https://www.brainyquote.com/quotes/pete_carroll_670246, accessed September 2, 2024.

24. Branka Vuleta, "14 Intriguing Divorce Statistics in 2023," Legaljobs, May 20, 2023, https://legaljobs.io/blog/divorce-statistics.

25. "Divorce Rate in America: 50+ Divorce Statistics [Updated 2024]," Divorce.com, January 6, 2024, https://divorce.com/blog/divorce-statistics/.

26. Christy Bieber, "Revealing Divorce Statistics in 2024," *Forbes*, January 8, 2024, https://www.forbes.com/advisor/legal/divorce/divorce-statistics/.

27. McGinty, "The Divorce Rate Is at a 40-Year Low, Unless You're 55 or Older."

28. Jessica Hall, "Gray Divorce Is Most Often Initiated by Women—Even Though It Can Crush Their Finances," MarketWatch, September 11, 2023, https://www.marketwatch.com/story/gray-divorce-is-most-often-initiated-by-women-even-though-it-can-crush-their-finances-4329540d.

29. Xenia P. Montenegro, "The Divorce Experience: A Study of Divorce at Midlife and Beyond." *AARP*, May 2004, https://assets.aarp.org/rgcenter/general/divorce.pdf.

30. "Own Your Worth: How Women Can Break the Cycle of Abdication and Take Control of Their Wealth," UBS, 2018, https://www.ubs.com/content/dam/WealthManagementAmericas/documents/2018-37666-UBS-Own-Your-Worth-report-R32.pdf.

31. "Fifth Annual Advisor Authority Study Shows Women Investors Less Optimistic about Market and Economy than Men Investors Regardless of Affluence or Access to a Financial Advisor," PR Newswire, July 22, 2019, https://www.prnewswire.com/news-releases/fifth-annual-advisor-authority-study-shows-women-investors-less-optimistic-about-market-and-economy-than-men-investors-regardless-of-affluence-or-access-to-a-financial-advisor-300888203.html.

32. "Bank of America Study Finds 94% of Women Believe They'll Be Personally Responsible for Their Finances at Some Point in Their Lives," PR Newswire, June 22, 2022, https://www.prnewswire.com/news-releases/bank-of-america-study-finds-94-of-women-believe-theyll-be-personally-responsible-for-their-finances-at-some-point-in-their-lives-301573161.html.

33. Suzanne Woolley, "Rise of 'Gray' Divorce Is Forcing a Financial Reckoning for 50-Plus Women," *Los Angeles Times*, April 20, 2018, https://www.latimes.com/business/la-fi-divorce-at-fifty-20180420-story.html.

34. Elizabeth Gravier, "Men Have over 3x More Retirement Savings than Women—7 Steps to Make Sure You Are Financially Secure," CNBC, January 2, 2024, https://www.cnbc.com/select/financial-steps-for-women/.

35. American Association of University Women, "The Simple Truth About the Gender Pay Gap," AAUW, 2020, https://www.aauw.org/app/uploads/2020/12/SimpleTruth_2.1.pdf.

214 ～ Notes

Chapter 1

1. Scott Galloway, "The Case to Rebrand 'Divorce,'" *Medium*, May 24, 2021, https://marker.medium.com/the-case-to-rebrand-divorce-c2e60f0922e3.

Chapter 2

1. Angela Moore, "This Is Why Baby Boomers Are Divorcing at a Stunning Rate," MarketWatch, October 20, 2018, https://www.marketwatch.com/story/your-failing-marriage-is-about-to-make-the-retirement-crisis-worse-2017-03-13.

2. Brigid Schulte, "Till Death Do Us Part? No Way. Gray Divorce on the Rise," *Washington Post*, October 8, 2014, https://www.washingtonpost.com/blogs/she-the-people/wp/2014/10/08/till-death-do-us-part-no-way-gray-divorce-on-the-rise/.

3. Wendy Wang, "The Share of Never-Married Americans Has Reached a New High," Institute for Family Studies, September 9, 2020, https://ifstudies.org/blog/the-share-of-never-married-americans-has-reached-a-new-high.

4. Rachel Epstein, "14 Weird-but-True Reasons Real People Have Gotten Divorced," *Marie Claire*, September 26, 2017, https://www.marieclaire.com/culture/a29603/weird-reasons-real-people-divorced/.

Chapter 3

1. Michael Paulson, "As Vatican Revisits Divorce, Many Catholics Long for Acceptance," *New York Times*, January 25, 2015, https://www.nytimes.com/2015/01/25/us/as-vatican-revisits-divorce-many-catholics-long-for-acceptance.html.

2. "Irish Divorce," Urban Dictionary, January 5, 2017, https://www.urbandiction-ary.com/define.php?term=Irish%2Bdivorce.

3. "How Seniors and Millennials Date," MedicareAdvantage.com, February 2023, https://www.medicareadvantage.com/senior-dating-survey.

Chapter 4

1. National Endowment for Financial Education®, "2 in 5 Americans Admit to Financial Infidelity against Their Partner," National Endowment for Financial Education®, November 18, 2021, https://www.nefe.org/news/2021/11/2-in-5-americans-admit-to-financial-infidelity-against-their-partner.aspx.

2. Mirza, Aisha. "Beyonce in GQ: All the Ladies! Put Your Hands up for Feminism." The Independent, January 18, 2013. https://www.independent.co.uk/voices/comment/beyonce-in-gq-all-the-ladies-put-your-hands-up-for-feminism-8456294.html.

Notes ~ 215

Chapter 5

1. Congress.gov, "H.R.8163—93rd Congress (1973–1974): Equal Credit Opportunity Act," May 29, 1973, https://www.congress.gov/bill/93rd-congress/house-bill/8163.

2. Lyle Denniston, "Opinion Analysis: Marriage Now Open to Same-Sex Couples," SCOTUSblog, June 26, 2015, https://www.scotusblog.com/2015/06/opinion-analysis-marriage-now-open-to-same-sex-couples/.

Chapter 6

1. "Emily Post," Encyclopedia Britannica, September 21, 2023, https://www.britannica.com/biography/Emily-Post.

2. Sarah Jane Glynn, "Breadwinning Mothers Are Critical to Families' Economic Security," Center for American Progress, September 8, 2022, https://www.americanprogress.org/issues/women/news/2021/03/29/497658/breadwinning-mothers-critical-familys-economic-security/.

3. Marta Murray-Close and Misty L. Heggeness, "Manning Up and Womaning Down: How Husbands and Wives Report Their Earnings When She Earns More," United States Census Bureau, June 6, 2018, https://www.census.gov/content/dam/Census/library/working-papers/2018/demo/SEHSD-WP2018-20.pdf.

4. "Average Wage Indexing (AWI) Series," Social Security Administration, accessed December 31, 2023, https://www.ssa.gov/OACT/COLA/awiseries.html.

5. Kevin Miller and Deborah J. Vagins, "The Simple Truth about the Gender Pay Gap," AAUW, 2018, https://www.aauw.org/resources/research/simple-truth/.

6. Rakesh Kochhar, "The Enduring Grip of the Gender Pay Gap," Pew Research Center, March 1, 2023, https://www.pewresearch.org/social-trends/2023/03/01/the-enduring-grip-of-the-gender-pay-gap/.

7. Emma Hinchliffe, "Women Run More than 10% of Fortune 500 Companies for the First Time," *Fortune*, January 12, 2023, https://fortune.com/2023/01/12/fortune-500-companies-ceos-women-10-percent/.

8. Victoria Masterson, "Here's What Women's Entrepreneurship Looks Like around the World," World Economic Forum, June 20, 2022, https://www.weforum.org/agenda/2022/07/women-entrepreneurs-gusto-gender/.

9. Emma Hinchliffe, "Funding for Female Founders Stalled at 2.2% of VC Dollars in 2018," *Fortune*, January 28, 2019, https://fortune.com/2019/01/28/funding-female-founders-2018/.

10. Gené Teare, "Q1 2019 Diversity Report: Female Founders Own 17 Percent of Venture Dollars," *Crunchbase News*, April 29, 2019, https://news.crunchbase.com/business/q1-2019-diversity-report-female-founders-own-17-percent-of-venture-dollars/.

11. US Bureau of Labor Statistics, "Median Usual Weekly Earnings of Full-Time Wage and Salary Workers by Age, Race, Hispanic or Latino Ethnicity, and Sex,

216 ∽ Notes

Fourth Quarter 2023 Averages, Not Seasonally Adjusted," Washington, DC: US Bureau of Labor Statistics, January 18, 2024.

12. Jo Craven McGinty, "The Divorce Rate Is at a 40-Year Low, Unless You're 55 or Older," *Wall Street Journal*, June 21, 2019, https://www.wsj.com/articles/the-divorce-rate-is-at-a-40-year-low-unless-youre-55-or-older-11561116601.

13. "9 Big Lies about Longevity," CBS News, December 18, 2011, https://www.cbsnews.com/pictures/9-big-lies-about-longevity/.

14. Howard S. Friedman and Leslie R. Martin, *The Longevity Project: Surprising Discoveries for Health and Long Life from the Landmark Eight-Decade Study* (New York: Plume, 2012).

15. Betsey Stevenson and Justin Wolfers, "Bargaining in the Shadow of the Law: Divorce Laws and Family Distress," *The Quarterly Journal of Economics* 121, no. 1 (February 1, 2006): 267–88, https://doi.org/https://doi.org/10.1093/qje/121.1.267.

16. Joyner-Kersee, Jackie. "Letter to My Younger Self: By Jackie Joyner-Kersee." The Players' Tribune, July 17, 2015. https://www.theplayerstribune.com/articles/jackie-joyner-kersee-letter-to-my-younger-self.

17. "Gender: Beyond the Binary," Bigeye, February 17, 2021, https://lp.bigeyeagency.com/hubfs/Gender_BeyondtheBinary.pdf.

18. "Own Your Worth: How Women Can Break the Cycle of Abdication and Take Control of Their Wealth," UBS, 2018, https://www.ubs.com/content/dam/WealthManagementAmericas/documents/2018-37666-UBS-Own-Your-Worth-report-R32.pdf.

19. Karen DeMasters, "Women Hold Majority of Personal Wealth, but Still Minorities in Advisory Field," *Financial Advisor*, March 25, 2020, https://www.fa-mag.com/news/women-need-to-lead-in-finances--consultant-says-54850.html.

Chapter 7

1. P. Hemez, "Distributions of Age at First Marriage, 1960–2018," Family Profiles, FP-20-09 (Bowling Green, OH: National Center for Family & Marriage Research, 2020), https://doi.org/10.25035/ncfmr/fp-20-09.

2. Catey Hill, "This Common Behavior Is the No. 1 Predictor of Whether You'll Get Divorced," MarketWatch, January 10, 2018, https://www.marketwatch.com/story/this-common-behavior-is-the-no-1-predictor-of-whether-youll-get-divorced-2018-01-10.

3. "Money Ruining Marriages in America: A Ramsey Solutions Study," Ramsey Solutions, February 6, 2018, https://www.ramseysolutions.com/company/newsroom/releases/money-ruining-marriages-in-america.

4. Juliana Menasce Horowitz, "Marriage and Cohabitation in the U.S.," Pew Research Center's Social & Demographic Trends Project, November 6, 2019, https://www.pewresearch.org/social-trends/2019/11/06/marriage-and-cohabitation-in-the-u-s/.

5. Susan Pease Gadoua, "It's Okay to Stay Together for the Kids: The Co-parent Solution," *Psychology Today*, January 17, 2022, https://www.psychologytoday.com/us/blog/contemplating-divorce/202201/its-okay-stay-together-the-kids-the-co-parent-solution.

Notes ～ 217

Chapter 8

1. Joyner-Kersee, Jackie. "Letter to My Younger Self: By Jackie Joyner-Kersee." The Players' Tribune, July 17, 2015. https://www.theplayerstribune.com/articles/jackie-joyner-kersee-letter-to-my-younger-self.

2. "A Quote by Mark Twain." Goodreads. Accessed September 24, 2024. https://www.goodreads.com/quotes/219455-the-secret-of-getting-ahead-is-getting-started-the-secret.

3. Unknown. AZQuotes.com, Wind and Fly LTD, 2024. https://www.azquotes.com/quote/1457383, accessed September 24, 2024.

Chapter 9

1. Carolyn Gregoire, "How Money Changes the Way You Think and Feel," *Greater Good Magazine*, February 8, 2018, https://greatergood.berkeley.edu/article/item/how_money_changes_the_way_you_think_and_feel.2.   Rand, Ayn. Atlas shrugged. New York, NY: Signet Book, 1992.

Chapter 10

1. Bouchard, Dr. Norma. "Colin Powell." Colin Powell| Chapman Collection of Historical Figures Map | Chapman University, December 22, 2022. https://www.chapman.edu/about/our-home/busts-collection/powell.aspx.

2. Bouchard, Dr. Norma. "Colin Powell." Colin Powell| Chapman Collection of Historical Figures Map | Chapman University, December 22, 2022. https://www.chapman.edu/about/our-home/busts-collection/powell.aspx.

3. Emma Rubin, "Adults Report Feeling More Isolated in 2021," *Consumer Affairs*, January 19, 2023, https://www.consumeraffairs.com/health/elderly-loneliness-statistics.html.

4. LendingClub Corporation, "At 73%, Millennials Are the Most Likely Generation to Live Paycheck to Paycheck," PR Newswire, April 28, 2023, https://www.prnewswire.com/news-releases/at-73-millennials-are-the-most-likely-generation-to-live-paycheck-to-paycheck-301810428.html.

Chapter 11

1. Roger Babson. AZQuotes.com, Wind and Fly LTD, 2024. https://www.azquotes.com/quote/604455, accessed September 02, 2024.

Chapter 12

1. Benjamin Franklin Quotes. BrainyQuote.com, BrainyMedia Inc, 2024. https://www.brainyquote.com/quotes/benjamin_franklin_135836, accessed September 2, 2024.

218 ～ Notes

2. "A Penny Saved: Thrift Bears Name of a Founding Father." OCC.gov, March 14, 2019. https://www.occ.treas.gov/about/who-we-are/history/1863-1865/1863-1865-a-penny-saved.html.

Chapter 13

1. "24 Encouraging Quotes for a Rough Day." NursingHomeVolunteer.com, June 9, 2021. https://nursinghomevolunteer.com/24-encouraging-quotes-for-a-rough-day/.

Chapter 14

1. Eleanor Roosevelt Quotes. BrainyQuote.com, BrainyMedia Inc, 2024. https://www.brainyquote.com/quotes/eleanor_roosevelt_379411, accessed September 2, 2024.

Chapter 15

1. Alex Miller, "Credit Score Facts & Statistics: Average Credit Score, Range & More," UpgradedPoints.com, October 4, 2023, https://upgradedpoints.com/credit-cards/credit-score-facts-statistics/.

2. Lincoln, Abraham. Letter to Secretary of War Edward Stanton, 1864.

3. Federal Trade Commission, "In FTC Study, Five Percent of Consumers Had Errors on Their Credit Reports That Could Result in Less Favorable Terms for Loans," Federal Trade Commission, February 11, 2013, https://www.ftc.gov/news-events/news/press-releases/2013/02/ftc-study-five-percent-consumers-had-errors-their-credit-reports-could-result-less-favorable-terms.

4. Earhart, Amelia. Letter to June Pierson. "Advice from the Cockpit." Detroit, MI, 1933.

5. Ace Bagtas, "What Is a Good Debt-to-Income Ratio to Have in 2024?," Review42, February 13, 2024, https://review42.com/resources/what-is-a-good-debt-to-income-ratio/.

6. Washington, George. Letter to James Welch, April 7, 1799.

Chapter 17

1. The *curious case of Benjamin Button*. Film. Hollywood, CA: Paramount, 2008.

2. Jung, Carl. "A Quote by C.G. Jung." Goodreads. Accessed September 5, 2024. https://www.goodreads.com/quotes/50795-i-am-not-what-happened-to-me-i-am-what.

3. Benjamin Franklin Quotes. BrainyQuote.com, BrainyMedia Inc, 2024. https://www.brainyquote.com/quotes/benjamin_franklin_125394, accessed September 2, 2024.

Notes ～ 219

Chapter 18

1. Jim Puzzanghera, "36% of Adults Lack Retirement Savings, Including Many 65 or Older," *Los Angeles Times*, August 18, 2014, http://www.latimes.com/business/la-fi -retirement-savings-bankrate-20140818-story.html.

2. "Retirement & Survivors Benefits: Life Expectancy Calculator," Social Security Administration, accessed February 17, 2024, https://www.ssa.gov/oact/population/ longevity.html.

3. "About Benjamin Franklin." About Benjamin Franklin | Benjamin Franklin College. Accessed September 2, 2024. https://benjaminfranklin.yalecollege.yale.edu/ about-us/about-benjamin-franklin.

Chapter 19

1. Townsend, Tomaio & Newmark, "Do You Have to File for Divorce in the Same State as the Marriage?" Townsend, Tomaio & Newmark, March 30, 2022, https://www.bergencountyfamilylawyers.com/blog/do-you-have-to-file-for-divorce-in -the-same-state-as-the-marriage.

2. Dads Divorce, "The 12 Weirdest Marriage & Divorce Laws in the World," Dads Divorce, February 24, 2016, https://dadsdivorce.com/articles/the-12-weirdest -marriage-divorce-laws-in-the-world/.

Chapter 20

1. Assistant Secretary for Public Affairs (ASPA), "About the Affordable Care Act," US Department of Health and Human Services, March 17, 2022, https://www .hhs.gov/healthcare/about-the-aca/index.html.

2. US Department of Labor, "Continuation of Health Coverage (COBRA)," US Department of Labor, accessed February 11, 2024, https://www.dol.gov/general/topic /health-plans/cobra.

3. Terry Turner, "Essential Facts about Medicare Seniors Should Know in 2023," Retire Guide, October 24, 2023, https://www.retireguide.com/guides/facts-about -medicare/.

4. medicareresources.org, "A Brief History of Medicare in America," medicareresources.org, August 24, 2023, https://www.medicareresources.org/basic-medicare -information/brief-history-of-medicare/.

5. "Ranking the Least Expensive Luxury Cars to Maintain," CarEdge, accessed February 11, 2024, https://caredge.com/ranks/maintenance/luxury/10-year/best #models.

6. Andrew Lisa, "How Much Does It Cost to Maintain a Luxury Car," GOBankingRates, September 9, 2022, https://www.gobankingrates.com/saving-money/car/ how-much-does-it-cost-to-maintain-a-luxury-car/.

Chapter 21

1. Sager, Mike. "Carrie Fisher Interview - Princess Leia Actress - Quotes on Rehab and Drugs." *Esquire,* January 29, 2007. https://www.esquire.com/entertainment/interviews/a2053/esq0102-jan-fisher/.

2. King, Martin Luther. "Keep Moving from This Mountain." *Founder's Day Address at Spelman College.* Speech presented at the Founder's Day Address at Spelman College, April 10, 1960.

Chapter 22

1. Joe Dillon, "Equitable Distribution: Who Gets What in a Divorce?," Equitable Mediation Services, accessed August 30, 2023, https://www.equitablemediation.com/divorce-mediation/equitable-distribution.

2. Joe Dillon, "Community Property California: Not Always 50-50 in Divorce," Equitable Mediation Services, accessed August 30, 2023, https://www.equitablemediation.com/blog/california-community-property-divorce.

3. Jeffrey Johnson, "What Is Equitable Distribution?," Free Advice, July 18, 2023, https://www.freeadvice.com/legal/what-is-equitable-distribution/.

4. Jeffrey Johnson, "What Is Community Property?," Free Advice, July 19, 2023, https://www.freeadvice.com/legal/what-is-community-property/.

5. Monk Kidd, Sue. *The secret life of bees.* New York, NY: Penguin Publishing Group, 2003.

6. Jade Chounlamountry, Esq., "Inheritance and Divorce," FindLaw, July 13, 2023, https://family.findlaw.com/divorce/inheritance-and-divorce.html.

7. Jason Crowley, CFA, CFP, CDFA, "A Guide to Social Security Benefits after Divorce," Survive Divorce, September 6, 2021, https://www.survivedivorce.com/social-security.

8. Mark P. Cussen, "Divorce and Social Security Rules: What to Know," Investopedia, December 10, 2023, https://www.investopedia.com/articles/financial-advisor/112216/divorce-and-new-social-security-rules-what-know.asp.

9. Brette Sember, J.D., "Divorce and Life Insurance: Understanding Your Rights," WomansDivorce.com, accessed February 11, 2024, https://www.womansdivorce.com/divorce-and-life-insurance.html.

10. LongTermCare.gov, "How Much Care Will You Need?," ACL Administration for Community Living, February 18, 2018, https://acl.gov/ltc/basic-needs/how-much-care-will-you-need.

11. "Protecting Your Finances during a Divorce," Wiser Women, February 16, 2023, https://wiserwomen.org/resources/divorce-fact-sheets/protecting-your-finances-during-a-divorce/.

12. "In a Divorce, Who Gets the 401k?," 401khelpcenter.com, accessed August 30, 2023, http://www.401khelpcenter.com/401k_education/divorce_and_your_401k.html.

Notes ～ 221

13. Eric Reed, "Is Alimony Taxable?," SmartAsset, November 8, 2022, https://smartasset.com/taxes/is-alimony-taxable.

14. US Department of Labor, "Continuation of Health Coverage (COBRA)," DOL.gov, accessed August 30, 2023, https://www.dol.gov/general/topic/health-plans/cobra.

15. Digital Communications Division (DCD), "What Is the Affordable Care Act?," HHS.gov, April 20, 2023, https://www.hhs.gov/answers/health-insurance-reform/what-is-the-affordable-care-act/index.html.

16. Loftus, Geoff. "If You're Going through Hell, Keep Going - Winston Churchill." Forbes, May 9, 2024. https://www.forbes.com/sites/geoffloftus/2012/05/09/if-youre-going-through-hell-keep-going-winston-churchill/.

Chapter 23

1. Grossman, Samantha. "Joan Rivers Dead: Cameo with Louis CK on Louie." Time, September 4, 2014. https://time.com/3270472/joan-rivers-dead-louie/.

2. Hicks, Saidah. "Do One Thing Every Day That Scares You! - UCF Business Incubation Program - University of Central Florida." UCF Business Incubation Program, June 21, 2023. https://incubator.ucf.edu/do-one-thing-every-day-that-scares-you/.

Chapter 24

1. Annie Nova, "Growing Debt among Older Americans Threatens Their Retirement," CNBC, April 5, 2018, https://www.cnbc.com/2018/04/04/growing-debt-among-older-americans-threatens-retirement.html.

2. Amelia Josephson, "What Is the Average American's Debt by Age Group?," SmartAsset, August 10, 2023, https://smartasset.com/credit-cards/the-average-debt-by-age.

3. Alessandra Malito, "Seniors Have More Household Debt Now than They Did during the Financial Crisis," MarketWatch, August 13, 2019, https://www.market-watch.com/story/seniors-have-more-household-debt-now-than-they-did-during-the-financial-crisis-2019-08-13.

4. National Council on Aging, "Get the Facts on Economic Security for Seniors," National Council on Aging, June 8, 2023, https://www.ncoa.org/article/get-the-facts-on-economic-security-for-seniors.

5. UnitedHealth Group, "The 2015 United States of Aging Survey National Findings," UnitedHealth Group, 2015, https://www.unitedhealthgroup.com/content/dam/UHG/PDF/2015/USofAging-2015-Fact-Sheet.pdf.

6. National Council on Aging, "Get the Facts on Economic Security for Seniors."

7. Stephen Kates, CFP®, "50+ Essential Retirement Statistics for 2024: Demographics," Annuity.org, January 10, 2024, https://www.annuity.org/retirement/retirement-statistics/.

222 ～ Notes

8. S. 1098 (117th), GovTrack § (2022), https://www.govtrack.us/congress/bills/117/s1098/text.

9. Allison Martin, "Medical Debt Consolidation," Bankrate, October 30, 2023, https://www.bankrate.com/personal-finance/debt/medical-debt-consolidation/.

10. National Council on Aging, "Benefits for Older Adults," National Council on Aging, accessed August 30, 2023, https://www.ncoa.org/economic-security/benefits/.

11. National Council on Aging, "Supplemental Nutrition Assistance Program (SNAP)," Food and Nutrition Service, US Department of Agriculture, February 5, 2024, https://www.fns.usda.gov/snap/supplemental-nutrition-assistance-program.

12. US Department of Agriculture, "Seniors Farmers Market Nutrition Program," Food and Nutrition Service, US Department of Agriculture, February 5, 2024, https://www.fns.usda.gov/sfmnp/senior-farmers-market-nutrition-program.

13. BeMedWise, "Prescription Assistance Programs," BeMedWise.org, accessed February 11, 2024, https://bemedwise.org/documents/paps.pdf.

14. Internal Revenue Service, "2023 Publication 524," Internal Revenue Service, December 19, 2023, https://www.irs.gov/pub/irs-pdf/p524.pdf.

15. Internal Revenue Service, "2023 Publication 502," Internal Revenue Service, December 21, 2023, https://www.irs.gov/pub/irs-pdf/p502.pdf.

16. US Department of Housing and Urban Development, "Rental Assistance," HUD.gov/US Department of Housing and Urban Development (HUD), December 8, 2021, https://www.hud.gov/topics/rental_assistance.

17. Anna Helhoski and Eliza Haverstock, "How Many Americans Have Student Loan Debt?," NerdWallet, January 19, 2023, https://www.nerdwallet.com/article/loans/student-loans/how-many-americans-have-student-loan-debt.

18. David Brancaccio, Chris Farrell, and Alex Schroeder, "Older People Also Face Student Loan Debt Burden with Payments Looming," Marketplace, September 14, 2023, https://www.marketplace.org/2023/09/14/older-people-also-face-student-loan-debt-burden-with-payments-looming/.

19. Business Wire, "Fidelity's® Annual Snapshot of America's Student Debt: Boomers Burdened with the Most Student Debt," Business Wire, October 27, 2020, https://www.businesswire.com/news/home/20201027005163/en/.

20. Andy Markowitz and Tracy Thompson, "Can Social Security Be Garnished?," AARP, November 15, 2023, https://www.aarp.org/retirement/social-security/questions-answers/social-security-garnished.html.

21. Wikipedia, "Equal Credit Opportunity Act," Wikipedia, January 21, 2024, https://en.wikipedia.org/wiki/Equal_Credit_Opportunity_Act.

Chapter 25

1. Urban Institute, "Housing Finance at a Glance: A Monthly Chartbook," Urban Institute, June 2022, https://www.urban.org/sites/default/files/2022-08/Housing_Finance_At_A_Glance_Monthly_Chartbook_August%202022.pdf.

Chapter 26

1. John Waggoner, "What to Know about Reverse Mortgages," *AARP*, November 16, 2022, https://www.aarp.org/money/credit-loans-debt/info-2019/reverse-mortgage-loan-advice.html.

Chapter 27

1. UBS, "UBS Investor Watch: Own Your Worth," UBS, 2019, https://www.ubs.com/it/en/wealth-management/our-approach/investor-watch/2019/own-your-worth.html.

2. Cassie Werber, "Wealthy Millennial Women Are More Likely to Defer to Their Husbands on Investing," Quartz, March 15, 2019, https://qz.com/work/1573457/wealthy-millennial-women-are-deferring-to-their-husbands-on-financial-planning/.

3. Joel Anderson, "Many Americans Are Stressed about Money—And This Is the No. 1 Reason Why," Yahoo! Finance, March 15, 2019, https://finance.yahoo.com/news/americans-choose-money-over-love-100000571.html.

4. American Psychological Association, "Stress in America 2022: Concerned for the Future, Beset by Inflation," American Psychological Association, October 2022, https://www.apa.org/news/press/releases/stress/2022/concerned-future-inflation.

5. N. Guan, A. Guariglia, P. Moore, F. Xu, and H. Al-Janabi, "Financial Stress and Depression in Adults: A Systematic Review," PLoS One, February 22, 2022, doi:10.1371/journal.pone.0264041.

6. Laura J. Herpolsheimer, "Financial Stress: How Older Adults' Health Is Affected," SOAR, May 1, 2015, https://soar.wichita.edu/handle/10057/11596.

7. Ogden Nash Quotes. BrainyQuote.com, BrainyMedia Inc, 2024. https://www.brainyquote.com/quotes/ogden_nash_386629, accessed September 2, 2024.

8. Alina Comoreanu, "Credit Card Debt Statistics for 2024," WalletHub, January 8, 2024, https://wallethub.com/edu/cc/credit-card-debt-study/24400.

9. Meghan Alard, "How Much Credit Card Debt Is Too Much?," Consolidated Credit, October 5, 2023, https://www.consolidatedcredit.org/credit-card-debt/how-much-debt-is-too-much/.

10. Rachel Bogardus Drew, "New Census Data Show Growing Share of Americans Struggling to Pay Rent," Enterprise Community Partners, September 15, 2022, https://www.enterprisecommunity.org/blog/new-census-data-show-growing-share-americans-struggling-pay-rent.

11. Bureau of Labor Statistics, "Annual Expenditures by Occupation," bls.gov, 2020, https://www.bls.gov/cex/tables/calendar-year/mean-item-share-average-standard-error/reference-person-occupation-2020.pdf.

12. United States Census Bureau, "Week 50 Household Pulse Survey: October 5–October 17," Census.gov, October 26, 2022, https://www.census.gov/data/tables/2022/demo/hhp/hhp50.html.

224 ~ Notes

Chapter 28

1. Neale Godfrey, "Never Own Anything Bigger Than Your Hat," *Forbes*, October 26, 2014, https://www.forbes.com/sites/nealegodfrey/2014/10/26/never-own-anything-bigger-than-your-hat/.

Chapter 29

1. UBS, "Own Your Worth: How Women Can Break the Cycle of Abdication and Take Control of Their Wealth," UBS, 2018, https://www.ubs.com/content/dam/WealthManagementAmericas/documents/2018-37666-UBS-Own-Your-Worth-report-R32.pdf.

2. Mandela, Nelson. "Acceptance and Nobel Lecture." Nobel Peace Prize 1993. Speech presented at the Nobel Lecture, December 10, 1993.

3. Steinem, Gloria. "Keynote Address." *Stanford University's "Herstory" Event.* Speech, 1998.

4. Lincoln, Abraham. "A Quote by Abraham Lincoln." Goodreads. Accessed September 8, 2024. https://www.goodreads.com/quotes/328848-the-best-way-to-predict-your-future-is-to-create.

Chapter 31

1. Fidelity Investments, "2021 Women and Investing Study," Fidelity Investments, 2021, https://www.fidelity.com/bin-public/060_www_fidelity_com/documents/about-fidelity/FidelityInvestmentsWomen&InvestingStudy2021.pdf.

2. Bakke, David. "The Top 25 Investing Quotes of All Time." Investopedia, September 15, 2023. https://www.investopedia.com/financial-edge/0511/the-top-17-investing-quotes-of-all-time.aspx.

3. Downie, Ryan. "This Is the 8th Wonder of the World, According to Albert Einstein. and Utilizing It Correctly Can Help Make Saving for Retirement an Absolute Breeze." Nasdaq, March 16, 2024. https://www.nasdaq.com/articles/this-is-the-8th-wonder-of-the-world-according-to-albert-einstein.-and-utilizing-it.

Chapter 32

1. Kaitlyn Koterbski, "30% of Women Say They Don't Know Enough to Start Investing. Here's How They Can Get Started," *Fortune*, July 14, 2022, https://fortune.com/2022/07/14/how-women-can-start-investing-for-retirement/.

2. "Snapshot of Older Consumers and Student Loan Debt," Consumer Financial Protection Bureau, January 2017, https://files.consumerfinance.gov/f/documents/201701_cfpb_OA-Student-Loan-Snapshot.pdf.

3. Zhe Li, "Household Debt among Older Americans, 1989–2016," Congressional Research Service, September 11, 2019, https://crsreports.congress.gov/.

Notes ～ 225

4. Cäzilia Loibl, Stephanie Moulton, Donald Haurin, and Chrisse Edmunds, "The Role of Consumer and Mortgage Debt for Financial Stress," *Aging & Mental Health* 26, no.1 (2022): 116–29, DOI: 10.1080/13607863.2020.1843000.

Chapter 33

1. J. Cruz, "Marriage: More than a Century of Change (FP-13-13)," National Center for Family & Marriage Research, 2013, retrieved from http://ncfmr.bgsu.edu/ pdf/ family_profiles/ file131529.pdf.

2. Sam M. Huisache, "Is Marriage Popularity Declining? Insights from a National Survey of Americans (2023 Data)," Clever Real Estate, June 27, 2023, https:// listwithclever.com/research/marriage-decline-survey-2023/.

3. L. Reynolds, "The U.S. Remarriage Rate, 2019: Trends and Geographic Variation by Gender," Family Profiles, FP-21-18, Bowling Green, OH: National Center for Family & Marriage Research, 2021, https://doi.org/10.25035/ncfmr/fp -21-18.

4. I.R.C. § 6013(d)(3).

5. Kaylene, "14 Celebrities and Their Insane Prenups," TheTalko, April 26, 2016, https://www.thetalko.com/15-celebrities-and-their-insane-prenups/.

6. Ryan Davis, "The Most Scandalous Rumored Details of Celebrity Prenups," Ranker, September 23, 2021, https://www.ranker.com/list/celebrity-prenup-details/ rydavis.

7. Rachel Dinning, "Queen Elizabeth II and Prince Philip: 8 Milestones in Their Marriage," HistoryExtra, November 20, 2020, https://www.historyextra .com/period/20th-century/queen-elizabeth-prince-philip-milestones-marriage -relationship/.

8. James Hockaday, "Why Prince Philip Changed His Surname before He Married the Queen," Metro, April 9, 2021, https://metro.co.uk/2021/04/09/why-prince-philip -did-prince-philip-change-his-surname-14385063/.

9. Jason Brow, "Did Prince Harry & Meghan Markle Sign $500 Mil Prenup? The Queen Reportedly Demanded It," Hollywood Life, December 9, 2022, https:// hollywoodlife.com/2018/06/13/prince-harry-meghan-markle-prenup-wedding-queen -elizabeth/.

Chapter 34

1. Victor Hugo Quotes. BrainyQuote.com, BrainyMedia Inc, 2024. https://www. brainyquote.com/quotes/victor_hugo_132467, accessed September 2, 2024.

2. Nonprofits Source, "2018 Online Giving Statistics, Trends & Data: The Ultimate List of Giving Stats," Nonprofits Source, 2023, https://nonprofitssource.com/ online-giving-statistics/.

3. Frank, Anne. *The diary of Anne Frank.* West Haven, CT: Pendulum Press, 1979.

226 ～ Notes

4. Nonprofits Source, "2018 Online Giving Statistics, Trends & Data, Nonprofits Source.

5. Julia Kagan, "Charitable Remainder Trust: Definition, How It Works, and Types," Investopedia, January 5, 2023, https://www.investopedia.com/terms/c/charita bleremaindertrust.asp.

6. Internal Revenue Service, "Seniors Can Reduce Their Tax Burden by Donating to Charity through Their IRA," Internal Revenue Service, November 8, 2022, https://www.irs.gov/newsroom/seniors-can-reduce-their-tax-burden-by-donating-to -charity-through-their-ira.

7 Winston Churchill Quotes. BrainyQuote.com, BrainyMedia Inc, 2024. https:// www.brainyquote.com/quotes/winston_churchill_131192, accessed September 2, 2024.

Chapter 35

1. Roth, Allan. "Compound Interest - the Most Powerful Force in the Universe?" CBS News, June 7, 2011. https://www.cbsnews.com/news/ compound-interest-the-most-powerful-force-in-the-universe/.

2. John J. Havens, and Paul G. Schervish, "Millionaires and the Millennium," Chestnut Hill, MA: Social Welfare Research Institute, Boston College, October 19, 1999, http://hdl.handle.net/2345/bc-ir:104110.

3. Neale S. Godfrey, *Money Doesn't Grow on Trees: A Parent's Guide to Raising Financially Responsible Children* (New York: Simon & Schuster, 2006).

Chapter 36

1. Lane Gillespie, "Survey: 68% of Parents Have Made a Financial Sacrifice to Help Their Adult Children with Money," Bankrate, April 10, 2023, https://www .bankrate.com/personal-finance/financial-independence-survey/.

2. Wikipedia, "Boomerang Generation," Wikipedia, January 31, 2024, https://en .wikipedia.org/wiki/Boomerang_Generation.

3. Thrivent, "How to Build a Healthy Financial Relationship with Your Boomerang Child," Thrivent, December 6, 2023, https://www.thrivent.com/insights/ financial-planning/build-a-healthy-financial-relationship-with-your-boomerang -child.

4. Gillespie, "Survey: 68% of Parents Have Made a Financial Sacrifice to Help Their Adult Children with Money."

5. Coolidge, Calvin, Amity Shlaes, and Matthew Denhart. The autobiography of Calvin Coolidge authorized, expanded, and annotated edition. New York, NY: Regnery Publishing, 2021.

Chapter 37

1. Richard Fry, "A Majority of Young Adults in the U.S. Live with Their Parents for the First Time since the Great Depression," Pew Research Center, September 4, 2020, https://www.pewresearch.org/fact-tank/2020/09/04/a-majority-of-young-adults -in-the-u-s-live-with-their-parents-for-the-first-time-since-the-great-depression/.

2. Jenn Hatfield, "Young Adults in the U.S. Are Less Likely Than Those in Most of Europe to Live in Their Parents' Home," Pew Research Center, May 3, 2023, https://www.pewresearch.org/short-reads/2023/05/03/in-the-u-s-and-abroad-more -young-adults-are-living-with-their-parents/.

3. Richard Fry, "Young Adults in U.S. Are Much More Likely than 50 Years Ago to Be Living in a Multigenerational Household," Pew Research Center, July 20, 2022, https://www.pewresearch.org/short-reads/2022/07/20/young-adults-in-u-s-are -much-more-likely-than-50-years-ago-to-be-living-in-a-multigenerational-house-hold/.4. Adams, Abigail. If you want your children to turn out well,... Accessed September 2, 2024. https://www.quotery.com/quotes/want-children-turn-well-spend.

Bibliography

"2 in 5 Americans Admit to Financial Infidelity against Their Partner." National Endowment for Financial Education®, November 18, 2021. https://www.nefe.org/news/2021/11/2-in-5-americans-admit-to-financial-infidelity-against-their-partner.aspx.

"9 Big Lies about Longevity." CBS News, December 18, 2011. https://www.cbsnews.com/pictures/9-big-lies-about-longevity/.

"The 12 Weirdest Marriage & Divorce Laws in the World." Dads Divorce, February 24, 2016. https://dadsdivorce.com/articles/the-12-weirdest-marriage-divorce-laws-in-the-world/.

"26 Surprising Statistics on Cheating Spouses." HRF, January 6, 2015. https://healthresearchfunding.org/26-surprising-statistics-cheating-spouses/.

"36% of Adults Lack Retirement Savings, Including Many 65 or Older." Los Angeles Times, August 18, 2014. http://www.latimes.com/business/la-fi-retirement-savings-bankrate-20140818-story.html.

"The 2015 United States of Aging Survey National Findings." UnitedHealth Group, 2015. https://www.unitedhealthgroup.com/content/dam/UHG/PDF/2015/USofAging-2015-Fact-Sheet.pdf.

"2018 Online Giving Statistics, Trends & Data: The Ultimate List of Giving Stats." Nonprofits Source, 2023. https://nonprofitssource.com/online-giving-statistics/.

"2021 Women and Investing Study." Fidelity, 2021. https://www.fidelity.com/bin-public/060_www_fidelity_com/documents/about-fidelity/FidelityInvestmentsWomen&InvestingStudy2021.pdf.

"2023 Publication 524." Internal Revenue Service, December 19, 2023. https://www.irs.gov/pub/irs-pdf/p524.pdf.

230 ⌒ Bibliography

"2023 Publication 502." Internal Revenue Service, December 21, 2023. https://www.irs.gov/pub/irs-pdf/p502.pdf.

Alard, Meghan. "How Much Credit Card Debt Is Too Much?" Consolidated Credit, October 5, 2023. https://www.consolidatedcredit.org/credit-card-debt/how-much-debt-is-too-much/.

Anderson, Joel. "Many Americans Are Stressed about Money - and This Is the No. 1 Reason Why." Yahoo! Finance, March 15, 2019. https://finance.yahoo.com/news/americans-choose-money-over-love-100000571.html.

Assistant Secretary for Public Affairs (ASPA). "About the Affordable Care Act." U.S. Department of Health and Human Services, March 17, 2022. https://www.hhs.gov/healthcare/about-the-aca/index.html.

"Average Wage Indexing (AWI) Series." Social Security Administration. Accessed December 31, 2023. https://www.ssa.gov/OACT/COLA/awiseries.html.

Bagtas, Ace. "What Is a Good Debt-to-Income Ratio to Have in 2024?" Review42, February 13, 2024. https://review42.com/resources/what-is-a-good-debt-to-income-ratio/.

"Bank of America Study Finds 94% of Women Believe They'll Be Personally Responsible for Their Finances at Some Point in Their Lives." PR Newswire, June 22, 2022. Bank of America Corporation. https://www.prnewswire.com/news-releases/bank-of-america-study-finds-94-of-women-believe-theyll-be-personally-responsible-for-their-finances-at-some-point-in-their-lives-301573161.html.

"Benefits for Older Adults." The National Council on Aging. Accessed August 30, 2023. https://www.ncoa.org/economic-security/benefits/.

Bieber, Christy. "Revealing Divorce Statistics in 2024." *Forbes*, January 8, 2024. https://www.forbes.com/advisor/legal/divorce/divorce-statistics/.

Bill, GovTrack § (2022). https://www.govtrack.us/congress/bills/117/s1098/text.

Bluedorn, John C, Francesca Caselli, Niels-Jakob H Hansen, Ippei Shibata, and Marina Mendes Tavares. "Gender and Employment in the COVID-19 Recession: Evidence on 'She-Cessions.'" International Monetary Fund, March 31, 2021. https://www.imf.org/en/Publications/WP/Issues/2021/03/31/Gender-and-Employment-in-the-COVID-19-Recession-Evidence-on-She-cessions-50316.

Bogardus Drew, Rachel. "New Census Data Show Growing Share of Americans Struggling to Pay Rent." Enterprise Community Partners, September 15, 2022. https://www.enterprisecommunity.org/blog/new-census-data-show-growing-share-americans-struggling-pay-rent.

"Boomerang Generation." Wikipedia, January 31, 2024. https://en.wikipedia.org/wiki/Boomerang_Generation.

Brancaccio, David, Chris Farrell, and Alex Schroeder. "Older People Also Face Student Loan Debt Burden with Payments Looming." Marketplace, September 14, 2023. https://www.marketplace.org/2023/09/14/older-people-also-face-student-loan-debt-burden-with-payments-looming/.

Bibliography 231

"A Brief History of Medicare in America." medicareresources.org, August 24, 2023. https://www.medicareresources.org/basic-medicare-information/brief-history-of-medicare/.

Brow, Jason. "Did Prince Harry & Meghan Markle Sign $500 Mil Prenup? The Queen Reportedly Demanded It." Hollywood Life, December 9, 2022. https://hollywoodlife.com/2018/06/13/prince-harry-meghan-markle-prenup-wedding-queen-elizabeth/.

Brown, Susan L., and I-Fen Lin. "Gray Divorce: A Growing Risk Regardless of Class or Education." Council on Contemporary Families, 2024. https://sites.utexas.edu/contemporaryfamilies/2014/10/08/growing-risk-brief-report/.

Bureau of Labor Statistics, "Annual Expenditures by Occupation." https://www.bls.gov/cex/tables/calendar-year/mean-item-share-average-standard-error/reference-person-occupation-2020.pdf.

Cäzilia Loibl, Stephanie Moulton, Donald Haurin & Chrisse Edmunds (2022) The role of consumer and mortgage debt for financial stress, Aging & Mental Health, 26:1, 116-129, DOI: 10.1080/13607863.2020.1843000.

Chounlamountry, Esq., Jade. "Inheritance and Divorce." FindLaw, July 13, 2023. https://family.findlaw.com/divorce/inheritance-and-divorce.html.

Coffey, Rebecca. "Have We Discovered a Prime Reason Why Some Men Cheat?" Psychology Today, June 1, 2015. https://www.psychologytoday.com/us/blog/the-bejeezus-out-me/201506/have-we-discovered-prime-reason-why-some-men-cheat.

Comoreanu, Alina. "Credit Card Debt Statistics for 2024." WalletHub, January 8, 2024. https://wallethub.com/edu/cc/credit-card-debt-study/24400.

Congress.gov. "H.R.8163 - 93rd Congress (1973-1974): Equal Credit Opportunity Act." May 29, 1973. https://www.congress.gov/bill/93rd-congress/house-bill/8163.

"Continuation of Health Coverage (COBRA)." DOL.gov. Accessed August 30, 2023. https://www.dol.gov/general/topic/health-plans/cobra.

Craven McGinty, Jo. "The Divorce Rate Is at a 40-Year Low, Unless You're 55 or Older." Wall Street Journal, June 21, 2019. https://www.wsj.com/articles/the-divorce-rate-is-at-a-40-year-low-unless-youre-55-or-older-11561116601.

Crowley, CFA, CFP, CDFA, Jason. "A Guide to Social Security Benefits After Divorce." Survive Divorce, September 6, 2021. https://www.survivedivorce.com/social-security.

Cruz, J. (2013). Marriage: More than a Century of Change (FP-13-13). National Center for Family & Marriage Research. Retrieved from http://ncfmr. bgsu.edu/p df/ family_profiles/ file131529.pdf

Cussen, Mark P. "Divorce and Social Security Rules: What to Know." Investopedia, December 10, 2023. https://www.investopedia.com/articles/financial-advisor/112216/divorce-and-new-social-security-rules-what-know.asp.

Davis, Ryan. "The Most Scandalous Rumored Details of Celebrity Prenups." Ranker, September 23, 2021. https://www.ranker.com/list/celebrity-prenup-details/rydavis.

232 ∽ Bibliography

DeMasters, Karen. "Women Hold Majority of Personal Wealth, but Still Minorities in Advisory Field." Financial Advisor, March 25, 2020. https://www.fa-mag.com/news/women-need-to-lead-in-finances--consultant-says-54850.html.

Denniston, Lyle. "Opinion Analysis: Marriage Now Open to Same-Sex Couples." SCOTUSblog, June 26, 2015. https://www.scotusblog.com/2015/06/opinion-analysis-marriage-now-open-to-same-sex-couples/.

Digital Communications Division (DCD). "What Is the Affordable Care Act?" HHS .gov, April 20, 2023. https://www.hhs.gov/answers/health-insurance-reform/what -is-the-affordable-care-act/index.html.

Dillon, Joe. "Community Property California: Not Always 50-50 in Divorce." Equitable Mediation Services. Accessed August 30, 2023. https://www.equitable-mediation.com/blog/california-community-property-divorce.

Dillon, Joe. "Equitable Distribution: Who Gets What in a Divorce?" Equitable Mediation Services. Accessed August 30, 2023. https://www.equitablemediation .com/divorce-mediation/equitable-distribution.

Dinning, Rachel. "Queen Elizabeth II and Prince Philip: 8 Milestones in Their Marriage." HistoryExtra, November 20, 2020. https://www.historyextra.com/period /20th-century/queen-elizabeth-prince-philip-milestones-marriage-relationship/.

"Divorce Rate in America: 50+ Divorce Statistics [Updated 2024]." Divorce.com, January 6, 2024. https://divorce.com/blog/divorce-statistics/.

"Do You Have to File for Divorce in the Same State as the Marriage?" Townsend, Tomaio & Newmark, March 30, 2022. https://www.bergencountyfamilylawyers .com/blog/do-you-have-to-file-for-divorce-in-the-same-state-as-the-marriage.

Ellyatt, Holly. "Arguing with Your Partner over Covid? You're Not Alone, with the Pandemic Straining Many Relationships." CNBC, January 21, 2022. https://www .cnbc.com/2022/01/21/covid-has-put-pressures-and-strains-on-relationships.html.

"Emily Post." Encyclopedia Britannica, September 21, 2023. https://www.britannica .com/biography/Emily-Post.

Epstein, Rachel. "14 Weird-but-True Reasons Real People Have Gotten Divorced." Marie Claire Magazine, September 26, 2017. https://www.marieclaire.com/culture /a29603/weird-reasons-real-people-divorced/.

"Equal Credit Opportunity Act." Wikipedia, January 21, 2024. https://en.wikipedia .org/wiki/Equal_Credit_Opportunity_Act.

Ewing-Nelson, Claire. "All of the Jobs Lost in December Were Women's Jobs." National Women's Law Center, January 2021. https://nwlc.org/wp-content/ uploads/2021/01/December-Jobs-Day.pdf.

"Fidelity's® Annual Snapshot of America's Student Debt: Boomers Burdened with the Most Student Debt." Business Wire, October 27, 2020. https://www.business-wire.com/news/home/20201027005163/en/.

Field, Emily, Alexis Krivkovich, Sandra Kügele, Nicole Robinson, and Lareina Yee. "Women in the Workplace 2023." McKinsey & Company, October 5, 2023. https://www.mckinsey.com/featured-insights/diversity-and-inclusion/women-in -the-workplace.

Bibliography ⁓ 233

"Fifth Annual Advisor Authority Study Shows Women Investors Less Optimistic about Market and Economy than Men Investors Regardless of Affluence or Access to a Financial Advisor." PR Newswire, July 22, 2019. Nationwide. https://www.prnewswire.com/news-releases/fifth-annual-advisor-authority-study-shows-women-investors-less-optimistic-about-market-and-economy-than-men-investors-regardless-of-affluence-or-access-to-a-financial-advisor-300888203.html.

Friedman, Howard S., and Leslie R. Martin. *The Longevity Project: Surprising Discoveries for Health and Long Life from the Landmark Eight-Decade Study.* New York: Plume, 2012.

Fry, Richard. "A Majority of Young Adults in the U.S. Live with Their Parents for the First Time since the Great Depression." Pew Research Center, September 4, 2020. https://www.pewresearch.org/fact-tank/2020/09/04/a-majority-of-young-adults-in-the-u-s-live-with-their-parents-for-the-first-time-since-the-great-depression/.

Fry, Richard. "Young Adults in U.S. Are Much More Likely than 50 Years Ago to Be Living in a Multigenerational Household." Pew Research Center, July 20, 2022. https://www.pewresearch.org/short-reads/2022/07/20/young-adults-in-u-s-are-much-more-likely-than-50-years-ago-to-be-living-in-a-multigenerational-household/.

Galloway, Scott. "The Case to Rebrand 'Divorce.'" *Medium*, May 24, 2021. https://marker.medium.com/the-case-to-rebrand-divorce-c2e60f0922e3.

"Gender: Beyond the Binary." Bigeye, February 17, 2021. https://lp.bigeyeagency.com/hubfs/Gender_BeyondtheBinary.pdf.

"Get the Facts on Economic Security for Seniors." The National Council on Aging, June 8, 2023. https://www.ncoa.org/article/get-the-facts-on-economic-security-for-seniors.

Gillespie, Lane. "Survey: 68% of Parents Have Made a Financial Sacrifice to Help Their Adult Children with Money." Bankrate, April 10, 2023. https://www.bankrate.com/personal-finance/financial-independence-survey/.

Glynn, Sarah Jane. "Breadwinning Mothers Are Critical to Families' Economic Security." Center for American Progress, September 8, 2022. https://www.americanprogress.org/issues/women/news/2021/03/29/497658/breadwinning-mothers-critical-familys-economic-security/.

Godfrey, Neale S. *Money Doesn't Grow on Trees: A Parent's Guide to Raising Financially Responsible Children.* New York: Simon & Schuster, 2006.

Godfrey, Neale. "Never Own Anything Bigger than Your Hat." *Forbes*, October 26, 2014. https://www.forbes.com/sites/nealegodfrey/2014/10/26/never-own-anything-bigger-than-your-hat/.

Gravier, Elizabeth. "Men Have over 3x More Retirement Savings than Women - 7 Steps to Make Sure You Are Financially Secure." CNBC, January 2, 2024. https://www.cnbc.com/select/financial-steps-for-women/.

Gregoire, Carolyn. "How Money Changes the Way You Think and Feel." Greater Good Magazine, February 8, 2018. https://greatergood.berkeley.edu/article/item/how_money_changes_the_way_you_think_and_feel.

234 ～ Bibliography

Guan N., Guariglia A., Moore P., Xu F., Al-Janabi H. "Financial stress and depression in adults: A systematic review." *PLoS One*. February 22, 2022. doi:10.1371/journal.pone.0264041.

Hall, Jessica. "Gray Divorce Is Most Often Initiated by Women - Even Though It Can Crush Their Finances." MarketWatch, September 11, 2023. https://www.marketwatch.com/story/gray-divorce-is-most-often-initiated-by-women-even-though-it-can-crush-their-finances-4329540d.

Hatfield, Jenn. "Young Adults in the U.S. Are Less Likely than Those in Most of Europe to Live in Their Parents' Home." Pew Research Center, May 3, 2023. https://www.pewresearch.org/short-reads/2023/05/03/in-the-u-s-and-abroad-more-young-adults-are-living-with-their-parents/.

Havens, John J., and Paul G. Schervish. "Millionaires and the millennium", Chestnut Hill, Mass.: Social Welfare Research Institute, Boston College, October 19, 1999. http://hdl.handle.net/2345/bc-ir:104110.

Helhoski, Anna, and Eliza Haverstock. "How Many Americans Have Student Loan Debt?" NerdWallet, January 19, 2023. https://www.nerdwallet.com/article/loans/student-loans/how-many-americans-have-student-loan-debt.

Hemez, P. (2020). "Distributions of age at first marriage, 1960-2018." Family Profiles, FP-20-09. Bowling Green, OH: National Center for Family & Marriage Research. https://doi.org/10.25035/ncfmr/fp-20-09.

Herpolsheimer, Laura J. "Financial Stress: How Older Adults' Health Is Affected." SOAR, May 1, 2015. https://soar.wichita.edu/handle/10057/11596.

Hill, Catey. "This Common Behavior Is the No. 1 Predictor of Whether You'll Get Divorced." MarketWatch, January 10, 2018. https://www.marketwatch.com/story/this-common-behavior-is-the-no-1-predictor-of-whether-youll-get-divorced-2018-01-10.

Hinchliffe, Emma. "Funding For Female Founders Stalled at 2.2% of VC Dollars in 2018." *Fortune*, January 28, 2019. https://fortune.com/2019/01/28/funding-female-founders-2018/.

Hinchliffe, Emma. "Women Run More than 10% of Fortune 500 Companies for the First Time." Fortune, January 12, 2023. https://fortune.com/2023/01/12/fortune-500-companies-ceos-women-10-percent/.

Hockaday, James. "Why Prince Philip Changed His Surname before He Married the Queen." Metro, April 9, 2021. https://metro.co.uk/2021/04/09/why-prince-philip-did-prince-philip-change-his-surname-14385063/.

"Housing Finance at a Glance: A Monthly Chartbook." Urban Institute, June 2022. https://www.urban.org/sites/default/files/2022-08/Housing_Finance_At_A_Glance_Monthly_Chartbook_August%202022.pdf.

"How to Build a Healthy Financial Relationship with Your Boomerang Child." Thrivent, December 6, 2023. https://www.thrivent.com/insights/financial-planning build-a-healthy-financial-relationship-with-your-boomerang-child.

"How Much Care Will You Need?" ACL Administration for Community Living, February 18, 2018. https://acl.gov/ltc/basic-needs/how-much-care-will-you-need.

Bibliography ～ 235

"How Seniors and Millennials Date." MedicareAdvantage.com, February 2023. https://www.medicareadvantage.com/senior-dating-survey.

Huisache, Sam M. "Is Marriage Popularity Declining? Insights from a National Survey of Americans (2023 Data)." Clever Real Estate, June 27, 2023. https://listwithclever.com/research/marriage-decline-survey-2023/.

"In a Divorce, Who Gets the 401k?" 401khelpcenter.com. Accessed August 30, 2023. http://www.401khelpcenter.com/401k_education/divorce_and_your_401k.html.

"In FTC Study, Five Percent of Consumers Had Errors on Their Credit Reports That Could Result in Less Favorable Terms for Loans." Federal Trade Commission, February 11, 2013. Federal Trade Commission. https://www.ftc.gov/news-events/news/press-releases/2013/02/ftc-study-five-percent-consumers-had-errors-their-credit-reports-could-result-less-favorable-terms.

I.R.C. § 6013(d)(3).

"Irish Divorce." Urban Dictionary, January 5, 2017. https://www.urbandictionary.com/define.php?term=Irish%2Bdivorce.

"Is Divorce Seasonal? UW Research Shows Biannual Spike in Divorce Filings." University of Washington, August 21, 2016. University of Washington. https://www.washington.edu/news/2016/08/21/is-divorce-seasonal-uw-research-shows-biannual-spike-in-divorce-filings/.

Johnson, Jeffrey. "What Is Community Property?" Free Advice, July 19, 2023. https://www.freeadvice.com/legal/what-is-community-property/.

Johnson, Jeffrey. "What Is Equitable Distribution?" Free Advice, July 18, 2023. https://www.freeadvice.com/legal/what-is-equitable-distribution/.

Josephson, Amelia. "What Is the Average American's Debt by Age Group?" SmartAsset, August 10, 2023. https://smartasset.com/credit-cards/the-average-debt-by-age.

Kagan, Julia. "Charitable Remainder Trust: Definition, How It Works, and Types." Investopedia, January 5, 2023. https://www.investopedia.com/terms/c/charitableremaindertrust.asp.

Kates, CFP®, Stephen. "50+ Essential Retirement Statistics for 2024: Demographics." Annuity.org, January 10, 2024. https://www.annuity.org/retirement/retirement-statistics/.

Kaylene. "14 Celebrities and Their Insane Prenups." TheTalko, April 26, 2016. https://www.thetalko.com/15-celebrities-and-their-insane-prenups/.

Kochhar, Rakesh. "The Enduring Grip of the Gender Pay Gap." Pew Research Center, March 1, 2023. https://www.pewresearch.org/social-trends/2023/03/01/the-enduring-grip-of-the-gender-pay-gap/.

Koterbski, Kaitlyn. "30% of Women Say They Don't Know Enough to Start Investing. Here's How They Can Get Started." Fortune, July 14, 2022. https://fortune.com/2022/07/14/how-women-can-start-investing-for-retirement/.

Li, Zhe. "Household Debt Among Older Americans, 1989-2016." Congressional Research Service, September 11, 2019. https://crsreports.congress.gov/.

236 〜 Bibliography

Lisa, Andrew. "How Much Does It Cost to Maintain a Luxury Car." GOBankingRates, September 9, 2022. https://www.gobankingrates.com/saving-money/car/how-much-does-it-cost-to-maintain-a-luxury-car/.

Malito, Alessandra. "Seniors Have More Household Debt Now than They Did during the Financial Crisis." MarketWatch, August 13, 2019. https://www.marketwatch.com/story/seniors-have-more-household-debt-now-than-they-did-during-the-financial-crisis-2019-08-13.

Markowitz, Andy, and Tracy Thompson. "Can Social Security Be Garnished?" AARP, November 15, 2023. https://www.aarp.org/retirement/social-security/questions-answers/social-security-garnished.html.

Martin, Allison. "Medical Debt Consolidation." Bankrate, October 30, 2023. https://www.bankrate.com/personal-finance/debt/medical-debt-consolidation/.

Masterson, Victoria. "Here's What Women's Entrepreneurship Looks like around the World." World Economic Forum, June 20, 2022. https://www.weforum.org/agenda/2022/07/women-entrepreneurs-gusto-gender/.

McManus, Darragh. "How You Can Cope with Competitive Marriage Syndrome." Independent.ie, April 11, 2014. https://www.independent.ie/lifestyle/how-you-can-cope-with-competitive-marriage-syndrome-30175393.html.

"Median Usual Weekly Earnings of Full-Time Wage and Salary Workers by Age, Race, Hispanic or Latino Ethnicity, and Sex, Fourth Quarter 2023 Averages, Not Seasonally Adjusted." Washington, DC: U.S. Bureau of Labor Statistics, January 18, 2024.

Menasce Horowitz, Juliana. "Marriage and Cohabitation in the U.S." Pew Research Center's Social & Demographic Trends Project, November 6, 2019. https://www.pewresearch.org/social-trends/2019/11/06/marriage-and-cohabitation-in-the-u-s/.

Miller, Alex. "Credit Score Facts & Statistics: Average Credit Score, Range & More." UpgradedPoints.com, October 4, 2023. https://upgradedpoints.com/credit-cards/credit-score-facts-statistics/.

Miller, Kevin, and Deborah J. Vagins. "The Simple Truth about the Gender Pay Gap." AAUW, 2018. https://www.aauw.org/resources/research/simple-truth/.

"Money Ruining Marriages in America: A Ramsey Solutions Study." Ramsey Solutions. The State of Finances in the American Household, February 6, 2018. Ramsey Solutions. https://www.ramseysolutions.com/company/newsroom/releases/money-ruining-marriages-in-america.

Montenegro, Xenia P. "The Divorce Experience: A Study of Divorce at Midlife and Beyond." AARP, May 2004. https://assets.aarp.org/rgcenter/general/divorce.pdf.

Moore, Angela. "This Is Why Baby Boomers Are Divorcing at a Stunning Rate." MarketWatch, October 20, 2018. https://www.marketwatch.com/story/your-failing-marriage-is-about-to-make-the-retirement-crisis-worse-2017-03-13.

Murray-Close, Marta, and Misty L. Heggeness. "Manning up and Womaning down: How Husbands and Wives Report Their Earnings When She Earns More." United States Census Bureau, June 6, 2018. https://www.census.gov/content/dam/Census/library/working-papers/2018/demo/SEHSD-WP2018-20.pdf.

Nova, Annie. "Growing Debt among Older Americans Threatens Their Retirement." CNBC, April 5, 2018. https://www.cnbc.com/2018/04/04/growing-debt-among-older-americans-threatens-retirement.html.

Novotney, A. "In brief: Snapshots of some of the latest peer-reviewed research within psychology and related fields." *Monitor on Psychology*, 44(10), November 1, 2013. https://www.apa.org/monitor/2013/11/inbrief.

"Own Your Worth: How Women Can Break the Cycle of Abdication and Take Control of Their Wealth." UBS, 2018. https://www.ubs.com/content/dam/WealthManagementAmericas/documents/2018-37666-UBS-Own-Your-Worth-report-R32.pdf.

Pandey, Erica. "Marriage Is on the Decline in the U.S." Axios, February 25, 2023. https://www.axios.com/2023/02/25/marriage-declining-single-dating-taxes-relationships.

Paulson, Michael. "As Vatican Revisits Divorce, Many Catholics Long for Acceptance." *New York Times*, January 25, 2015. https://www.nytimes.com/2015/01/25/us/as-vatican-revisits-divorce-many-catholics-long-for-acceptance.html.

Pease Gadoua, Susan. "It's Okay to Stay Together for the Kids: The Co-Parent Solution." *Psychology Today*, January 17, 2022. https://www.psychologytoday.com/us/blog/contemplating-divorce/202201/its-okay-stay-together-the-kids-the-co-parent-solution.

Picchi, Aimee. "More Women Are Now Outearning Their Husbands – and Emotions Can Be Big." *USA Today*, March 3, 2020. https://www.usatoday.com/story/money/2020/03/03/gender-wage-gap-more-women-out-earning-husbands/4933666002/.

"Prescription Assistance Programs." BeMedWise. Accessed February 11, 2024. https://bemedwise.org/documents/paps.pdf.

"Protecting Your Finances during a Divorce." Wiser Women, February 16, 2023. https://wiserwomen.org/resources/divorce-fact-sheets/protecting-your-finances-during-a-divorce/.

"Provisional Number of Marriages and Marriage Rate: United States, 2000–2021." Centers of Disease Control and Prevention, 2021.

"Ranking the Least Expensive Luxury Cars to Maintain." CarEdge. Accessed February 11, 2024. https://caredge.com/ranks/maintenance/luxury/10-year/best#models.

Reed, Eric. "Is Alimony Taxable?" SmartAsset, November 8, 2022. https://smartasset.com/taxes/is-alimony-taxable.

"Rental Assistance." HUD.gov / U.S. Department of Housing and Urban Development (HUD), December 8, 2021. https://www.hud.gov/topics/rental_assistance.

"Retirement & Survivors Benefits: Life Expectancy Calculator." Social Security Administration. Accessed February 17, 2024. https://www.ssa.gov/oact/population/longevity.html.

Reynolds, L. (2021). The U.S. remarriage rate, 2019: Trends and geographic variation by gender. Family Profiles, FP-21-18. Bowling Green, OH: National Center for Family & Marriage Research. https://doi.org/10.25035/ncfmr/fp-21-18

238 ～ Bibliography

Schulte, Brigid. "Till Death Do Us Part? No Way. Gray Divorce on the Rise." *Washington Post*, October 8, 2014. https://www.washingtonpost.com/blogs/she-the -people/wp/2014/10/08/till-death-do-us-part-no-way-gray-divorce-on-the-rise/.

Sember, J.D., Brette. "Divorce and Life Insurance: Understanding Your Rights." WomansDivorce.com. Accessed February 11, 2024. https://www.womansdivorce .com/divorce-and-life-insurance.html.

"Seniors Can Reduce Their Tax Burden by Donating to Charity through Their IRA." Internal Revenue Service, November 8, 2022. https://www.irs.gov/news-room/seniors-can-reduce-their-tax-burden-by-donating-to-charity-through-their -ira.

"Seniors Farmers Market Nutrition Program." Food and Nutrition Service U.S. Department of Agriculture, February 5, 2024. https://www.fns.usda.gov/sfmnp/ senior-farmers-market-nutrition-program.

"The Simple Truth About the Gender Pay Gap." American Association of University Women, 2020. https://www.aauw.org/app/uploads/2020/12/SimpleTruth _2.1.pdf.

Smith, Sylvia. "5 Potential Signs of Miserable Husband Syndrome & How to Deal." Marriage.com, December 12, 2023. https://www.marriage.com/advice/relationship /miserable-husband-syndrome/.

"Snapshot of Older Consumers and Student Loan Debt." Consumer Financial Protection Bureau, January 2017. https://files.consumerfinance.gov/f/documents /201701_cfpb_OA-Student-Loan-Snapshot.pdf.

Stevenson, Betsey, and Justin Wolfers. "Bargaining in the Shadow of the Law: Divorce Laws and Family Distress." *The Quarterly Journal of Economics* 121, no. 1 (February 1, 2006): 267–88. https://doi.org/https://doi.org/10.1093/qje/121.1.267.

"Stress in America 2022: Concerned for the Future, Beset by Inflation." American Psychological Association, October 2022. https://www.apa.org/news/press/releases /stress/2022/concerned-future-inflation.

"Supplemental Nutrition Assistance Program (SNAP)." Food and Nutrition Service, U.S. Department of Agriculture, February 5, 2024. https://www.fns.usda.gov/snap/ supplemental-nutrition-assistance-program.

Teare, Gené. "Q1 2019 Diversity Report: Female Founders Own 17 Percent of Venture Dollars." *Crunchbase News*, April 29, 2019. https://news.crunchbase.com /business/q1-2019-diversity-report-female-founders-own-17-percent-of-venture -dollars/.

Tuckman, Ari. "Will a Partner Who Cheated Cheat Again?" *Psychology Today*, February 28, 2021. https://www.psychologytoday.com/us/blog/sex-matters/202102/will -partner-who-cheated-cheat-again.

Turner, Terry. "Essential Facts about Medicare Seniors Should Know in 2023." Retire Guide, October 24, 2023. https://www.retireguide.com/guides/facts-about -medicare/.

"UBS Investor Watch: Own Your Worth." UBS, 2019. https://www.ubs.com/it/en/ wealth-management/our-approach/investor-watch/2019/own-your-worth.html.

Bibliography ～ 239

United States Census Bureau, "Week 50 Household Pulse Survey: October 5 - October 17." Census.gov, October 26, 2022. https://www.census.gov/data/tables/2022/demo/hhp/hhp50.html.

Vuleta, Branka. "14 Intriguing Divorce Statistics in 2023." Legaljobs, May 20, 2023. https://legaljobs.io/blog/divorce-statistics.

Waggoner, John. "What to Know about Reverse Mortgages." AARP, November 16, 2022. https://www.aarp.org/money/credit-loans-debt/info-2019/reverse-mortgage-loan-advice.html.

Wang, Wendy. "The Share of Never-Married Americans Has Reached a New High." Institute for Family Studies, September 9, 2020. https://ifstudies.org/blog/the-share-of-never-married-americans-has-reached-a-new-high.

Werber, Cassie. "Wealthy Millennial Women Are More Likely to Defer to Their Husbands on Investing." Quartz, March 15, 2019. https://qz.com/work/1573457/wealthy-millennial-women-are-deferring-to-their-husbands-on-financial-planning/.

"When Women Earn More Than Their Husbands." The University of Chicago Booth School of Business, February 18, 2013. The University of Chicago. https://www.chicagobooth.edu/media-relations-and-communications/press-releases/when-women-earn-more-than-their-husbands.

Woolley, Suzanne. "Rise of 'gray' Divorce Is Forcing a Financial Reckoning for 50-plus Women." *Los Angeles Times*, April 20, 2018. https://www.latimes.com/business/la-fi-divorce-at-fifty-20180420-story.html.

Index

AAML. *See* American Academy of Matrimonial Lawyers

AARP, xxvi

Abzug, Bella, xxiv

ACA. *See* Patient Protection and Affordable Care Act

accountant, 85–86

Adjustable-Rate Mortgage (ARM), 142

Adjusted Gross Income (AGI), 196

adultery. *See* cheating

adult kids, xxii, 205–7, 208

Advance Health Care Directive, 39

advice: financial advisor, 85, 95–99; gender roles and, 35

Aetna, xxv

affairs. *See* cheating

"affluenza," 55

Affordable Care Act. *See* Patient Protection and Affordable Care Act

age: full retirement, 122; of marriage, median, 37

AGI. *See* Adjusted Gross Income

AIG, xxv

Airbnb, 66

alimony: determining amount and duration of, 116–17; permanent, 116–17, 123; rehabilitative, 115, 117; retirement and, 116; tax laws on, 126

allowance system, 200

American Academy of Matrimonial Lawyers (AAML), 91

American Bankers Association, xxv

American Dream, 205

American Psychological Association (APA), xix, 149

American Sociological Review (journal), xix

Angelou, Maya, xv

annuity, 175

annulment, 23

antique appraiser, 86

APA. *See* American Psychological Association

Apple Music, 155

appraisal, of home, 142

appraisers, 86

appreciation, 175

ARM. *See* Adjustable-Rate Mortgage

242 ~ Index

art appraiser, 86
assets: allocation of, 174; defined, 174; marital, 190–91; premarital, 190–91
assets and income division, 119; checklist, 120; inheritances, 121; life insurance, 123–24; pension plans, 125–26; retirement accounts, 125–26; Social Security, 121–23; tax considerations, 126–27
Associated Press, xxv
attorney: basic personal information for, 92; checklist for, 91–93; fees for, 91, 97–98; mediation versus, 87–88; more information for, 92–93; for prenup, 187–88, 192–93; selecting, 89–91

Babson, Roger, 59
Baby Boomers, xvii, 9, 76, 199, 204; charity by, 195; long-term financial planning and, 95; prenups and, 179; retirement and, 96; student loan debt of, 139
Babylon, 23
baggage: gender stereotypes and, 34; for kids, 37–40; money patterns as, 14–15
"Bag Lady Syndrome," 147, 153; credit card debt and, 150, 150–52; financial stress and, 149; money FOG and, 148
Bank of America, xxvii
Bankrate.com, 95, 203
Barbarito, Pat, 90
basic personal information, for attorney, 92
the Beatles, 97
beneficiary, 176
Beyoncé, 19, 188
Bezos, Jeff, xviii
bias: gender, xxii, 30; sexual, xxii
Bill & Melinda Gates Foundation, 127
bills: credit card debt and, 152; paying, 103–4

Black women, 30
Boleyn, Anne, 23
The Book of Choice (DeYoung), 131
Boomerang Generation, 203
Booth School of Business, at University of Chicago, xix
Boston College, 199
boundaries, setting with kids, 203–4
Bowling Green State University, 9
breadwinners: men as, 28; women as, xix
Brines, Julie, xvi
brokerage accounts, 167
Brown, Susan L., 9, 11
Buddha Gautama, 50
budgets, 58, 67; chart, 63–64; monthly, 61–65
Bureau of Labor Statistics, 30, 151

California, 104, 119
capital gains, 110, 175
Cappiello, Rose-Marie, 67
Carroll, Pete, xxii
cars, 154; insurance for, 65; leased, 112–13
"The Case to Rebrand 'Divorce'" (Galloway), 3
Catherine of Aragon, 23
Catholic Church, 11, 23
CDC. See Center for Disease Control
Census Bureau, United States, 28
Center for Disease Control (CDC), xvii
Center on Wealth and Philanthropy, 199
Centers for Medicare & Medicaid Services, 111
certified financial planner (CFP), 98
Certified Financial Planning Board of Standards, 98
CFP. See certified financial planner
CFPB. See Consumer Financial Protection Bureau
Chan, Priscilla, 189

Index ~ 243

charitable giving, 195; grandchildren and, 201–2; ways to donate, 196–97

charitable remainder trust, 196

Chase Manhattan Bank, xxiii, 29

cheating, xix, 23, 37, 180; emotional dissatisfaction and, xx; financial infidelity, 16, 18–19; women hanging on and, xx–xxi

Chicago, University of, xix

children. See kids

China, xvi

choice, 131

Christie, Chris, 30

Churchill, Winston, 128, 197

Church of England, 23

Clarke, Denis, 23

Clement VII (Pope), 23

CNBC, xvi, xxv, 135

CNN, xxv

COBRA. See Consolidated Omnibus Budget Reconciliation Act

Coca-Cola, xxv

coffee, 66

COLA. See Cost of Living Adjustment

"cold sweat test," 97, 167, 174

collectible appraiser, 86

college: graduates, 30; student loans, 113, 136–37, 138–40, 177, 205

Columbia Graduate School of Business, xxv

Columbia University, xxiv

combined income, 127

commission-based structures, 98

common-law marriage, 24, 39

communication, xiv, 38

community property, 119

Competitive Marriage Syndrome, xviii–xix

complaining, xv–xvi

compound interest, 168–69, 174, 199

confidence, 174–76

conflict-of-interest rules, 90

Congressional Research Service, 177

"conscious uncoupling," 3

Consolidated Omnibus Budget Reconciliation Act (COBRA), 110, 128

consumer debt, 37

Consumer Financial Protection Bureau (CFPB), 177

Consumer Price Index (CPI), 200

Coolidge, Calvin, 204

cost, median, 3

Cost of Living Adjustment (COLA), 122

Council on Contemporary Families, xvii

coverture, 23

coverture fraction, 126

COVID-19 pandemic, xvi, 37

CPA, 85–86

credentials, of financial advisors, 98

credit card debt, 102, 140; "Bag Lady Syndrome" and, 150, 150–52; compound interest and, 169; dividing, 104; medical debt and, 137; ratio, 82

credit cards, 78, 82; freezing, 66; opening new, 103; secured, 83, 103; for women, xxiv

credit history, 76, 82–83

credit mix, 76

credit-monitoring services, 103

credit owed, 75–76

credit reports, 74, 102–3

credit score, 75, 141, 174; importance of, 76–77; improvement of, 77–80

credit utilization ratio, 79

DAF. See donor-advised fund

dating, online, 11–12

death benefits, 123

debt, 135; consumer, 37; listing, 120; marital, 191; medical, 137; mortgage,

244 ～ Index

116; premarital, 190; prenups and, 182; student loan, 113, 136–37, 138–40; taking on more, 176–77. *See also* credit card debt

debt-consolidation loans, 139–40

debt-to-income ratio (DTI), 79–82, *81*, 141

deception, financial, 18

default divorce, 26

defined-benefit plan, 175

defined-contribution plan, 175

denial, xiii–xiv

Department of Housing and Urban Development (HUD), 138

depression, financial stress and, 149

detanglement list, 71–72

Detroit, Michigan, 104

DeYoung, Kim, 131, 180

Diana (Princess), xxiv

Dimon, Jamie, 29

discovery, for divorce, 26

diversification, 175

dividends, 175

divorce. *See specific topics*

Divorce and Matrimonial Causes Act, 23

divorce decree, 71

"divorce month," January as, xvii

divorce rate, xviii, 3, 9, 31; COVID-19 and, xvi; declining, xxvi; holiday season and, xvii

"The Divorce Rate Is at a 40-Year Low, Unless You're 55 or Older," xvii

Divorce Reform Act, 24

documents: estate-planning, 102; income, 101; for kids and loved ones, 73; real estate, 101; tax, 101

domestic partnerships, 24–25, 39

donor-advised fund (DAF), 196–97

downsizing, 153

DTI. *See* debt-to-income ratio

Earhart, Amelia, 79

ecdysis, 131

education, 147, 168. *See also* college

Einstein, Albert, 169, 199

Elizabeth II (Queen), 189–90

emotional dissatisfaction, xx

empowerment, financial, 38

empty-nest syndrome, 205

entrepreneurship, 30

Equal Credit Opportunity Act, 21, *22*, 140, 141

Equal Pay Act, *22*

Equifax, 75, 102

equitable distribution, 119

equity: defined, 175; in home, 141; investment, 167

escrow, 175

estate planning, 102, 175, 191–92

etiquette training, 28

expenses, 61–62, 65, 67

Experian, 75, 102

Fair Credit Reporting Act, xxiv, 78

Fair Isaac Corporation (FICO), 75, 174; score importance, 76–77; score improvement, 77–80

family: attorney selection and, 91; finances, *17*, 18; financial goals and, 164–65; home, 73–74, 109, 116; loans to, 137; money issues, 147. *See also* kids; parents

Family Court system, 24

FAO Schwarz, xxiv

Fear, Obligation, and Guilt (FOG), 148

Federal Insurance Contributions Act (FICA), 121

federal poverty level (FPL), 135

Federal Trade Commission (FTC), 78, 140

fee-only financial planner, 175

fees, for attorney, 91, 97–98

feminism, 27

FICA. *See* Federal Insurance
Contributions Act
FICO. *See* Fair Isaac Corporation
Fidelity Investments, xxv, 167, 168
filing for divorce, 25
finances: arguments about, 37; family,
17, 18
financial advisors, 85; choosing, 95–99;
credentials of, 98; traditional, 98
financial deception, 18
financial education, 147
financial empowerment, 38
financial goals: family and loved ones
and, 164–65; mapping, 163; Money
Map and, 165–66, *166*
financial independence, 19, 163
financial infidelity, 16, 18–19
financial information, 102
financial personality, 51, *52–54*, 55–56
financial planner, fee-only, 175
financial planning, long-term, 95
financial responsibilities, marital, 191
financial rights of women, 21; history of
divorce and, 23–25; milestones for,
22; rules and steps for divorce, 25–26
financial security, 57–58
financial situation, 12
Financial Sock Drawer, 44, 47, 58
financial stress, 149
Financial Tips from Grandma Jewel (radio
segment), 87
financial wellness, 171; confidence and,
174–76; quiz for, *172–73*; what not
to do, 176–77
The First Children's Bank, xxiv
The First Women's Bank, xxiv
Fisher, Carrie, 115
fixed expenses, 62, 67
FOG. *See* Fear, Obligation, and Guilt
Forbes (magazine), xxv, 153
foreign laws, 105
forensic accountant, 86
401(k) account, 110, 119, 125–26

403(b) account, 126
Fox, xxv
FPL. *See* federal poverty level
Francis (Pope), 11
Frank, Anne, 195
Franklin, Benjamin, 62, 65, 91, 99
freedom, 154
Friedan, Betty, xxiv
Friedman, Howard S., 31
friends: attorney selection and, 91;
loans to, 137; as support structure,
xxii
Frozen (film), 10
FTC. *See* Federal Trade Commission
full retirement age, 122

Galloway, Scott, 3–4
Gates, Bill, xviii, 127
Gates, Melinda, xviii, 127
gender: bias, xxii, 30; disparity, 29–30;
stereotypes, 34. *See also* men;
women
gender roles, 27, 36; advice and, 35;
gender disparity and, 29–30; men as
breadwinners, 28; stereotypes and,
34; women living longer and, 31–34;
women pulled in many directions,
28–29
Gen X, 179
Gen Z, 34, 179
gifts, setting limits for, 66
giving. *See* charitable giving
Global Credit Training Program, 29
goals, 158. *See also* financial goals
GoBankingRates, 148
Godfrey, Neale S., 29
"golden years," xi
Gone with the Wind (film), 34–35
Good Morning America (TV program),
xxv
Gore, Al, xviii
Gore, Tipper, xviii
grandchildren, 199–202

246 ～ Index

gray divorce: defining, 3–4; readiness for, 4, 5–7. *See also specific topics*
"Groundhog Day," xii
grounds for divorce, 25
Guest Bedroom Syndrome, xiv
guilt, 9, 148, 204
guilt-free spending, 66

Habitat for Humanity, 201
Hammurabi (King), 23
happiness, 67–68, 157
Harris Poll, 18
Harry (Prince), 190
Hartford Insurance, xxv
health, financial stress and, 149
health benefits, 39
health insurance: domestic partnerships and, 24; long-term, 124–25; loss of, 127–28; money mistake with, 110
health proxy, 176
Health Savings Account (HSA), 111
heating, 138
Henry VIII (King), 23
high-earning wives, xix
higher-cost investment, 98
Hispanic women, 30
history, of divorce, 23–25
holidays, xvi–xvii
home: appraisal of, 142; equity in, 141; family, 73–74, 109, 116. *See also* mortgage
homeowners insurance, 65
honesty, xix–xx
Hong Kong, 105
household duties, 29
house phone, 138
houses, 39. *See also* home
housing costs, 205
HSA. *See* Health Savings Account
HUD. *See* Department of Housing and Urban Development
Huffington Post (news outlet), xxv

Hugo, Victor, 195
human nature, xiii

identity: changing, xii; for men, xix
Illinois, 119
income, 61; combined, 127; disparity, 181; documents, 101; DTI, 79–82, 81, 141; net, 82; total gross monthly, 80. *See also* assets and income division
incompletions, 43–45
independence, financial, 19, 163
infidelity. *See* cheating
inflation, 151
inheritances, 121
Instagram, xxiii
Institute for Youth Entrepreneurship, xxiv
insurance: car, 65; homeowners, 65; life, 65, 123–24; long-term health care, 124–25; permanent, 123. *See also* health insurance
interest, compound, 168–69, 174, 199
International Monetary Fund, xvi
Internet, 12
interview, for attorney, 90–91
intimacy, Guest Bedroom Syndrome and, xiv
investments: big deal about, 168–69; equity, 167; higher-cost, 98; joint accounts, 103; low-cost, 98; medium-cost, 98; time and, 169; women and, 167–69
Iowa University, 37
IRAs, 125, 167, 176
Irish Divorce, 11
IRS, 28, 39, 138, 182, 190–91
Irving, Amy, 189

January, as "divorce month," xvii
Jay-Z, 189
joint accounts, 103
Jordan, Tera R., 37

Index ⌢ 247

JPMorgan Chase, 29
Judge Judy, 10

Kansas, 104
Kidd, Sue Monk, 120
kids: adult, xxii, 205–7, 208; baggage
for, 37–40; documents for, 73;
grandchildren, 199–202; from
previous marriages, 191; setting
boundaries with, 203–4; special
needs, 116
Kindle, 155
Kiplinger Magazine, xxv
knee-jerk reactions, 7
Kruesi, Oscar, 115

Landmark Eight-Decade Study, 31
lawyer. *See* attorney
lease, with adult kids, 205–7, 208
leased cars, 112–13
legal decisions, 176
liabilities, 174
library books, 138
life goals, 158
life insurance, 65, 123–24
LifeLock, 103
Life's Incompletion List, 45
lifestyle aspects, 49
Lin, I-Fen, 9
Lincoln, Abraham, 78, 161
Lincoln, Kate, 115
Lincoln Financial, xxv
liquidity, 176
living together, 38–39
living will, 176
loans, 83; debt-consolidation, 139–40;
to friends and family, 137; payday,
176; student, 113, 136–37, 138–40,
177, 205
Longevity Project (Friedman),
31
long-term capital gain, 110
Long-Term Care (LTC), 124–25

long-term financial planning, 95
long-term health care insurance,
124–25
low-cost investment, 98
LTC. *See* Long-Term Care
luxury cars, 112–13

Madonna, xxiv
Mandela, Nelson, 43
Manhattan Bank, 202
"Manning up and Womaning down"
(Census Bureau), 28
Marie Claire (magazine), 10
marital assets and debt, 191. *See also*
assets and income division
marital financial responsibilities, 191
MarketWatch, 135
Markle, Meghan, 190
marriage: common-law, 24, 39;
Competitive Marriage Syndrome,
xviii–xix; kids from previous, 191;
median age of, 37; rate, xviii;
remarriages, 180; same-sex, 24;
standard, 24; traditional, xix. *See also*
specific topics
Married Women's Property Acts, 23
Martins, Eric, 131, 180
Maryland, 104
masculinity, xix
Massachusetts, 104
Massachusetts Bay Colony, 23
MasterCard, xxv
McKinsey & Company, xvi
median age of marriage, 37
median cost, of divorce, 3
median retirement savings, 136
mediation, 87–88
Medicaid, 138
medical costs, 137
medical debt, 137
Medicare, 110–12, 127, 137
Medium (website), 3
medium-cost investment, 98

248 ～ Index

men: as breadwinners, 28; identity for, xix; investments and, 167; prenups and, 180; self-esteem of, xix; women earning less than, xxvii, 29–30
mental excuses, for Miserable Husband Syndrome, xv
mental health, financial stress and, 149
Michelangelo, 209
Michigan: Detroit, 104; University of, xviii
Microsoft, xxv
military, 77
Millennials, xvii, xxvi, 9, 11, 38
Miserable Husband Syndrome, xiv–xvi
Miserable Wife Syndrome, xv
mixed messages, for women, xviii
Mom, Inc. (Godfrey), 29
Monaco, 105
"Money" (the Beatles), 97
money habits, 47–48, 51
money issues, 37, 39, 44; family, 147; prenups and, 179
Money Map, xxi, 44, 58, 165–66, *166*
money marriage myths, 13, 16; family finances and, *17*, 18; patterns, *14–15*
money mistakes, 107–13; with health insurance, 110; with prenup, 187–88
"money talk," 188
monthly budget, 61–65
monthly fees, 97–98
mortgage: debt, 116; refinancing, 141–42; reverse, 143–45, *144*
motherhood, 30
multigenerational living, 205

Nash, Ogden, 151
National Center for Biotechnology Information, 149
National Council on Aging (NCOA), 135, 137
National Endowment for Financial Education, 18
National Library of Medicine, 149

Nationwide Advisory Solutions, xxvi
Native American women, 30
NCOA. *See* National Council on Aging
negativity, xv
net income, 82
net worth, 174
new credit, 76
New Jersey, 119
New Jersey Gender Parity Committee, 30
New York, 119; no-fault divorce and, 24; property ownership in, 23
New York Times (newspaper), xxiv
no-fault divorce, 24
No Magic Money Log, 58, 59–62, 60, 165
Nordegren, Elin, 189

Obama, Michelle, xix
Obergefell v. Hodges, 24
obligation (money FOG), 148
online dating, 11–12
online financial-planning services, 98
online self-help divorce agreements, xvi
Oprah, 38, 56, 66, 183
Oprah (TV program), xxv, 180

pandemic, COVID-19, xvi, 37
Pandora (music app), 155
PAPs. *See* prescription drug assistance programs
Parenting Marriage, 40
parents: divorce of, xiii; money patterns and, *14–15*
Parks, Rosa, xxi
Patient Protection and Affordable Care Act (ACA), 110, 128
payday loans, 176
payment history, 75
Pay On Death (POD), 72
PBS, xxv
Pennsylvania, 119
pension plans, 125–26

Index ~ 249

permanent alimony, 116–17, 123
permanent insurance, 123
personality, financial, 51, *52–54*, 55–56
personal property information, 102
petition for divorce, serving, 26
Pew Research Center, 30, 38, 205
Philip (Prince), 189–90
Philippines, 105
phone, house, 138
physical health, financial stress and, 149
physical infidelity, 18
Picasso, Pablo, xxi
"Please Pass the Butter" syndrome, xii, xvi, xxi, xxiii, 3, 25, 40, 43
POA. *See* power of attorney
POD. *See* Pay On Death
Post, Emily, 28
postnups, 187
potlucks, 66
Powell, Colin, 57
power of attorney (POA), 176
premarital assets and debt, 190
premium, 176
prenups (prenuptial agreements), 89, 183–86, *185*; attorney for, 188, 193; Baby Boomers and, 179; basic elements of, 190–91; cost of, 183; debt and, 182; men and, 180; money issues and, 179; money mistakes with, 188–89; need for, 182; talk about getting, 191–93; taxes and, 182; topics to discuss, 186; when to get, 187–88
preparation, for divorce, 26
prescription drug assistance programs (PAPs), 138
present value (PV), 125
property: community, 119; division of, 191; ownership, 23; personal property information, 102
psychological impact, xxi
Psychology Today (magazine), xx, 40

pure life insurance, 123
PV. *See* present value

QDRO. *See* qualified domestic relations order
qualified charitable distribution (QCD), 197
qualified domestic relations order (QDRO), 126
Quartz at Work, 148

Rand, Ayn, 56
rate-and-term refinancing, 141–42
real estate: appraiser, 86; documents, 101. *See also* home
reasons for divorce, weird, 10
Reed v. Reed, 22
referral services, 91
rehabilitative alimony, 115, 117
remarriages, 179
rental assistance, 138
respect, xiv
response, to divorce, 26
retainers, for attorney, 91
retirees, 151, 199–201
retirement: accounts, 125–26; alimony and, 116; Baby Boomers and, 96; downsizing and, 153; 401(k) account, 110, 119, 125–26; full retirement age, 122; savings, 95, 136, 138
reverse mortgage, 143–45, *144*
revolving credit accounts, 78–79
rights: of survivorship, 39; of women, 21–26, *22*
risk tolerance, 97, 174–75
Rivers, Joan, 132
robo-advisors, 98
Rockefeller, David, 202
rollover, 176
Roman Catholic Church, 23
Roosevelt, Eleanor, 72, 133
Roth IRA, 176

250 ~ Index

"same old, same old," xii
same-sex marriages, 24
Samoa, 105
Saudi Arabia, 105
Saver (financial personality), 55–56
savings: HSA, 111; retirement, 95, 136, 138; small, 65–66
Scaramucci, Anthony, 10
Scarlett O'Hara (fictional character), 34–35, 148
Scott, MacKenzie, xviii
Seattle Seahawks (football team), xxii
The Secret Life of Bees (Kidd), 120
secured credit card, 83, 103
security, financial, 57–58
self-esteem: of men, xix; of women, xx
self-reflection, 7
self-reliance, 210
self-worth, 209
senior citizens, xviii
senior discounts, 138
Seniors Farmers Market Nutrition Program (SFMNP), 138
Sennott, Laurie, 57
separation, 25
Serafini, Brian, xvi
settlement, divorce, 26
sexual bias, xxii
SFMNP. See Seniors Farmers Market Nutrition Program
shame, 4
"she-cession," xvi
Shields, Brooke, 67
shopping list, 138
short-term capital gain, 110
Siebert, Muriel, xxiv
Silent Generation, 76
Slacker (music app), 155
"Slaves" (Michelangelo), 209
small savings, 65–66
SmartAsset, 135
SNAP. See Supplemental Nutrition Assistance Program

Social Security, xviii, xxvii, 24, 30, 71, 139; assets and income division and, 121–23; student loans and, 177; taxes and, 127
Social Security Administration (SSA), 122
socks, 45–46
specialization, of attorneys, 90
special needs children, 116
Spender (financial personality), 55
spending, 59–60, 66
Spielberg, Stephen, 189
Spotify, 155
spouse, relationship with, xi–xii
SSA. See Social Security Administration
standard marriage, 24
state laws, 104
status quo, 34
Steinem, Gloria, xxiv, 158
stereotypes, xix, 34
Stewart, Martha, xii, 107
stigma, 4, 11, 28
stocks, 110
stress, financial, 149
"Stress in America Survey 2022" (APA), 149
student loans, 113, 136–37, 138–40, 205; of Baby Boomers, 139; Social Security and, 177
suicides, xvii, 31
Supplemental Nutrition Assistance Program (SNAP), 137
Supreme Court, 22
survivorship, right of, 39
Sweden, xvi
Syracuse University, xxv

taxes: on alimony, 126; assets and income division and, 126–27; charitable giving and, 196; documents, 101; prenups and, 182; Social Security and, 127

Index ～ 251

TD Ameritrade, xix
team, divorce: attorney checklist,
91–93; attorney interview, 90–91;
attorney selection, 89–91; finding,
87–93; mediation versus lawyer,
87–88; putting together, 85–86
temporary hearings, 26
tenancy-in-common, 39
"termination of domestic partnership"
form, 25
term life insurance, 123
Texas, 104
Thoreau, Henry David, 210
Thrivent, 203
TikTok, xxiii
"time out," 35–36
TOD. See Transfer On Death
The Today Show (TV program), xxv
Tolle, Eckhart, xvi
total gross monthly income, 80
traditional financial advisors, 98
traditional marriage, xix
Transfer On Death (TOD), 73
transparency, 38
TransUnion, 75, 102
trial, divorce, 26
Truman, Harry, 111
Trump, Donald, 10
Truro, Massachusetts, 104
trusts, 176, 196
Twain, Mark, 45

UBS Global Wealth Management,
xxvi, 28, 34, 125, 147, 157
United States Census Bureau, 28
United States of Aging Survey for
Low- & Moderate-Income, 135
universal life insurance, 123
University of Chicago, Booth School of
Business, xix
University of Michigan, xviii
University of Washington, xvi
unmarried couples, 39

UPS, xxv
Urban Dictionary, 11
USA Today (newspaper), xix
utilization rate, 75

value, 25, 120
Van Buren, Abigail, 207
variable expenses, 62, 67
Vatican, 105
venture capital (VC), 30
Vermont, 104
victimhood, xv–xvi
Vision Board, 67
Visioning Model, 157, 158, 159–61,
204
volunteering, 195
V-WISE, xxv

Wage Index, 29
WalletHub, 151
Wall Street Journal (newspaper), xvii
warning signs, for divorce, xiv
Washington (state), 119
Washington, George, 83
Washington, University of, xvi
wealth, women controlling, 35
Whitman School of Business, xxv
whole life insurance, 123
Wichita, Kansas, 104
Wichita State University, 149
wills, 39
Winfrey, Oprah, 38, 56, 66, 183
wish list, 69
women, 57; Black, 30; as breadwinners,
xix; Competitive Marriage Syndrome
and, xviii–xix; credit cards for,
xxiv; earning less than men, xxvii,
29–30; economic cost of divorce
and, xxvi; family money issues
and, 147; financial independence
of, 19; financial rights of, 21–26,
22; hanging on, xx–xxi; Hispanic,
30; household duties and, 29;

252   ~   Index

investments and, 167–69; living longer, 31–34; mixed messages for, xviii; during pandemic, xvi; pulled in many directions, 28–29; self-esteem of, xx; suicides of, 31; wealth controlled by, 35

women of color: earning less than men, xxvii, 30; during pandemic, xvi

Woods, Tiger, 189

work, 191

yield, 175

Your Money, Your Children, Your Life (PBS special), xxv

Zuckerberg, Mark, 189